Camera Obscura 106

Feminism, Culture, and Media Studies

Editors: Lalitha Gopalan, Lynne Joyrich, Homay King, Bliss Cua Lim, Constance Penley, Tess Takahashi, Patricia White, and Sharon Willis

Advisory Editors: Paula Amad, Aubrey Anable, Joanne Bernardi, Shohini Chaudhuri, Michelle Cho, Rey Chow, Wendy Hui Kyong Chun, Mary Desjardins, Mary Ann Doane, Rosa-Linda Fregoso, Bishnupriya Ghosh, Jennifer González, Elena Gorfinkel, Roger Hallas, Amelie Hastie, Jennifer Horne, Dina Iordanova, Ana López, Yosefa Loshitzky, Kathleen McHugh, Mandy Merck, Meaghan Morris, Frances Negrón-Muntaner, Kathleen Newman, Lisa Parks, B. Ruby Rich, Julie Levin Russo, Ella Shohat, Janet Staiger, Sasha Torres, and Mimi White

Managing Editor: Sarah Lerner

Editorial Assistants: Casey Coffee, Kyna McClenaghan, Charlotte Orzel, Anita Raychawdhuri, and Megan Reilly

Camera Obscura is published three times a year by Duke University Press, 905 W. Main St., Suite 18B, Durham, NC 27701.

Thanks to the University of California, Santa Barbara, College of Letters and Science and Department of Film and Media Studies for their generous support of the editorial office. *Camera Obscura* also benefits from the generous support of the following institutions: the University of Rochester, Brown University, Bryn Mawr College, Swarthmore College, the University of Texas at Austin, and the School of Humanities, University of California, Irvine.

Send correspondence to *Camera Obscura*, Department of Film and Media Studies, University of California, Santa Barbara, CA 93106-4010.

Visit Duke University Press Journals at dukeupress.edu/journals.

Direct all orders to Duke University Press, Journals Customer Relations, 905 W. Main St., Suite 18B, Durham, NC 27701. Volume 36 of *Camera Obscura* corresponds to issues 106–8. Annual subscription rates: print-plus-electronic institutions, $286; print-only institutions, $267; e-only institutions, $218; e-only individuals, $15; individuals, $30; students, $20. For information on subscriptions to the e-Duke Journals Scholarly Collections, contact libraryrelations@dukeupress.edu.

Print subscriptions: add $11 postage and applicable HST (including 5% GST) for Canada; add $14 postage outside the US and Canada. Back volumes (institutions): $267. Single issues: institutions, $89; individuals, $12. For more information, contact Duke University Press Journals at 888-651-0122 (toll-free in the US and Canada) or 919-688-5134; subscriptions@dukeupress.edu.

Camera Obscura provides a forum for scholarship and debate on

feminism, culture, and media studies. The journal encourages

contributions in areas such as the conjunctions of gender, race,

class, and sexuality with audiovisual culture; new histories

and theories of film, television, video, and digital media; and

politically engaged approaches to a range of media practices.

Contributor Information

Camera Obscura seeks essays (approximately 6,500–9,000 words, including endnotes) that engage with current academic and popular debates in feminism, culture, and media studies. We encourage potential contributors to browse recent issues of the journal for examples of the types of scholarship we currently seek.

Camera Obscura is also interested in short pieces (750–2,500 words) on current media practices, practitioners, resources, events, or issues for the section "In Practice: Feminism/Culture/Media." The editors encourage authors to use the short format to experiment with form in a critical context. The section includes solicited contributions and open submissions, with the intention of enriching dialogue between feminist media scholarship and the practices—production, distribution, exhibition, organizing, curating, archiving, research, etc.—that sustain it.

Please submit an electronic copy of the manuscript (as a Microsoft Word email attachment) with a cover letter to the managing editor at cameraobscura@ filmandmedia.ucsb.edu. Manuscripts should be double-spaced and use endnotes. Authors should declare all sources of funding (if applicable) in the cover letter. *Camera Obscura*'s documentation style follows *The Chicago Manual of Style*, 17th ed., chap. 14.

Camera Obscura, Department of Film and Media Studies, University of California, Santa Barbara, Santa Barbara, CA 93106-4010; fax: 805-893-8630; email: cameraobscura@filmandmedia.ucsb.edu.

Indexing and Abstract Listings

For a list of sources in which *Camera Obscura* is indexed and abstracted, see dukeupress.edu/camera-obscura.

Introduction: Future Varda

Rebecca J. DeRoo and Homay King

Agnès Varda achieved success with award-winning films span-
ning a directorial career of more than six decades; in the last
years of her life she became a major public figure in the global
press and on social media. Retrospectives following her death in
March 2019 have further sparked interest and acclaim across generations. Her final film, *Varda by Agnès* (*Varda par Agnès*, France,
2019), continues to be screened globally. Varda has attracted
important scholarly and critical attention not only for her prolific
cinematic career but also for her work across visual media, from
photography to installation art. Moreover, people view her as
someone who surmounted obstacles—creating her own production company and making work largely outside the mainstream
industry—and who also confronted those obstacles on behalf of
others, participating in women's demonstrations and public activism into the final years of her life. Now is a moment when everyone is discovering or looking anew at Varda.

We contend that this is also the time to look at what is most
extreme, innovative, and challenging in Varda's work, at what
speaks to the future. Building on generations of important scholarship about Varda and her work, we continue the dialogue across

Camera Obscura 106, Volume 36, Number 1
DOI 10.1215/02705346-8838505   © 2021 by *Camera Obscura*
Published by Duke University Press

disciplines and focus on some key areas of Varda's corpus. As well as appreciating underconsidered parts of her oeuvre, "Future Varda" offers a reflection on the living issues her work illuminates. Our aim is not to offer a comprehensive survey, or a final word. Rather, we pursue concerns her work raises that challenge us now and that are relevant for the future of feminism, film and media studies, and Varda's own legacy. Varda was engaged with these issues of feminist filmmaking until the last. We believe it is especially fitting to do so in *Camera Obscura*, with its history of commitment to these concerns and early attention to Varda's oeuvre.[1]

The articles in this special issue trace diverse strands in Varda's work that we identify as central to understanding her feminist vision for the future: her work across artistic media; her radical portraiture and self-portraiture that rethinks the relation of self and world; her taboo-breaking examination of maternity and eroticism; her symbolic engagement with politics and historical trauma; her development of her own production company, Ciné-Tamaris; her recent political activism at Cannes and importance to contemporary feminism; and her innovative marketing bridging international film festivals and social media. We have organized this issue into three sections, using terms that, as she states in *Varda by Agnès*, served as Varda's own guiding principles: *inspiration/création* and *partage* (sharing), followed by an In Practice section.

Inspiration, Création

In "Floating Roots: Agnès Varda's *Uncle Yanco*," Homay King traces one source of Varda's artistic inspiration to Jean "Yanco" Varda, the subject of her 1967 short film *Uncle Yanco*. Jean Varda was a peripatetic artist who lived on a houseboat and was part of a bohemian circle that included Henry Miller, Anaïs Nin, Alan Watts, and other luminaries of the San Francisco counterculture. Both Vardas were gleaners and artists. King argues that both saw the imagination as a place where matter and spirit were reconciled. The article builds on previous work about Varda's *The Gleaners and I* (*Les glaneurs et la glaneuse*, France, 2000), exploring Varda's materialist feminism and her use of earthly and tactile materials. "Floating Roots" focuses not only on matter but also on the imagination and the intangible images, colors, and forms that are prominent in her oeuvre, arguing that Yanco served as a muse to his niece.

Emma Wilson turns to another less studied film from earlier in Varda's career, *Kung-fu Master!* (*Le petit amour*, France, 1988). She draws on the work of Adriana Cavarero to analyze the feminist ethics of Varda's taboo-breaking representation of maternal eroticism, which has been long understudied in Varda's corpus. In "Agnès Varda, Jane Birkin, and *Kung-fu Master!*," Wilson analyzes how the film arose from Varda's collaboration with actress Jane Birkin and starred both Birkin's and Varda's children. She eloquently illuminates how Varda uses a fairy-tale motif to depict a complex story of a relationship between a teenage boy and an adult mother, framing the film as part of Varda's larger investigations of the imaginative and emotional worlds of women and children.

In "She Listened: Vardian Self-Portraiture and Auto-Refrains of Sea, Wind, and Sand," Nadine Boljkovac examines (self-)portraiture in *The Beaches of Agnès* (*Les plages d'Agnès*, France, 2008), *Agnès de ci de là Varda* (*Agnès Varda: From Here to There*, France, 2011), and *Visages Villages* (*Faces Places*, France, 2017)—and the process of intertwining the individual and the world, the detail and the environment, the visual and sensual. These intertwinings take shape in the recurring motifs of sand, sea, and wind in *The Beaches of Agnès*, as well as in Varda's late films and installations in general. Boljkovac helpfully turns to the audio register of Varda's work to explore these refrains.

A number of articles in "Future Varda" address important yet previously underexplored feminist ethics in Varda's films and artwork, as well as in her public actions, models for engaged filmmakers today and going forward. In "Passion, Commitment, Compassion: *Les Justes au Panthéon* by Agnès Varda," Sandy Flitterman-Lewis carefully documents and insightfully analyzes Varda's 2007 multimedia installation *Les Justes*, honoring the "Righteous," individuals who protected Jewish children during World War II. She analyzes how Varda moves between cinematic reconstruction and physical photographs, immortalizing the ephemeral. By addressing the Occupation as a woman artist in the French monument the Pantheon, where so few women have been honored, Varda also opens questions of national reflection on gender and historical commemoration.

Partage

Varda was not only a brilliant creator but also a shrewd business-woman who made most of her work outside the mainstream film industry. In "Agnès Varda, Producer," Kelley Conway analyzes Varda as both artist and entrepreneur who found creative ways to make, finance, and later restore her films. From forming a cooperative of artists and technicians to make her first film, *La Pointe Courte* (France, 1954), to founding the production company Tamaris Films, which would come to be Ciné-Tamaris, Varda created films prolifically with limited resources. Drawing on material from the Ciné-Tamaris archive and conducting new interviews with producers at Ciné-Tamaris, Conway expands our knowledge of how Varda ran her company.

Varda's work in production and distribution is in many ways inseparable from her feminist politics. In "Agnès Varda and Le Collectif 50/50 en 2020: Power and Protest at the Cannes Film Festival," Rebecca J. DeRoo provides a new analysis of Varda's late career activism. Weaving together recent documents, including an interview with Varda, DeRoo shows how Varda used honorary award speeches at the Cannes festival and then joined with the feminist collective 50/50 en 2020 to suggest that retrospective tributes obscure the career obstacles she encountered and the under-representation of women directors at Cannes more broadly. DeRoo shows that Varda was willing to use her platform to advocate for others; together with 50/50 en 2020, Varda made broader calls for parity and equity in the festival and film industry.

In "From Cannes to Cardboard: The Circulation and Promotion of *Visages Villages* and the Auteur on Instagram," Matt St. John offers original research on Varda's strategies for presenting and publicizing her film *Visages Villages*, leading up to its Oscar nomination for best documentary and other awards. Varda screened the film at film festivals, fundraised with the crowdsourcing platform KissKissBankBank, and publicized on Instagram. He presents this publicity as a twenty-first-century extension of Varda's filmmaking practice, which combines her own presence on the screen, her characteristic humor, and details of her working process. *Visages Villages* also reflects on its own making, beginning with the meeting of the two artists and portraying their adventures traveling across France to interview locals and create photographic murals. St. John shows how Varda continually adapted her creative strategies to new media technologies and platforms, up to the end of her career.

Varda was an artist with many lives, as she put it, working in and across film, video, photography, and installation art. Such crossovers among media are common in contemporary art and filmmaking, though Varda began doing so in the 1950s. Although she documented much of her work across visual media herself, for many years this documentation was inaccessible, fragmentary, or overlooked. Dominique Bluher, who has curated exhibitions of Varda's work, illuminates what Varda termed her "third life," or move to create multimedia art in the twenty-first century at age seventy-five. Bluher draws important connections between Varda's cinema and artwork: "Her movies were already invitations to posing questions; her photographic and videographic installations further these invitations to a voyage of personal reflections, emotional responses, or active reveries." Bluher examines these exhibitions as personal and emotional, both for the creator and for the spectators who experience the installations' multimodal means of address in a range of physical spaces.

"Future Varda" concludes with two "In Practice" pieces, the first of which continues the work of attending to Varda's archival documentation of her practice across media. In "Agnès Varda: Photography and Early Creative Process," Rebecca J. DeRoo brings to light primary sources from Varda's archives to explore how she used photography to develop her first film, *La Pointe Courte* (France, 1954), and her 1958 short film *L'Opéra Mouffe* (*Diary of a Pregnant Woman*, France). Photography, DeRoo demonstrates, provided a creative way of drawing on her training and work as a photographer and was also economically beneficial, when working with minimal budgets. DeRoo's article also challenges long-held myths of Varda as inexperienced at the beginning of her directorial career, showing the extent of Varda's careful use of photography to plan cinematic shots and deliberate aesthetics in her early work, opening avenues for future research and creative work.

The second and final "In Practice" piece looks toward another aspect of the future: virtual presence and remote intimacy. Colleen Kennedy-Karpat co-organized a symposium originally titled "Gender Equality and Sustainability: Agnès Varda's Sustaining Legacy," which was to take place at Bilgi University in Istanbul in March 2020. Due to the coronavirus pandemic, it was retitled "Virtual Varda" and hosted via Zoom teleconference. In "'Virtual Varda': Sustainable Legacies, Digital Communities, and Scholarly Postcards," Kennedy-Karpat reflects on the appropriateness of online scholarly presentations to Varda and her work, noting that Varda herself moved between media, fostered interpersonal and international connections, and created engaged global work. Varda's own example supports the conditions of scholarly work on her oeuvre in the present and helps us generate productive models of future scholarly collaboration.

This journal issue brings together Varda scholars of different generations, building on earlier scholarly insights, analyzing underacknowledged aspects of Varda's work in activism, art, film, and media, and opening avenues for the feminist future she worked to make possible. Varda was a renaissance woman who produced complex creative work within economic arrangements that she herself innovated, who was consistently feminist in her life and work, moving among aesthetic forms and modalities, incorporating new technologies, and reflecting on the poetics and politics of visual art. Here is an incredible example for the present and future, as so many female and feminist directors are working to make inroads. Her range truly is stunning—and it is still being understood.

Note

1. Agnès Varda is mentioned in *Camera Obscura*'s inaugural issue in 1976, in an interview with Yvonne Rainer conducted by Janet Bergstrom and signed by the editorial collective. "Yvonne Rainer: Interview," *Camera Obscura*, no. 1 (1976): 96. In a piece describing the journal's beginnings, the collective mentions a Varda retrospective at the Pacific Film Archive as a key factor that prompted the formation of the *Camera Obscura* collective in December 1974. "Chronology: *The Camera Obscura Collective*," *Camera Obscura*, nos. 3–4 (1979): 6.

Rebecca J. DeRoo is associate professor in the School of Communication at the Rochester Institute of Technology. She cocurated the 2016 retrospective *Agnès Varda: (Self-)Portraits Facts and Fiction* at the Dryden Theatre, George Eastman Museum. Her book *Agnès Varda between Film, Photography, and Art* (2018) was a finalist for the Kraszna-Krausz Book Award. This research was supported by grants from the American Association of University Women, the American Philosophical Society, and the National Endowment for the Humanities. Her first book, *The Museum Establishment and Contemporary Art* (2006, 2014), received the Laurence Wylie Prize in French Cultural Studies.

Homay King is professor and Eugenia Chase Guild Chair in the Humanities in the Department of History of Art at Bryn Mawr College, where she cofounded the Program in Film Studies. She is the author of *Virtual Memory: Time-Based Art and the Dream of Digitality* (2015) and *Lost in Translation: Orientalism, Cinema, and the Enigmatic Signifier* (2010). Her work has appeared in *Afterall, Discourse, Film Quarterly, October,* and edited collections, including the exhibition catalog for the Metropolitan Museum of Art's *China: Through the Looking Glass*. She is a member of the *Camera Obscura* editorial collective.

Figure 1. "Heavenly cities float": San Francisco in the establishing shot of *Uncle Yanco* (US/France, 1967)

Floating Roots:
Agnès Varda's *Uncle Yanco*

Homay King

Agnès Varda's 1967 short portrait film *Uncle Yanco* (US/France) begins with an image of San Francisco at dawn. From a distance, the city appears to hover over the water. Yanco Varda speaks in voice-over: "Heavenly cities float. They have no top or bottom. They call San Francisco the Holy City. It's the city of love." This image was taken in October, a time of year that, due to the San Francisco Bay's unique microclimate, tends to be clear and warm. In the summer months an opaque morning fog funnels through the Golden Gate, blanketing the city's hills and spilling into its valleys, obscuring the skyline, evaporating only during a narrow window of afternoon sun. On the day depicted in this image, though, the morning view was translucent, and the city is shrouded in pink. In voice-over, Agnès Varda invokes "rosy-fingered dawn," a Homeric epithet that links this image to the *Odyssey* and the Varda family's Greek roots, signaling that this film will be in some way connected to ancient myth.

In this article I attempt to trace some of Agnès Varda's "floating roots," as she calls them, primarily through Jean "Yanco" Varda, the uncle of this film (who was in fact her second cousin).

Camera Obscura 106, Volume 36, Number 1
DOI 10.1215/02705346-8838517   © 2021 by *Camera Obscura*
Published by Duke University Press

I argue that Yanco served as a muse to his niece and that they shared a similar philosophy: the idea that the imagination is the place where matter and spirit are reconciled. This work builds on an argument I made in my book *Virtual Memory* about Varda's *The Gleaners and I* (*Les glaneurs et la glaneuse*, France, 2000), in which I read that film as a supreme example of materialist feminism, stressing her use of earthly and tactile materials and interpreting her as an artist committed to what Siegfried Kracauer called "the redemption of physical reality," despite the fact that the film is shot entirely with a digital camera.[1] Here I focus not only on matter but also on the immaterial and its significance in Agnès Varda's oeuvre. For the sake of clarity, I refer to her primarily as *Varda* and to her uncle primarily as *Yanco*, a longtime nickname that he instructs his niece to call him by in her film.

Like Gaston Bachelard, Varda's mentor at the Sorbonne, Yanco found inspiration in the elemental matter of the world and the forms it wondrously assumes. But both also insisted on the primacy of the intangible, frequently stressing words like *transcendence, myth, heavenly,* and *sacred.* This insistence can be puzzling, since their mystical tendencies cannot be fully explained in religious terms. Bachelard's writings frequently invoke the idea of spirit, but not any particular theological system. And although Jean Varda claimed that he could not help but be *croyant* (believing), given his Greek Orthodox upbringing, his notion of the divine was extremely syncretic, even heretical.[2] In addition, neither the artist nor the philosopher can rightfully be described as proponents of Platonic, idealist, or Cartesian principles. They are both worldly sensualists, disdaining the disciplinary connotations of mind-over-matter subjectivity, elevating the enjoyment of aesthetic pleasure to a kind of Epicurean ethical practice. Furthermore, while both attribute redemptive powers to creativity and the imagination, neither of them understands these faculties as related to individual authority or the products of human will and agency. At the same time, they are definitely not structuralists: while they put little stock in notions of individual agency or self-sovereignty, they do not dismiss culture as merely the by-product of abstract, impersonal systems like language and kinship structures that imprint themselves in an ideologically determinative way on subjects. Finally, the deep human psyche is also not the true wellspring of imagination for either one, as in a psychoanalytic account. While Bachelard wrote of the power of dreams and reverie, his version of these does not square fully with the Freudian concepts of fantasy or sublimation, nor did he describe them as by-products of the unconscious or repression. Jean Varda, for his part, openly disdained psychoanalysis: as he quips in *Uncle Yanco*, "For me, the only way not to succumb to life's supreme indignity, which is being psychoanalyzed, is to go sailing once a week with no motor."

How, then, are we to understand this worldview, which I argue is visible in the work of Agnès Varda, too? What kind of creative imagination has its source not in the divine, in the human mind, in abstract structures like language, in the unconscious, or, finally, as one might expect, in a phenomenological or vitalist account, but solely in the physical and vital properties of matter? I hope to begin to answer this question in a provisional way in this article, through analysis of Varda's film, an account of Jean Varda's life and artistic oeuvre, and commentary on Bachelard's writings on the image. It is a question that I hope will illuminate not only the work of these three figures but also the California mindset as it took hold of the San Francisco Bay Area in the mid-twentieth century, in its least hypocritical form. This way of understanding the creative imagination is related to the utopian, visionary prong of what Fred Turner called "the Californian Ideology"—a blend of "libertarian politics, countercultural aesthetics, and techno-utopian visions."[3] I would call it a form of Romantic phenomenology.

The Meeting of Two Vardas
Uncle Yanco's opening shot of the floating city at dawn is followed by a quick montage of images introducing San Francisco as it was in 1967: the Golden Gate Bridge seen by car, psychedelic artwork and posters from the legendary Fillmore music venue, photographs documenting protests of the Vietnam War, and similar images. The next shots return to Yanco, who appears in his natural habitat: the *SS Vallejo*, a patchwork quilt of a houseboat built

from the shell of a retired passenger ferry. Yanco acquired this boat in 1949 with his friend Gordon Onslow Ford, a British surrealist who fronted $500 for the purchase. Together they refurbished it for use as a home, artist studio, and social gathering site. They docked in Sausalito, California, a small bayside community just north of San Francisco's Golden Gate Bridge, where dozens of floating homes sit tucked in a corner of the bay sheltered by Mount Tamalpais. During the 1950s and 1960s, through Yanco's death in 1971, the *Vallejo* hosted various luminaries of the California counterculture movement. Alan Watts (1915–73), a founder of the California Institute of Integral Studies and author of over twenty books on Eastern mysticism, largely responsible for popularizing Zen Buddhism in the Western world, visited the ship and soon became Varda's roommate there.[4] Watts convened the famous Houseboat Summit of February 1967 on the ship, which gathered Timothy Leary, Allen Ginsburg, Gary Snyder, and others.[5] Artists, poets, and scholars who visited or had studio space on the *Vallejo* included Maya Angelou, the Chilean painter Roberto Matta, Ruth Asawa (whom Yanko had taught at Black Mountain College), the Austrian painter and theorist Wolfgang Paalen, Luchita Hurtado, and Grace McCann Morley, then director of San Francisco's Museum of Modern Art.[6] Sabro Hasegawa, who introduced Eastern calligraphy to the Bay Area and Western abstract art to Japan, produced work on the ship.[7] Yanco Varda collaborated with these and other Bay Area artists and filmmakers, appearing in a role in James Broughton's *The Bed* (US, 1968). The *Vallejo* is still intact and currently hosts an invitation-only artists' residency.

Uncle Yanco provides a short tour of this community and its unusual architecture through a series of mobile images, filmed as if we were gliding around its piers on a skimmer. The 35mm film stock reveals a fairyland of saturated colors and quirky shapes: boats of red, blue, and brown, some half-sunken, some geodesic, one floating alone like a tiny island, others docked in cozy groups bridged by narrow wooden walkways, many of which are lined with pots of cultivated herbs and succulents. "Sausalito," Yanco explains in voice-over, "is what they call 'aquatic suburbia' . . . the aquatic

Figure 2. The *SS Vallejo*, with *The Owl* in the background, in Varda's *Uncle Yanco* (US/France, 1967)

Figure 3. "Aquatic suburbia": Sausalito docks in *Uncle Yanco* (US/France, 1967)

suburbs represent a certain intelligence. It's people who aren't rebels with guns, but rebels against the system, against the American obsession with making money." A notable icon appears in this sequence: a pagoda-like structure with pointed eaves for wings and large round windows, resembling a sort of half-bird, half–sea creature. Nicknamed *The Owl*, the boat was constructed by architect Chris Roberts, who built a second floating residence called *The Madonna* that towered over the marina until it was destroyed by a fire in 1975.

Soon the film introduces a set of mythological references that will be activated throughout its brief duration—many of which Varda would continue to work with in later work. Yanco proclaims: "It's important to always be by the sea. The sea is the element of love. The Greeks say so. Aphrodite emerged from the water." A tracking shot reveals more floating homes, accompanied by the sound of Greek lyra music. Varda picks up the voice-over where Yanco has left off: "This Greek who says so lives on the water in this floating house right out of a cartoon, in this ark worthy of Noah, off this island worthy of a Greek . . . a painter, my ancestor, my floating root." On this houseboat with its collection of fantastic creatures, including his pet cat Melanesia, Uncle Yanco seems Noah-like: a savior figure in times of war and destruction. Yanco was known for telling tall tales about himself: he claimed that his mother was a seal and that he was from the island of Cythera, the mythical birthplace of Aphrodite and home to her archaic temple.[8] Like Mona in *Vagabond* (*Sans toit ni loi*, France, 1985), it seems as though Yanco came from the sea, a semiaquatic being emerging like Venus from a shell. One legend about San Francisco imagines it as the resurrection of the lost city of Atlantis.[9] Yanco clearly lives in a world steeped in myth and ancient imagery, and the film opens in such a way that we feel we are stepping into this world. Varda refers to Yanco as a member of her "imaginary family," suggesting that, to her, kinship to him involves more than a chance fact of birth. As Yanco quips, "The family is what we mustn't be." In a later interview, Varda referred to Yanco as "this father of my dreams."[10] Theirs is a chosen, fantasy kinship in addition to being a biological one.

Figure 4. Yanco (left) and Tom Luddy (right),
in *Uncle Yanco* (US/France, 1967)

The next segment of the film, labeled "How Uncle Yanco
Met His Niece Agnès," consists of a montage of reenacted takes of
the two Vardas meeting each other. Agnès approaches the *SS Vallejo*
via its wooden walkway and pretends to be meeting Yanco for the
first time, introduced by her friend Tom Luddy. Their encounter is
shown a total of seven times, with the dialogue repeated in French,
English, and Greek, sometimes as a complete action, sometimes in
fragments. A clapperboard snaps between takes, showing the date
as 29 October 1967, a Sunday and their second day of filming.
The inclusion of the date and the repetitions produce an alienation effect, clearly marking their meeting as a fictional reenact-
ment. As Rebecca J. DeRoo notes, Varda often practiced feminism
through Brechtian methods.[11] Similar repetitions and breaks with
illusionism are to be found in *Le bonheur* (*Happiness*, France, 1965),
where color takes on a Sirkian unreality, as well as *Lions Love* (. . .
and Lies) (US, 1969) and *One Sings, the Other Doesn't* (*L'une chante,
l'autre pas*, France/Belgium, 1977). Varda had served as the official
photographer of the Théâtre National Populaire under the direc-

tion of Brechtian Jean Vilar and imported alienation effects into her filmmaking.[12]

Agnès appears in a bright violet top and trousers, and Yanco in a pink jersey tinted with the inexpensive Rit dyes that he was known for. These colors, against the backdrop of the *Vallejo*'s cheery pink and yellow windowpanes, lend a painterly effect to the scene. Color was already a prominent element in Agnès Varda's practice, evidenced in the stunning, anti-illusionist palette of *Le Bonheur*. Sandy Flitterman-Lewis writes that in that film "Varda implicitly evokes impressionist painting theory in her use of analytic color shading (violet as the shadow of orange, for example)" and notes that, throughout her career, Varda's use of color continued to be influenced by "her painter-hippie Greek relative."[13] Varda's use of color here verges on extradiegetic: in *Le bonheur* she inventively fades to monochromes of blue or red rather than to black or white, and in *Uncle Yanco*, too, there is a sense that color assumes a life of its own, independent of the objects that serve as its canvas, producing what Gilles Deleuze calls an absorbent "color-image."[14]

At the conclusion of the repetition montage, children hold yellow and red cellophane hearts up to frame the pair, anticipating Varda's use of the heart motif in later work, notably the heart-shaped potatoes in *The Gleaners and I*. The images of their embrace also look backward, to Jacopo Pontormo's *Visitation* (1528–30), the Mannerist painting that inspired Bill Viola's *The Greeting* (US, 1995). Pontormo's image depicts a meeting between the Virgin Mary and her elderly relative Elizabeth, who is also miraculously pregnant with a son who will become John the Baptist. It captures the moment in the story when they approach each other, embrace, and are filled with the Holy Spirit. While Varda's film gestures only obliquely at this iconography, she would surely have known of it from her art historical training, and even if it is not a direct quotation, affinities between the two images are worth observing: the matching bright hues of pink, orange, and blue, the two attendants flanking the pair, and the joyful meeting of two relatives, one young and one old, who are kindred spirits. The positioning of Yanco in Elizabeth's place has feminist implications, as though he were both an uncle and a maternal figure. While conventionally

Figure 5. Embrace with cellophane heart in *Uncle Yanco* (US/
France, 1967)

masculine and even sexist in some of his behaviors, Yanco appears
in his niece's film as a chimerical, fluidly gendered figure, aligned
with Aphrodite and feminine creative potential, a point I return
to later in this article.

Through all these devices—the repetitions, the colors, the
iconographic references—the meeting of two Vardas is placed
under the sign of the imaginary many times over. We are presented with an uncle and niece, who are in reality second cousins
(Yanco explains that he is actually the cousin of Agnès's father
Eugène), who repeatedly pretend to meet for the first time onboard
a polychromatic floating home, when in fact, as Varda states in her
final film, *Varda by Agnès* (*Varda par Agnès*, France, 2019), they had
been introduced by Luddy the previous Wednesday. The scene is
of course no less touching for its lack of facticity. Varda imbues it
with a fairy-tale quality and makes clear the visit is not motivated
by family obligation or filial duty. Their kinship is not defined by
a single arboreal line of descent; rather, it goes by multiple names
and reaches into the future as well as the past.

Figure 6. Jacopo Pontormo, *Visitation* (ca. 1528–30). Oil
on panel, 80 × 61 in. The Church of San Michele e San
Francesco, Carmignano, Italy

The Artist as Sublime Ragpicker

Agnès Varda had come to the Bay Area to present *The Creatures* (*Les créatures*, France/Sweden, 1966) at the San Francisco Film Festival. Tom Luddy, who arranged her meeting with Yanco, was a programmer at the Pacific Film Archive, and soon-to-be cofounder of the Telluride Film Festival.[15] Varda and Jacques Demy had temporarily moved to Los Angeles that year, as Demy had a contract with Columbia Pictures, during which time he made the 1969 film *Model Shop*.[16] Due to this residency, Varda and Demy missed May 1968 in France but were in California for the Summer of Love, the Bobby Kennedy assassination, and the beginnings of the Black Panthers movement, which Varda documented in her 1968 short film of that title.

Yanco, for his part, had been living in California since the 1940s. Born in 1893 in Smyrna, of Greek and French heritage, he and his family moved to Athens in 1905.[17] He left Greece for Paris in 1913 to study at the École des Beaux Arts; there he kept a studio in a Montmartre building owned by Georges Braque. He crossed paths with Picasso, who insultingly called him "a classical painter, not a modern painter" (22). According to his biographer Elizabeth Leavy Stroman, Yanco dropped out shortly after this encounter, perhaps as a result of it, and gave up painting for years. He turned his attention instead to dance: after seeing a production of Stravinsky's *Rite of Spring* around 1916, he began to study ballet, joining Margaret Morris's dance club (22). During the 1920s he moved between the art worlds of Paris, Cassis in the south of France, and London, where he was a member of the short-lived Omega Workshops design movement. In this decade, Yanco also had his first solo show and married Dorothy Varda, with whom he had a daughter named Dominica. It was the first of five committed romantic relationships he had throughout his life, many of them contentious due to Yanco's self-proclaimed nature as "a cat who walks by himself" (108). In his final years he would surround himself with a retinue of young women he called his "graces": dancers and young hippies who lived with him on the *Vallejo*, four or five at a time (54). As an artist in her own right, Agnès Varda seems to have escaped being slotted by Yanco into this problematically gendered category.

Yanco's nymphets may rightly strike the contemporary viewer as antifeminist, given their youth, their devotion to him, and the fact that they appear utterly replaceable and interchangeable with one another. Still, it is important to remember the context of 1967 San Francisco: *Uncle Yanco* was filmed immediately after the Summer of Love, at the height of the free love movement and its radical sexual politics, but before Stonewall and the women's liberation movement.

By the early 1930s, Yanco had begun to experiment with a mosaic technique using mirrors, which involved scratching their backs, painting over the scratches, and embedding the pieces on boards covered with gesso such that the paint would show through the scored areas. Inventive use of materials characterized his entire career. He continued to produce mosaic-like assemblages made from glass, textiles, paper, metal, and other found fragments, usually embedded on wood. As he states in *Uncle Yanco*, "I don't like people calling them 'collages.' I use all sorts of durable materials: plastics, fabrics, like a mosaicist. Stone, glass." Later, he would return to painting for practical reasons, stating that it made the work "easier to carry around." But even then, his supports and canvases were often scavenged from discarded materials. Anaïs Nin, who befriended him in the early 1940s, dubbed him "a sublime ragpicker who turns everything into an object of beauty."[18] Yanco, like his niece, was a gleaner, turning salvaging into an art form.

Yanco's first journey to the United States took place in 1939, during which he visited New York, Chicago, and finally San Francisco, for a showing of his work at the Courvoisier Galleries. He fell in love with Northern California, and by 1942 he had moved to the coastal town of Monterey after a stint in nearby Big Sur. He and his third partner, Virginia Barclay, a textile designer, purchased a home that would come to be known as the Red Barn. The interior was gaudily decorated with odds and ends: pieces of polished driftwood, bits of broken marble, and a child-sized mannequin named Phoebe, who had straw hair, red and blue legs, and a dress dotted with tin foil.[19] He taught at various colleges, including Black Mountain, the San Francisco Art Institute (then known as the California School of Fine Arts), and the California College of the Arts

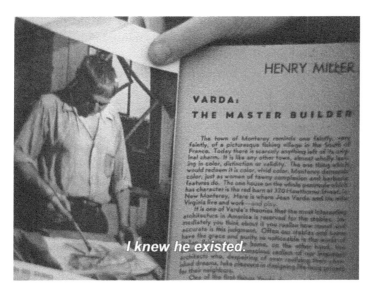

Figure 7. Agnès Varda holds a copy of Henry Miller's *Varda: The Master Builder* in *Uncle Yanco* (US/France, 1967)

in Oakland, while also working occasionally as a cook on a Yugoslavian sardine boat.[20]

One notable local commission in Monterey was for a restaurant called Angelo's, built out of salvaged lumber and recycled wood, which, in typical fashion, Varda painted in garish hues of blue, pink, and black. Its opening was celebrated with a costume party attended by local author John Steinbeck, at which several guests came dressed as characters from Varda's mosaics.[21] The building has a flattened, facade-like look, making it seem almost like one of Varda's mosaics come to life. The restaurant's name is painted in a Greek-looking font, a reference to the other seaside country that Varda associated in his mind with the Northern California landscape and climate.

Friends and party guests at the Red Barn during this period in the 1940s included Henry Miller, who had moved to Big Sur at Yanco's suggestion, and Anaïs Nin, the writer's friend and former lover. Like many, Miller found a muse in Yanco. His short volume titled *Varda: The Master Builder* was the text that provided Agnès with knowledge of Yanco prior to their meeting. Miller described the Red Barn as "a house made entirely of refuse: bottles, tin boxes, rockers, lead pipe, rope, dismantled hulls and masts of wrecked ships."[22] Miller drew a portrait of the artist as a Neptunian magician whose chief power is to create beauty from foraged debris: "He takes delight in plundering the refuse heaps and from the plunder creating veritable mansions of light and joy. One of the first things I was instructed in, on coming to stay with him, was never to throw away tin cans or empty bottles—nor rags, nor paper, nor string, nor buttons, nor corks, nor even dollar bills."[23]

Anaïs Nin used one of Yanco's untitled collages as the cover image for her 1961 book *Seduction of the Minotaur.* In her diaries she wrote eloquently of his work *Women Reconstructing the World*, which he had gifted to her, in a passage that merits quoting at length:

One morning . . . appeared . . . a big square package, one yard around. I opened it and it was a collage by Jean Varda. He calls it "Women Reconstructing the World." Against a background of sand the color of champagne, with its tiny grains of sparkling glass, five women in airy cutouts. The middle one is the strongest, with her abstract labyrinth of black-and-red stripes; on her left walks an Ophelia in a trailing white dress of clouds and lace, dancing not walking. And on her right a sturdy woman in white and blue, carrying a piece of music on her head. . . . In the back are four small houses, all façades, pierced with smiling, askew windows; one can easily walk in and out of them . . . They are made of intangibles, lights and space, labyrinths, and molecules which may change as you look at them. Elusive and free of gravity. They bring freedom by transcendence.[24]

Indeed, these footless women appear "free of gravity"; they seem to float toward us from the distant city, despite the fact that they are made of mixed materials of varying thicknesses. The "piece of music" that the figure on the left carries on her head is a collaged, cut-out slice of an actual musical score. The middle figure wears a pale apron that drapes and folds slightly, behaving like a moving piece of fabric. They approach on white welcome mats, as if inviting us to join them. They cross a desert of indeterminate scale, bringing all the shapes, colors, and bits of material they have sal-

Figure 8. Jean Varda, *Women Reconstructing the World* (1944). Courtesy of the Anaïs Nin Foundation

vaged and will use to reconstruct the world. They do not appear burdened by this task; rather, in Nin's words, they are airy and transcendent.

Where other artists at this time were exploring the material, factual qualities of paint and the objecthood of paintings, Yanco emphasized the ethereal, insubstantial qualities of matter. Perhaps this is why Picasso could not recognize his work as "modern": he reversed the quintessential modernist gesture of reflexivity, insisting instead on matter's capacity to be etherized into scenes of the imagination. This insistence must have struck Picasso as naive, or even semi-illiterate. For this final point, compare Jean Varda's use of the musical score fragment in *Women Reconstructing the World* with Picasso's use of newspaper in the 1913 collage *Bowl of Fruit, Violin, and Wineglass*. Writing about this painting, Rosalind Krauss famously argued that Picasso uses the collage medium in a proto-postmodern way, "setting up discourse in place of presence": words, letters, and violin *f*-holes are not so much figural elements as signifiers deployed as such.[25] Rather than referring to "predicates" like

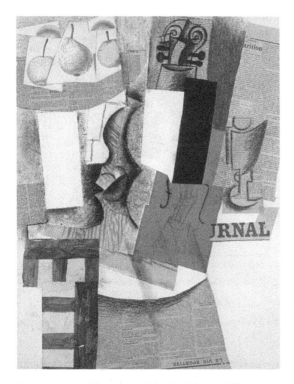

Figure 9. Pablo Picasso, *Bowl of Fruit, Violin, and Wineglass* (1913). Charcoal, black chalk, watercolor, oil paint, coarse black wash, and collage of printed and colored papers on board, 25^{11}/$_{16}$ × 19^{3}/$_{4}$ in. © 2021 Estate of Pablo Picasso / Artists Rights Society (ARS), New York

actual newspapers or violins, they invoke "the very system of form" itself; in this way, Krauss argued, the subject of Picasso's collage becomes not the objects in the still life but "the various resources for the visual illusion of spatial presence."[26] Form itself, representational systems as such, are what this image is about and what it interrogates.

Women Reconstructing the World, though, does the opposite. The clipped piece of musical score is not a sign as sign, nor is it even "itself," presented literally as a found object. It is meant to invoke music as a whole, all the music in the world, not as an abstract generalization (as in Music with a capital *M*), but as actual music that this woman is carrying to the new world that is being prepared, as if she were Noah, stocking an ark not with generalized concepts or signifiers of things but with real things. It is not meant to derealize the image and interrogate its illusionism; rather, Jean Varda wanted to create hyperreal images, dreamscapes, that would operate like archaic myths. He stubbornly and anachronistically insisted on the thingliness of representations, effectively declaring, "This *is* music; this *is* a pipe." His art involves a two-stage transmutation: salvaged scraps of matter are dematerialized into an image, and then that image assumes a reality of its own. In this way, its magic is not unlike that of film, although it has roots in a much earlier epoch.

Heavenly Cities

During his time in London, Jean Varda spent time in the British Library reading room, where he recalled immersing himself in texts by Byzantine mystics. One of these, Joannes Bardas, supplied him with one of his favorite quotations: "To the eye that is pure, the world is transparent. If there is still opacity, this is not a defect in matter, but an infirmity in the eye of the onlooker."[27] However, there is no known documentation of the existence of any Joannes Bardas or any volumes by him housed in the library; he seems to have been invented by Yanco as a kind of alter ego. A clue to this is offered by the similarity of their names. Another Byzantine mystic he quoted, Emanuel Mavroulas, is also likely fictional; there is no record of his existence, and the name is suspiciously similar to the

Figure 10. Two Vardas in profile in *Uncle Yanco* (US/France, 1967)

But feel free to call me your uncle if you like.

Figure 11. Yanco as "rich American uncle" in *Uncle Yanco* (US/France, 1967)

word "marvelous."[28] It is fitting that Yanco would use make-believe scholars to illustrate his philosophy about the pliability and transparency of worldly matter. He understood plasticity in the Eisensteinian sense of potential and malleability, that is, in terms of its capacity for transformation rather than its obdurateness.[29]

Agnès Varda films portions of her conversation with her uncle in sharp profiles edited in shot–counter shot, her uncle against a golden yellow wall, and herself, still clothed in purple, against a burgundy background, one silver earring dangling beneath her bobbed hair. These images have an icon-like quality, with their flat outlines and jewel tones: she composes their portraits with a nod to the Byzantine forms that influenced her uncle. As if to emphasize the suitableness of these forms, Varda inserts a second, contrasting portrait of Yanco in a wholly different guise, that of the rich American uncle. He poses seated in an ill-fitting checked suit jacket, a too-wide red tie, and white cowboy hat, his hand resting on a stuffy-looking book called *The Bible of the World*. His expression is wary, even slightly terrified: the role, pose, clothing, and genre of portrait are a bad fit for him. "I'm not really American,"

Figure 12. The dinner party scene in *Uncle Yanco* (US/
France, 1967)

Yanco says, "I was naturalized at fifty. And I'm not rich." Here, the
film signals again that this dream uncle will not be the caricature
we might expect from clichés, even if his persona is archetypal in
a different way.

Varda quickly restores her uncle to his preferred habitat: a
casual celebratory dinner party on the *Vallejo*. The film's images of
the composition—Henry Miller noted that Yanco always referred
to parties as "compositions"—reveal an inventory of objects.[30] At
the center are steamed mussels in a giant bowl made of reclaimed
wood. Works on paper fill the back wall. Flowers, both real and silk,
decorate the dinner table and ornament the ship's mismatched
wooden columns. A documentary photo by Bob Greensfelder
reveals Yanko's second daughter, Vagadu, among the group, leaning against one of these supports in the back; in the upper left corner is an electric lamp that was likely used to provide illumination
for the film shoot; its cord is visible in the film. Present here are the
many colorfully clad guests in Yanco's social milieu.

The next segment of the film takes the form of a sort of studio visit. Yanco describes his methods and principles while standing

Figure 13. "Some cities": one of Jean Varda's Heavenly Cities mosaics in *Uncle Yanco* (US/France, 1967)

before a work in progress on an easel. Reiterating his commitment to the transcendent, he states that "the goal of painting is to have light penetrate matter and dematerialize it." Again, his metaphors establish a link between his own art forms and his niece's, the cinema. The film continues to a sequence of shots of Yanco speaking in front of his work as if giving an artist's lecture, intercut with more examples of his images, sometimes filmed statically, sometimes panning or zooming in to close-ups of details.

One group of images to which Agnès devotes particular attention is his Heavenly Cities series. "I did a series of heavenly cities," Yanco intones. "The walls were emeralds and precious stones and so forth. . . . I did 30 of them. They're all hanging in houses now. Some cities are blue, red, gold, black—every color." Extradiegetic celestial music plays. Yanco continues his narration: "Gold—more childhood memories, of course. Mosaics, the gold backgrounds. Gold is the color of revelation." But the splendor Yanco describes does not fully match up to what we see on-screen, at least not at first glance. While the images do reveal some of the Byzantine and Islamic architectural forms that Yanco invokes, they are expressed loosely, through simplified approximations of shape.

The emeralds, precious stones, and gold he describes are suggested by the bright colors and decorative details but are far from expensive looking. No gems or even gem substitutes are inlayed here: the city is built from scraps of glued-together paper, fabric, and paint. Their patchwork look recalls quilting. They might easily be dismissed as kitsch outsider art; indeed, to this day, Stroman's is the sole monograph on Jean Varda's artistic oeuvre, and he is remembered equally if not more as a countercultural persona, teacher, and social hub as for his art.

However, this is precisely where it makes sense to return to Yanco's counterintuitive declaration that the purpose of art is to "dematerialize matter." It has nothing to do with denying the worldly objecthood of the found materials with which he builds his images; rather, it is about the marvelous capacity for a magnificent city to arise from what is in reality only bits of trash. This is poiesis in its highest form. To make a luxurious emerald city out of luxurious emeralds is no great feat. What Yanco does is more magical, akin to transubstantiation or alchemy. This explains why he called his works "mosaics" rather than collages, even when using only paper, textiles, or paint: like Byzantine mosaics, his images are meant to function as miraculous objects, exceeding the sum of their parts and conjuring up the presence of another world. "Painting rivals the splendor of a bird, the opulence of the sea or any landscape, but it surpasses them," says Yanco to his niece. Again, this is not because the bird or the sea is any less wondrous but, rather, because they already exist as such and do not require any transformation.

However roughshod one finds Jean Varda's artistic work, one cannot deny that it illustrates this power of the imagination, a faculty that allows visions of things to appear that do not in fact yet exist. It is not a negation of reality, like a lie or falsehood. Nor does it entail the destruction of the existing physical world. But it does require that the matter of this world be transformed, a capacity that Yanco attributed at times to light and at times to color, facilitated but not solely enacted by the artist. "Art is the last refuge of magic," he once wrote, "and the artist the modern alchemist, transmuting the refuse and scraps of civilization."[31] He was a pre-Reformation subject living in iconoclastic times.

Figure 14. A close-up of a mosaic by Jean Varda in
Uncle Yanco (US/France, 1967)

Shells Navigating the Water

Several of Yanco's Heavenly Cities are floating cities, like San Francisco. One of them that appears in *Uncle Yanco* contains a detail that Varda zooms in on: a structure with eaves and a large round window resembling *The Owl*, a floating home shown earlier in the film. Another of these aquatic cityscapes bears a slight resemblance to San Francisco. In the foreground, pink and red blocks are nested on a shimmering waterfront, while in the background, a row of taller structures in foggier colors juts skyward. One of these has twin spires reminiscent of the landmark Saints Peter and Paul Church in the city. A small boat appears ready to dock at a pier in the lower right corner, perhaps having just entered the bay via the gateway behind it, which, although it looks nothing like the Golden Gate Bridge, can be imagined as its analogue due to its position in the picture.

In *The Poetics of Space*, Gaston Bachelard, Varda's mentor at the Sorbonne, compares cities themselves to the ocean. Specifically, he writes that the sound of city bustle and traffic mimics the rhythmic crash of ocean tides, producing a soothing effect. He writes:

"My bed is a small boat lost at sea; that sudden whistling is the wind in the sails. On every side the air is filled with the sound of furious klaxoning. . . . But there now, your skiff is holding its own, you are safe in your stone boat."[32] This relationship between city thrum and ocean rumble is more than a metaphor, in Bachelard's view; it is what he calls a true image: "Everything corroborates my view that the image of the city's ocean roar is in the very 'nature of things' . . . that it is a true image."[33] By *true image*, he seems to indicate something like what Varda called a "key image," which operates as a touchstone, in a stronger way than a mere metaphor.[34] Something ascends to the status of a true image of something else when the two are experientially and perceptually nearly indistinguishable, due to qualities that inhere in their very matter and spatial organization. Bachelard elaborates on this idea in an anecdote about Gustave Courbet, who wanted to paint a view of Paris as seen from the top floor of the Sainte-Pélagie prison where he was confined, and to paint it "the way I do my marines: with an immensely deep sky, and all its movement, all its houses and domes, imitating the tumultuous waves of the ocean."[35]

Figure 15. Sailing party aboard the *Cythera* in *Uncle Yanco* (US/France, 1967)

The Poetics of Space contains a long chapter on the image of the seashell used poetically. Bachelard suggests that the shell-house is also a "primal" or true image in this sense (140). Shells, he writes, are "rough and rocky on the outside" but "highly polished" and "enamel-like" on the inside (149, 126). They are the very evocation of what he calls "the tranquility of inhabiting" (151). He describes the myth of Aphrodite's emergence from her shell as the opposite of the Medusa myth: whereas Medusa petrifies her victims with fear, turning flesh into stone, shellfish exude stone-like dwellings from their soft bodies (128). The birth of a creature from an eggshell or a sapling from a seed, too, inverts the Medusa curse: vitality breaks forth from an inanimate, sculptural hard casing.

The penultimate section of *Uncle Yanco* depicts a sailing party onboard Yanco's boat the *Cythera*, named, of course, for the island of Aphrodite and his self-appointed birthplace. Many of the same vividly clothed guests from the dinner party board the vessel for a merry outing. They bring their dogs aboard and smoke joints. A Pan-like hippie in green crowned with a headband plays a bamboo woodwind instrument. Varda films the boat from several angles, high above, level with the party, and from another vessel as the boat sails, revealing its painted exterior and sail. Extradiegetic Greek lute music accompanies the scene. Later, in *Varda by Agnès*, she reenacted this sailing venture in a similarly painted boat.

Bachelard's chapter on shells contains a final example of this form's dwelling-like qualities, the image of the seashell as a sailboat. He describes a sixteenth-century engraving by Pieter van der Heyden after Hieronymus Bosch, alternately titled *Shell Navigating the Water, The Oyster Shell,* and *The Sailing Scale.* Like the boating party in *Uncle Yanco*, the sailors feast, play music, and kiss, and there is even a dog on board. The image is likely a copy of *The Concert in the Egg* (1561), once attributed to Bosch and now assigned to a follower. These sixteenth-century images belong to the "ship of fools" genre; their purpose is to warn of the dangers of overindulgence in drink, song, and merriment. As Bachelard put it, "The dream of inhabiting all the hollow objects in the world is accompanied by ludicrous scenes peculiar to Bosch's imagination. . . . The travelers are feast-

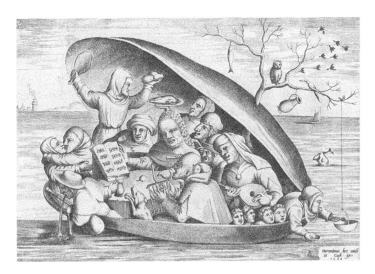

Figure 16. Pieter van der Heyden, *The Oyster Shell* (1562).
Engraving, 7.6 × 11.2 in.

ing and carousing, with the result that the dream of tranquility
we should like to pursue when we 'withdraw into our shells' . . .
is lost because of the insistence on frenzied joy that marks the
genius of this painter."[36]

Varda, though, is able to reconcile the ecstatic and the
tranquil. Her uncle's ship of fools is the very image of a floating
root, an understanding of what it means to cultivate a sense of
dwelling even in conditions of impermanence and instability.
Years later, in 2012, she would build one of her cinema-shacks, a
greenhouse-like installation made from recycled celluloid strips,
out of the final print of *Lions Love (. . . and Lies)* for an exhibition of her work at the Los Angeles County Museum of Art,
titled *Agnès Varda in Californialand*; *Uncle Yanco* was screened at
that exhibition. In an interview, she says, "I've been working all
my life, and I feel this is my private shack. This is where I live.
I live into cinema."[37] In the same interview, she suggests that
her movement between various media forms was also a kind of
migratory travel: "It's very exciting for me to go from one life
into another, and from one medium into another." Like a house-

boat, the cine-shack is semiweightless; it is made of light and airy materials that transmute into a vision of solid, inhabitable space. Both the French and English titles of her film *Vagabond* likewise convey a sense of being at home in itinerancy. One also thinks of the island of Noirmoutier that, like the mudflats of Sausalito where the *Vallejo* is docked, is connected to the land at low tide but floats separate from it when the tide rolls in. We might also recall the tomb of Varda's cat Zgougou adorned in seashells, and her *Cabane du chat* at the Fondation Cartier in Paris. And then, there is the concluding image of her final film *Varda by Agnès*, in which sea, sand, and sky blur together as one.

Varda describes what she learned from Bachelard in these words: he "had this dream of the *material* in people: a psychoanalysis of the material world related to people, wood, rivers, the sea, fire, wind, air. . . . He taught us to study writers not only by the stories they told but by the material things they mentioned."[38] Varda seems to have applied this principle to her uncle, who personified the element of water. "There is a distilling apparatus in every one of us," Yanco once quipped, one that "reduces all material, even the one of stark realism, into a parable or more often into a fable. In the beginning there was the Fable and in the end the Fable will be. . . . Nothing endures unless it has first been transposed into a myth."[39] Bachelard, a self-described phenomenologist of the imagination, shared this sense that matter requires myth to remove it from the stream of impermanence. And both of these men now find their transposition into myth, their endurance, in the work of a woman who studied them well, capturing them in images made of light.

Notes

My thanks to Patricia White for editorial wisdom, to Emily Leifer for assistance with images, and to the organizers of the "Virtual Varda" conference hosted by Bilgi University in March 2020, where I delivered a version of this article as a talk.

1.   Homay King, *Virtual Memory: Time-Based Art and the Dream of Digitality* (Durham, NC: Duke University Press, 2015), 71–88;

Siegfried Kracauer, *Theory of Film: The Redemption of Physical Reality* (Princeton, NJ: Princeton University Press, 1960).

2. Jean Varda studied with a nun and claimed at one point to have converted to Catholicism, but there is no evidence that he participated in organized religion later in life. See Elizabeth Leavy Stroman, *The Art and Life of Jean Varda* (Sausalito, CA: Purple Cottage, 2015), a comprehensive monograph that I rely on for much of Jean Varda's biography.

3. Fred Turner, *From Counterculture to Cyberculture: Stewart Brand, the Whole Earth Network, and the Rise of Digital Utopianism* (Chicago: University of Chicago Press, 2006), 208. Turner cited Richard Barbrook and Andy Cameron, who described *Wired* magazine as a purveyor of the Californian ideology, which Turner traced to the Whole Earth Network.

4. Watts also hosted a radio program on principles of Eastern thought called *Way beyond the West* on KPFA from 1959 to 1973.

5. Alan Watts, Gary Snyder, Tim Leary, and Allen Ginsberg, "Changes (The Houseboat Summit)," *San Francisco Oracle* 1, no. 7 (1967).

6. Stroman, *Art and Life of Jean Varda*, 6, 10, 92, 96, and 138.

7. David Keaton and Linda Keaton, "Ship of Dreams: Artists, Poets, and Visionaries of the *S.S. Vallejo*," in *Artists, Poets, and Visionaries of the S.S. Vallejo: 1949–1969*, ed. Fariba Bogzaran (Inverness, CA: Lucid Art Foundation, 2018), 5–6.

8. Stroman, *Art and Life of Jean Varda*, 15.

9. See, for example, Frona Eunice Wait, *Yermah the Dorado* (San Francisco: William Doxey, 1897), a science fiction novel that casts San Francisco as a resurrected Atlantis.

10. Jean Narboni, Serge Toubiana, and Dominique Villain, "*L'Une Chante, L'Autre Pas*: Interview with Agnès Varda," in *Agnès Varda: Interviews*, ed. T. Jefferson Kline (Jackson: University of Mississippi Press, 2014), 86.

11. Rebecca J. DeRoo, *Agnès Varda between Film, Photography, and Art* (Oakland: University of California Press, 2018), 75.

12. Gordon Gow, "The Underground River (1970)," in Kline, *Agnès Varda: Interviews*, 42.

13.   Sandy Flitterman-Lewis, *To Desire Differently: Feminism and the French Cinema* (New York: Columbia University Press, 1996), 233.

14.   Gilles Deleuze, *Cinema 1: The Movement-Image*, trans. Hugh Tomlinson and Barbara Habberjam (Minneapolis: University of Minnesota Press, 1986), 118.

15.   A graduate of the University of California, Berkeley, Luddy was also instrumental in bringing film studies to the university, hosting 16mm screenings in the basement of Alice Waters's home. Seymour Chatman, interview with the author, Berkeley, CA, 2001.

16.   Alison Smith, *Agnès Varda* (Manchester: Manchester University Press, 1998), 8.

17.   Jean Varda chronology from Stroman, *Art and Life of Jean Varda*, 6–11.

18.   Anaïs Nin, *The Diary of Anaïs Nin*, vol. 5, *1947–1945*, ed. Gunther Stuhlmann (New York: Harcourt Brace Jovanovich, 1971), 107.

19.   Elayne Wareing Fitzpatrick, *Traveling Backward: Curious Journeys and Quixotic Quests beyond the Youth of Old Age* (Bloomington, IN: Xlibris, 2009), 157.

20.   Fitzpatrick, *Traveling Backward*, 158.

21.   Catherine Coburn, "Monterey's Regional Cuisine Is Defined by Geographical Blessings and Cultural Influences," *Monterey County Weekly*, 16 July 1998, www.montereycountyweekly.com /news/local_news/monterey-s-regional-cuisine-is-defined-by -geographical-blessings-and/article_7c59b050-365c-53da-8f4e -4523ee51c9b6.html.

22.   Henry Miller, *Varda: The Master Builder* (Berkeley, CA: Circle Editions, 1947), 6–7.

23.   Miller, *Varda*, 4.

24.   Anaïs Nin, *The Diary of Anaïs Nin*, vol. 3, *1939–1944*, ed. Gunther Stuhlmann (Orlando: Harcourt Brace Jovanovich, 1969), 312–13.

25.   Rosalind Krauss, "In the Name of Picasso," *October*, no. 16 (1981): 20.

26. Krauss, "In the Name of Picasso," 19.

27. Quoted in Stroman, *Art and Life of Jean Varda*, 36.

28. Stroman, *Art and Life of Jean Varda*, 36.

29. Sergei Eisenstein defines *plasmaticness* as "like the primal protoplasm, not yet possessing a 'stable' form, but capable of assuming any form." Eisenstein, *Eisenstein on Disney*, trans. Alan Upchurch (New York: Methuen, 1988), 21.

30. Miller, *Varda*, 13.

31. Quoted in Stroman, "Jean 'Yanko' Varda: The Modern Alchemist," in Bogzaran, *Artists, Poets, and Visionaries of the S.S. Vallejo*, 31.

32. Gaston Bachelard, *The Poetics of Space*, trans. Maria Jolas (New York: Penguin Books, 1958), 49.

33. Bachelard, *Poetics of Space*, 49.

34. See Sandy Flitterman-Lewis, "The Gleaner and the Just," in *Situating the Feminist Gaze and Spectatorship in Postwar Cinema*, ed. Marcelline Block (Cambridge: Cambridge Scholars, 2008), 222.

35. Bachelard, *Poetics of Space*, 49.

36. Bachelard, *Poetics of Space*, 142.

37. "Agnès Varda Discusses Her Work in the Exhibition" (video), in *Agnès Varda in Californialand*, Los Angeles County Museum of Art, www.lacma.org/art/exhibition/agnes-varda-californialand (accessed 2 February 2020).

38. Quoted in Gow, "Underground River," 42.

39. Quoted in Stroman, *Art and Life of Jean Varda*, 4, 31.

Homay King is professor and Eugenia Chase Guild Chair in the Humanities in the Department of History of Art at Bryn Mawr College, where she cofounded the Program in Film Studies. She is the author of *Virtual Memory: Time-Based Art and the Dream of Digitality* (2015) and *Lost in Translation: Orientalism, Cinema, and the Enigmatic Signifier* (2010). Her work has appeared in *Afterall, Discourse, Film Quarterly, October,* and edited collections, including the exhibition catalog for the Metropolitan Museum of Art's *China: Through the Looking Glass* (2015). She is a member of the *Camera Obscura* editorial collective.

Figure 17. Varda Landing, Sausalito, California.
Photo by the author

Figure 1. Mary-Jane (Jane Birkin) and Lou (Lou Doillon)
in *Kung-fu Master!* (*Le petit amour*, France, 1988)

Agnès Varda, Jane Birkin, and *Kung-fu Master!*

Emma Wilson

White Flowers

In her documentary portrait of Jane Birkin, *Jane B. by Agnès V.* (*Jane B. par Agnès V.*, France, 1988), Agnès Varda included a sequence that explains the inspiration of her companion Birkin film, the fictional *Kung-fu Master!* (*Le petit amour*, France, 1988).[1] In the sequence in the documentary, Birkin talks about her own creative writing. She dreams up stories while she writes in the bathroom of her Paris house, the only place where she feels she is really alone. Birkin is heard speaking as the camera moves slowly round this wood-paneled Victorian bathroom, showing its monochrome photographs of her children, its perfume bottles (Penhaligon's Bluebell, Shalimar), and its vase of white flowers. This is an enclosed, regressive space, decorative and erotic.

The story inspiring *Kung-fu Master!* that Birkin recounts, composed in the bathroom, has the aura of erotic fantasy. Birkin relates: "C'est une femme comme moi, enfin moi, qui devient amoureuse d'un garçon" (The story is about a woman like me, in fact she is me. She falls in love with a very young man).[2] The faltering between a woman and herself, the imagining of a woman who is

Camera Obscura 106, Volume 36, Number 1
DOI 10.1215/02705346-8838529 © 2021 by *Camera Obscura*
Published by Duke University Press

herself, suggests how this is a story of wish fulfillment, fantasy, and the psyche. She says that the story finishes badly. This is part of its pleasure. She tells herself this story as if it were already in the past, "comme si c'était déjà un souvenir avant même d'avoir existé" (as though it were a memory before it happened). It is a lost love affair. These words are heard as the camera shows a photograph of Birkin and her daughters when they were younger. She says she likes the melancholy of the story. It is at a remove, relished peculiarly as if it is an event that is remembered. It is a story in the conditional, in the imperfect. It is a mirage, an island of memory.

Birkin daydreams about *cette fraîcheur* (translated oddly in the subtitles as "the spontaneity"), the freshness and youth of the boy. She is touched, troubled, by the boy's youngness. It seems loosely associated with the blossomy white flowers of the bathroom. The film lets her longing and her idealization of the boy be felt. But in *Jane B. by Agnès V.*, Varda, sitting beside Birkin on the stairs in her house, stroking a cat, says: "C'est ton enfance, c'est l'Angleterre que tu veux" (You want your family and England). Birkin's fantasy about a young boy is explained as part of her own nostalgia for her youth, her childhood in another country, which she seems to re-create in this Victorian house in France. "L'Angleterre," Albion, the world of Birkin's childhood, is conjured here as a rapturous, lost, *Alice in Wonderland* world.[3] It is recaptured in the bathroom, a little hothouse piece of England. Varda allows the fantasy to take shape; she lets it be nourished and nurtured in her film yet also lets the context, the root, of these feelings be glimpsed.

Birkin's imagined story was meant to be realized as one of the dramatized sequences of *Jane B. by Agnès V.*, but it grew large. It became its own parallel film. In prioritizing this story and pushing it to feature length, Varda opened it up for imagining with and beyond Birkin. She made it a fairy-tale, a feminist story about what women may imagine and eroticize, about the grief, pathos, damage, and beauty in this imagining.[4] The story was Birkin's, and the credits of the film remind us that this is made "d'après un récit de Jane Birkin" (from a story by Jane Birkin). But Varda wrote the script. She cites herself in the book *Varda par Agnès*: "Jane avait écrit la femme et rien d'autre. J'ai donc écrit le reste: l'adolescent (et le monde autour de lui)" (Jane had written the woman and nothing else. So I wrote the rest: the young boy [and the world around him]).[5] She created a narrative about very contemporary children caught between childhood and adulthood, absorbed by video games but encountering the realities of a world suddenly facing AIDS and its losses. This narrative became a vital part of Varda's film corpus and of her feminist investigations of different subjectivities and desires, of the affective worlds of contemporary women and children. It takes shape in her tenderness for Jane Birkin, but also in light of her own clearer thinking about childhood, nostalgia, and fantasy. In this film, Varda explored female-authored fantasies in delicate, unabashed, and queer ways. This is part of her feminist legacy for the future. *Kung-fu Master!* is key.

Me and You and Everyone We Know (2005)

At the time of the (belated) release of *Jane B. by Agnès V.* and *Kung-fu Master!* on DVD and in cinemas in the United States in 2015, Sandy Flitterman-Lewis described them as "two sparkling, exquisite mosaic-like objects that have been right in plain view all along, but practically unnoticed for several decades."[6] Writing about *Kung-fu Master!* previously, in 1996, she described it as "a film that neither advocates nor denigrates—but simply presents— the desire of a woman of thirty-nine for a fourteen-year-old boy."[7] Reviewing the films in the *New Yorker*, Richard Brody wrote of them as "two films that are as artistically audacious as they are original in their approach to sex and the female body."[8] If *Jane B.* has received more attention in the last few years, *Kung-fu Master!* is still less frequently discussed, its issues more radical and sensitive.

Varda spoke about the film in an interview with film-maker Miranda July in 2015.[9] July herself is a filmmaker who has explored the parallel lines of female sexuality and childhood subjectivities, notably in her debut feature film *Me and You and Everyone We Know* (US/UK, 2005). As she discusses *Kung-fu Master!* with Varda, it becomes clear that the earlier film was a point of reference for her own work. The alliance between the two films speaks of Varda's influential role for later female directors, in particular in her unorthodox, nonjudgmental take on female sexuality. The interview offers precious insight into the complexity and delicacy of Varda's feelings about the material she engaged with.

July begins: "Did you think that Jane's initial idea, and later the film, were really daring and that people would be shocked? Or was it so shrouded in Jane's kind of innocence that it didn't occur to either of you?" Varda replies, conceding about Jane: "She's totally innocent because she has the soul of a beautiful person." But she also continues, intriguingly: "I'm not proud, but I'm easy on what's happening, I don't know, I feel the way it goes, the way it goes about, I never really studied it, what effect the film had on me, on Jane. It happened, you know. And we felt it moving." She shows the film as an event, as something growing, moving, intuitive, that she and Jane were party to. This gives a vision of the film's strangeness. It happens like an encounter, an imaginary game. The film became possible as two different women worked together. Varda does not exclude the possibility that the effect of the film was difficult or damaging, but she is open to the film having happened. And she identifies "delicate feelings, things vaguely troubling and different." It is as if she opens her film to something uncertain and new.

July acknowledges a certain divide between fantasy and the world. She gives voice to the shock and liberation of the film, particularly viewed more recently: "I could totally understand how that woman would have that fantasy. Because I could relate in an intimate way it didn't seem daring, just very honest. But I live in the world and so it's almost like a horror movie, like 'Oh my goodness, is this allowed? How far can this love go?' And I was so impressed by how far it went without ever losing the beauty of it." The interview itself seems honest in its acknowledgment that the material is difficult and transgressive and in its recognition that the fantasy explored is familiar, delicate, painful, and angled toward beauty rather than toward violence or the violation of power. Varda and July together direct us to see the film as intuitive and freeing yet also disquieting, intimate, and fearless. I am interested here in how this is achieved and in the film's feminist future.

Inclinations

In her 2016 volume *Inclinations*, Adriana Cavarero offers an argument for thinking a relational ontology marked by a maternal and feminist critique of uprightness and rectitude.[10] Cavarero replaces rectitude with inclining, remarking that "to incline is to bend, to lean down, to lower" (3). For Cavarero, "inclination bends and dispossesses the *I*" (7), and she comments that "the most frequent and feared inclination, love, is an attack against the self's balance" (6). Her aims are vast as she moves against rectitude, uprightness, and their valuation in philosophical tradition, to envisage "a kind of subjectivity already caught up in folds, dependencies, exposures, dramas, knots, and bonds" (130). This is, for Cavarero, the maternal, and, developing a postural ethics, she highlights "maternal inclination—understood as a posture that is relational, originary, and asymmetrical, capable of evoking a common vulnerability" (127). A model for this is found in Leonardo da Vinci's painting *The Virgin and Child with Saint Anne* (ca. 1503–19), housed in the Louvre. Here the Virgin leans toward her child, inclining her body. Cavarero presents this image as a model for possibilities of involvement, interrelation, and attention to others. According to her, "Leonardo's painting gives the meaning of maternal inclination a special ethical density and a neat geometric linearity" (99). She continues, "The posture of self-sacrificing maternity thus becomes a figure that can keep in check the vertical system in general and the verticalized subject in particular" (102). She states clearly, "The interference of eros is out of the picture" (101).

Varda criticizes rectitude, at least posturally, as seen in her particular interest in the act of gleaning, bending over, and her interest more broadly in proneness and reclining.[11] Her work keeps the vertical in check and embraces a vulnerability similar to the kind illuminated by Cavarero.[12] Varda repeatedly shows us involved with one another in her films and conveys these relations as intricate, unexpected, and demanding. She looks toward embrace of these inclinations, this relationality. She is also a filmmaker who in her work turns to examples from painting to think of pose, ethics, and possibility.[13] Key to *Kung-fu Master!*, and to my argument about the film, are filmic images of women and children, images of maternity, of the Madonna and Child, that imagine different forms of interaction. This adoption of images of maternity is part of Varda's feminism. Her approach to these images is notably secular where she shows interest in the human emotions of love and pain they hold and locates her own work in a moving, formal, and aesthetic continuum with such images across time and media. If Varda pursues a feminist grappling with maternity, inclination, and involvement, one aspect of her work sets her apart from Cavarero. She does not bracket out sensuality and erotic love. She lets eros into the mix. She looks at the demands of a self-sacrificing maternity on women that exists at odds with the pursuit of their own affective and erotic lives. Varda is closer to the work of Jacqueline Rose, who argues in her essay "Mothers": "A mother is a woman whose sexual being must be invisible. She must save the world from her desire—a further projection that allows the world to conceal from itself the unmanageable nature of all human sexuality, and its own voraciousness."[14] It is this unmanageability that Varda makes her subject in *Kung-fu Master!* She presents it pictorially first in a reference to a surrealist painting and second in an extended exploration of images of the mother and child on film. Here she explores how maternal inclination and the interference of eros may coexist.

La Visite (1939)

Jane B. by Agnès V. offers a frame for *Kung-fu Master!* and shows Varda, as she sits on the stairs, revealing the boundaries she set around the production. Her own son, Mathieu Demy, actor in the film and Jane Birkin's fictional crush, will play a boy of his age and so will have his own world and language. Although the characters have a rendezvous at a hotel, there will be no sex. When *Jane B. by Agnès V.* alludes to the scene when the characters meet at the hotel, Varda cuts to a reproduction of a painting, *La Visite* (1939), by Belgian surrealist Paul Delvaux. The painting is seen against wallpaper or patterned fabric, with the effect that it seems, on the one hand, like an image on the wall of the hotel room we do not see and, on the other, like an image of what we do not see in the hotel room.

In the painting, a naked adolescent boy enters a room. He is small, and his still-smaller shadow is reflected against the wood of the open door. He has dark eyes and hair like Mathieu Demy. The room is strangely bare, except for a nineteenth-century chandelier, painted angels on the ceiling, and a naked adult woman sitting on a chair. She is shown as the larger figure, her presence emphasizing his littleness. She sits with her hands under her breasts as if she lays them out as gifts for him or touches them for her own pleasure. She is blonde and large eyed, alone in an anonymous room, crystallizing his fantasies. Her mature body and full hips, her adult femaleness, are in contrast to his youthful fragility. The room is strongly lit, the lighting throwing ethereal mauve shadows.

References to surrealist art appear frequently in Varda's work, and the inclusion of this image by Delvaux signals her interest in dream and reverie and its cross-media inspiration. The image is rare in Delvaux's corpus in showing within the frame a dreaming adolescent. The fantasies of this child self are materialized in Delvaux's dream images of a lost nineteenth-century world of naked women, railway tracks, moonlit cities, and forlorn interiors. More usually we see the dreams and not the dreamer. It is also unusual in surrealist art to show a male child, an *homme-enfant*, in contrast to the *femme-enfant* who so frequently offers a conduit to the unconscious. In cutting to the Delvaux painting, Varda pursues her engagement with interactions between film and the other arts. Delvaux offers a still, painted precursor image for her subject in *Kung-fu Master!* Her film is, like Delvaux's work, an exploration of reverie and fantasy, in spite of the film's apparent realist aesthetic.

The Delvaux image is enthralling. Cutting it into her film as she evokes *Kung-fu Master!*, Varda presents a still image that at once blocks and gives access to the feelings in her film.[15] If the painting apparently represents the fantasy of the male artist enraptured with the adult female body, Varda expands its meanings in alternate ways by aligning it with *Kung-fu Master!* The relay of looks between the woman and the boy in the painting is open to interpretation.[16] The surrealist dream painting can also figure the fantasy of an adult female, her eroticism, her maternity, as she feels her own breasts and receives the visit of this diminutive boy. She looks down at his body. This Felliniesque visit becomes, in the reframing of Delvaux by Varda, a female erotic fantasy.[17] This is to claim feminist film as a space to lay out different fantasies, to attend to conflicted feelings of pleasure and pain. Varda found a surrealist precursor for her subject and imagined new possibilities around the Delvaux scenario, already a variation on standard imagery of adult women with children.

Mother and Child

In *Kung-fu Master!* Julien (Mathieu Demy) is a visitor in Mary-Jane's (Jane Birkin's) house. The scenario of the Delvaux painting offers the coordinates of the film, but Varda also opens out to a further series of pictorial points of reference, creating in the house a *tableau vivant* of a modern Madonna and Child. It is the intrusion, the interference, of the visitor, Julien, in the house of a mother and her children that marks the subject and tension of the film.

Mary-Jane's smaller daughter, Lou (Lou Doillon), is ill in bed during the birthday party of her other, older daughter, Lucy (Charlotte Gainsbourg). Mary-Jane is in the house with her little girl but several times looks out the window at the teenagers partying outside in the courtyard. Varda cuts between the childhood interior, the shadowy house, and this outdoor space of adolescence, dancing, condoms, pranks, and drinking. Julien enters the house to go to the bathroom (a lavatory on the landing) and fill a condom as a water balloon. His act is at odds with the Victorian surroundings, the dark floral wallpaper, the painting of a naked woman with her lady's maid. He is an intruder in this antiquated, hyperfeminine space. The film cuts between the spaces of this Victorian family house, the bedrooms, the lavatory, showing different images of childhood and adolescence coexisting.

In one bedroom, in a Victorian storybook image, Mary-Jane comforts her littlest child. A fluted glass flower-shaded light casts honeyed shadows in the bedroom. There is a metal box with Snow White and the dwarves on the bedside table. Large stuffed bears and other soft creatures surround little Lou in bed. She is in helicopter-print pajamas. Her cheek appears flushed against the whiteness of her pillow. She seems glassy-eyed, feverish. Mary-Jane is seen close in the frame with her, whispering to her, stroking her hair. Soft in her paisley shirt, she is a living part of this benign space around Lou. Varda goes deep into the textures and threads of affection between mother and child, the fever and illness rarefying this moment and its drama. The images here resemble the interior imaginings of mothers and children in the work of the impressionists Mary Cassatt and Berthe Morisot, but Varda thinks spatially too, making this a moving, multisensory, nestling image (fig. 1).

The film cuts to Julien with his water balloon, adolescence and eroticism moving together in its bulbous watery form, its stretched glassy texture matching a crystal knob on the banisters. He climbs the stairs to Mary-Jane's perch at the window, dropping the full balloon on the head of a boy below. Mary-Jane is distracted by Julien. He is now sitting on the floor of her lavatory, queasy by the toilet bowl. He confesses that he drank too much. She kneels with him on the floor. A close-up image shows her two fingers reaching down his throat until he throws up in the toilet. His drunkenness and the odd intimacy of the fingers in the throat suggest a relationship that is more than maternal. She is complicit with him as she tells him to wash his face and offers him a clean shirt.

Framed by the bedroom door and the iron bed, the film now presents an image of Mary-Jane and Lou as a secular Madonna and Child, an image in its pose and composition recalling the tenderness of Duccio's images of the Virgin as Lou reaches for Mary-Jane's face. Yet the image of Lou at four also looks forward to Mary Cassatt's more prehensile capture of children held and sprawling. Mary-Jane is sitting up in bed and Lou is lying in her arms, reaching up to touch her. Birkin sings a lullaby, her sounds anticipating the loving lullaby to the dying Jacques Demy, "Démons et merveilles," in Varda's next film *Jacquot* (*Jacquot de Nantes*, France, 1991). Mary-Jane and Lou are seen by Varda's camera, caught on film in this image of maternity. Julien also watches them within the narrative (fig. 2).

He walks up the stairs and looks in on the pair from the doorway, hungover. He is a visitor to their world. His face softens as he watches Mary-Jane and Lou in their room together, Mary-Jane supporting her shoulder, Lou held, one leg resting on another. Her mother's fingertips graze her face. Mary-Jane looks up, glimpsing Julien. She sings to Lou the words of the lullaby, "Ô mon doux fiancé" (Oh my sweet love). They are words that speak to Julien, to this boy who visits their house, watching the maternal scenario in this idyllic room. Mary-Jane's awareness of him allows the Madonna image to open beyond the self-sacrificing maternity envisaged by Cavarero. Mary-Jane bends toward her child, inclines herself, and dandles her, but Julien's gaze ties Mary-Jane into a different nexus of relations, folds, and bonds. Mary-Jane, a young mother, sees how her love for her child is seen by an observer, an adolescent boy. She continues her cradling of Lou, but her acts are observed, and it seems that she feels this gaze upon her. And she is moved by it.

Julien continues watching as Lou settles down to sleep, Mary-Jane tucking her in and sliding out from under her, bringing Lou's legs around her body. The image is softly lit, its tones and mood matching the tenderness of Birkin's nursing. While inclined toward Lou, Mary-Jane speaks to Julien, telling him to go back to the others outside. She tells him not to say he was sick. Lou turns over, and Mary-Jane seems still fully focused on tucking in and cradling her child. But she is also arranging Julien's narrative, as if she already knows that something has happened. She has permitted his sickness, her intervention on his throat, his spellbound watching of her intimacy with Lou. But in encouraging him to pretend his visit did not happen, she prepares for it to pass as a secret, or a dream, or a dream within a dream.

Childhood Illness

This scene, the bedroom drama of the film, establishes the nurturing image of the Madonna as also amorous and erotic. The effect is achieved as the adolescent boy visits the house and remains poised at the doorway. The gentleness of Mary-Jane as loving mother is the source of his romantic and erotic feelings for her. The involvement of the maternal and the erotic is also indicated as part of a female fantasy, where Mary-Jane, while giving herself over to her ill child, can also become aware of and be troubled by the visitor to the house who observes this moment of intimacy. The feminism of the film comes in its claim that a mother may also feel desire and nourish fantasies. There is no sense that she is troubled by her own children. But an issue the film moves forward with is how far, for the mother, maternal energies, devotion, and sensory experience may also, in fantasy, become part of her desiring life. Varda takes an experience of tending and nursing, of intimacy, readily part of maternal experience, and asks what it means for this intensity to be pursued in a different, erotic context.

It is telling that the parameters of the film are established in two narratives of child and adolescent sickness and illness. Lou's fever keeps Mary-Jane at her bedside. Julien's vomiting makes him vulnerable, abashed, in Mary-Jane's house. Sickness and the sickbed are repeated motifs as the film continues and opens more spaces where scenarios of maternity and eroticism are explored. As the film goes on, Mary-Jane knocks Julien down in her car outside the school gates. She therefore has an excuse to take him to a café for their first exterior encounter together. She wants to take him to a pharmacy to treat his grazes. The pathos of his vulnerability, her damage of him, is part of their encounter. In a further example, he comes to visit Mary-Jane in her house on a Sunday, bringing jonquils, and she receives him with Lou. This time Mary-Jane is still in her pajamas, recalling bed and sleep. In a later scene, Julien is unwell and away from school. Mary-Jane finds an excuse to go visit him and enter his bedroom at his grandparents' house, where he lives because his parents are in Africa. A photograph of him with his mother is on the wall. Mary-Jane speaks to him with the tenderness she has used previously for Lou. She puts her arm around him and tells him not to be sad. She comments that he is in his pajamas and that she was in her pajamas when he came to visit. He puts his hand inside her blouse. She moves in toward him, and he puts his face against her breast, his cheek against her skin. She holds him in her arms, holding him close, maternal and erotic all at once, the scene sad and tender. He seems needy, pressed against her.

Georgiana M. M. Colville notes of this scene: "C'est la douceur maternelle de Mary-Jane envers la petite Lou malade qui attire d'abord Julien. Malade à son tour et recevant sa visite, il lui touche le sein et y enfouit son visage, geste plus évocateur d'un bébé voulant téter que des préliminaires de l'amour" (It is Mary-Jane's maternal tenderness toward little Lou when she is ill that first attracts Julien. Ill himself in turn and visited by her, he touches her breast and hides his face in it, a gesture more evocative of a baby that wants to suckle than the preliminaries of lovemaking).[18] If it is certainly Mary-Jane's maternal tenderness that attracts Julien, his move to touch her breast is more than a regressive, infant gesture. The scene holds exactly the tension of the film that takes a sacrosanct image of rapture between a mother and child, holds it up to the eye of an adolescent beholder, and repeats it with surreal persistence, where Julien seeks precisely to surpass Lou's dreamy attention to her mother and, as a lover, touch her breast. Varda opens up similarly structured scenes and shows Birkin's Mary-Jane walking mesmerized, as if drugged, from one to another. The sick-bed scene with Julien is followed immediately by a return to the bathroom where Birkin has said she tells herself this fantasy story. It may even be that this move undoes the reality of the scene that has just taken place, so it is framed as a fantasy Mary-Jane conjures in her bath. The cut to her naked, washing, crying, and hitting her own cheeks as if to wake herself up from this dream only underlines her own investment in this as love story.

In an interview included on the Ciné-Tamaris DVD edition of the film, Varda spoke about Birkin's fantasy involving "un adolescent maladif" (a sickly child), "tuberculeux si possible" (tubercular, if possible). She underlines the film as fantasy, the unwell boy as stereotype. In taking on this figure she also, unwittingly perhaps, recalls a motif of precursor works of maternal eroticism, in this case an incest narrative, Louis Malle's film of a mother and son, *Murmur of the Heart* (*Le souffle au coeur*, France/Italy/West Germany, 1971). Originally planned as an adaptation of Georges Bataille's 1966 novel *Ma mère*, Malle's film depicts a teenage son and his mother who inadvertently sleep with one another as they stay at a sanatorium, where he is treated for lung disease.[19] His Italian mother (Lea Massari) returns to the sanatorium drunk after an argument with her lover and makes love with her son. The film plays out as a critique of the bourgeois family, and also as a coming-of-age narrative where this transgression leads the boy to find a girl lover of his own and accede to manhood. Beyond Malle, the larger illness and issue of sexuality and terror that subtends *Kung-fu Master!* is AIDS, this new disease and risk.[20] Varda explores a fantasy of the tubercular boy but also looks out in the film to the imbrication of sexuality and illness in the contemporary world.[21]

"In This Kingdom by the Sea"

Murmur of the Heart takes mother/son incest as subject, where, by contrast, *Kung-fu Master!* plays out its maternal eroticism at one remove. Mary-Jane is a mother of daughters, and her house is a feminine space. Varda shows the mother and daughters somehow missing the masculine, the father and son. When Julien comes to the house with flowers sometime after the party, Mary-Jane and Lou are alone and lonely because Lucy is with her father and Lou's father has not come. In subsequent scenes, Julien is present with them in a new makeshift family. They go to video game arcades together and, in the film's most delirious flight of fantasy, depart for an island where, for a short summer, Mary-Jane and Julien, with Lou too, live out their love.

The strangest part of the film is this escape from reality to the island, a remote seaside space, a kingdom by the sea, associated with childhood and wildness.[22] Mary-Jane and Julien kiss in her parents' garden, in England. This location speaks of the nostalgic aspects of the affair, where Mary-Jane literally recovers a space of her own adolescence. She is denounced here for "détournement de mineur" (statutory rape) by her own adolescent daughter, Lucy. In this garden, the love between Mary-Jane and Julien is discovered, and its unlikely protector is Mary-Jane's mother, played by Birkin's own mother, actress Judy Campbell. Mary-Jane says: "I didn't do anything wrong, Ma," and her mother replies, "Of course you didn't." She continues, protective, "Let's not spoil the day for the little ones." And her solution is straight from an *Alice in Wonderland* childhood: "You must go to the island, of course. I'll give you the keys." For Flitterman-Lewis, "an almost breathtaking intimacy is created by these half-whispered words."[23] For Mary-Jane's mother, "love's the biggest mystery in life." For Varda, in her introduction to the film on the Ciné-Tamaris DVD: "Le désir a mille formes, mille ruses, mille mensonges" (Desire has a thousand forms, a thousand ruses, a thousand lies). She adds, closing the introduction, "Le désir est une île isolée dans la mer" (Desire is an island lost at sea).

In an opening to a new dimension in the film, Mary-Jane escapes to the island. She lives out her love here, forming with Julien and Lou together a strange recomposed family. They sleep in sleeping bags, Julien and Mary-Jane zipped in one. They cry like birds on the beach and make omelets from the eggs they find on the rocks. This is a wild, seashore world, salty, windblown, remote, barren, an idyllic adventure space where the boundaries between adult and child are crossed. This is a childhood holiday remembered in adult retrospection, in fantasy. For Colville, in Varda's films, "ses couples font l'amour hors champ. L'idylle entre Mary-Jane et Julien reste crédible et poétique, car ils n'échangent que des baisers, même dans l'île" (her couples make love off-screen. The idyll between Mary-Jane and Julien remains credible and poetic, because they only exchange kisses even on the island).[24] In this enchanted space, nothing beyond a kiss is seen, the film keeping true to a childish vision of love and romance, the fantasy skirting the erotic acts that make it taboo, and the film refusing to expose or compromise the adolescent actor Mathieu Demy. But, already, the dream is fraying at the edges on the island. Mary-Jane says to Julien that she is too old for him. Around this precarious family the tide comes in too quickly. An information leaflet about AIDS is thrown out into the sea, a message in a bottle.

This unraveling only moves more rapidly when they return from the island. The last part of the film undoes Mary-Jane's love and her own family. As Brody wrote: "The romance is filmed as if in the conditional tense, fusing its fantasy with a clear-eyed view of its recklessly dangerous impracticality."[25] As Mary-Jane recounts, as soon as they are back from the island Julien is snatched away from her. She is turned into a monster. In this transmogrification she is confronted by Julien's mother (Sabine Mamou, who also plays mother to the child Mathieu Demy in *Documenteur*), returned from

Africa. Mary-Jane loses Julien, and in part she loses her daughters: Lucy moves to live with her father, and Lou stays with Mary-Jane during the school year but not for vacations. It seems a deep tragedy that this family should come apart. And Mary-Jane is shown melancholy in Paris alone in the summer, wondering if Julien loved her and if he has now forgotten her. Even now she is oddly lovesick.

A Family Affair

In her Ciné-Tamaris introduction to the film, Varda acknowledged that her husband, Jacques Demy, Mathieu's father, had some qualms about the project: "Jacques Demy, son père, se posait des questions" (Jacques Demy, his father, wasn't sure). Her fourteen-year-old son also didn't immediately jump at the role: "Mathieu hésitait" (Mathieu was hesitant). But once Charlotte Gainsbourg, who was sixteen, signed up to play Lucy, and it was clear that Lou Doillon would act as well, Mathieu took the part. As Varda put it: "On a dit on va tourner en famille" (We decided to make it a family affair). Speaking about the experience for herself and Jane and what it meant to work with their own children, she said, disarmingly: "Il est magnifique d'avoir des images de nos enfants à des moments éphémères" (It's great to have footage of our children from those fleeting moments). The comment speaks of the pathos of a mother looking back, nostalgic for some living images of her once small children. The humility and craving here, the pleasure in images of fleeting moments from childhood, express some aspect of maternity. They let us glimpse the intoxication of working as a filmmaker. Lived, imagined childhood acts, caught on film, become their own island of memory. The film holds for Varda, and for Birkin, "des souvenirs extraordinaires" (wonderful memories). But Varda acknowledged too that the experience might have been different for the children: "Pour eux je ne sais pas" (For them I don't know). She also seemed willing to leave this question open.

   Kung-fu Master! is radical in its focus on a woman's erotic fantasy and also in its willingness to follow this through and see what it looks like. That fantasy is in strange ways bound up with memories from childhood, nostalgia for a lost, storybook world, and also with the intensities of maternity, with the acts of intimacy, love, and care that emerge in the specific embodied experience of motherhood. The film imagines a different family, without the father, with an adolescent boy offering a different, stranger, more transgressive relation to female maternity and to desire for the adult female subject. He is part of her family and plays with her children, and she remains magical, a fantasy figure bathed in his love.

Kung-fu Master!, with its focus on fantasy, dream, transgression, and desire, casts light on Varda as a daughter of the surrealists, of Delvaux and others, whose mad loves, dollhouses, lost-object worlds she rearranges in the feminine to teach us something about, in Rose's words, the unmanageable nature of all human sexuality. Varda's stringency and delicacy, her ability to pursue what may seem sick and strange and to see its beauty and its simultaneous unlivability, its truth and sadness, are unique. And, with her characteristic capaciousness of thinking, Varda also offers new pictorial imaginings of motherhood, new secular Madonna images, a new tenderness as her camera observes Jane Birkin with her own children. These images are an archive of her own and Birkin's feelings for their children, now all grown.

Childhoods are left behind. Mothers observe their children age and change with dizzying quickness. Varda's film pays attention to the grief, enchantment, and self-indulgent love around this. It dallies with taboo feelings, puts them in the open, to let them be visible, expressed, and overcome. *Kung-fu Master!* shows both maternity and love as attack on the self's balance. It shows what this feels like, for women, with unrepenting clarity.

Notes

1. The film is named for a video game played by Julien, the teenage boy protagonist.

2. Translations of film dialogue are taken directly from the subtitles on the Ciné-Tamaris editions of *Jane B. par Agnès V.* and *Kung-fu Master!*

3. Varda explores Jane's childhood memories in *Jane B. by Agnès V.* while showing her childhood photographs.

4. In this way, the film might be aligned with Jacques Demy's *Donkey Skin* (*Peau d'âne*, France, 1970) as a fairy-tale working-through of incestuous and intergenerational relations.

5. Agnès Varda, *Varda par Agnès* (Paris: Cahiers du cinéma et Ciné-Tamaris, 1994), 186.

6. Sandy Flitterman-Lewis, "Agnès Varda's Brilliant Alchemy," sleeve notes, *Two Films by Agnès Varda Starring Jane Birkin: Jane B. par Agnès V. / Kung-fu Master!* (1988; Los Angeles, CA, Cinelicious Pics, 2015), Blu-ray.

7. Sandy Flitterman-Lewis, *To Desire Differently: Feminism and the French Cinema*, expanded ed. (New York: Columbia University Press, 1996), 342.

8. Richard Brody, "Family Affair," *New Yorker*, 1 February 2016, 8.

9. "Agnès Varda in Conversation with Miranda July," sleeve notes, *Two Films by Agnès Varda.*

10. Adriana Cavarero, *Inclinations: A Critique of Rectitude* (Stanford, CA: Stanford University Press, 2016).

11. See Emma Wilson, *The Reclining Nude: Agnès Varda, Catherine Breillat, and Nan Goldin* (Liverpool: Liverpool University Press, 2019).

12. Varda also has an interest in images of the life of the Virgin Mary, notably images of the Annunciation.

13. In discussing Varda's reference to paintings in this article, I am inspired by Rebecca J. DeRoo's important study *Agnès Varda: Dialogues among Film, Photography, and Art* (Oakland: University of California Press, 2018).

14. Jacqueline Rose, "Mothers," *London Review of Books* 36, no. 12 (2014), www.lrb.co.uk/the-paper/v36/n12/jacqueline-rose /mothers/.

15. She uses the same strategy in *The Beaches of Agnes* (*Les plages d'Agnès*, France, 2008), where she cuts to a Picasso portrait of a weeping Dora Maar, *Femme en pleurs* (*Weeping Woman*, 1937), as she speaks of her period of separation from Jacques Demy. For discussion of this sequence, see Dominique Bluher, "Autobiography, (Re-)enactment and the Performative Self-Portrait in Varda's *Les Plages d'Agnès / The Beaches of Agnes*," *Studies in European Cinema* 10, no. 1 (2013): 59–69, 66.

16. For Georgiana M. M. Colville, "dans *Jane B.*, un tableau de
Paul Delvaux, où un jeune garçon et une femme mûre, nus,
se dévorent des yeux, annonce leur désir réciproque" (in *Jane
B.*, a painting by Paul Delvaux where a young boy and an adult
woman, naked, look intently at one another, announces their
reciprocal desire). Colville, "Autoportraits d'une autre: *Jane
B. par Agnès V.* et *Kung-fu Master!*," in *Agnès Varda: Le cinéma et
au-delà*, ed. Antony Fiant, Roxane Hamery, and Éric Thouvenel
(Rennes: Presses Universitaires de Rennes, 2009), 147;
translation mine.

17. My reference is to Fellini's *Amarcord* (Italy/France, 1973), where a
tobacconist (Maria Antonietta Beluzzi) lets the boy Titto (Bruno
Zanin) under the blind of her shop and shows him her breasts.

18. Colville, "Autoportraits d'une autre," 153.

19. See Justine Malle, "Amère victoire: Les projets non réalisés de
Louis Malle," *Positif*, no. 538 (2005): 103–6.

20. In a recent commemorative piece, Birkin pointed out that AIDS
entered the story at Varda's insistence: "At the time AIDS was in
the headlines and she insisted we deal with it in the film. This
was Agnès; she was very opinionated about things and if she was
working on something and there was an issue that was current,
she felt you had to mention it." "Agnès Varda Remembered by
Jane Birkin," *Guardian*, 16 December 2019, www.theguardian.com
/film/2019/dec/16/agnes-varda-remembered-by-jane-birkin/.

21. I'm grateful to Homay King for remarking on the ways Varda
may be offering new versions of the Oedipus myth, reminding
me of how Varda is also interested in antiquity. This interest is
evident in *Jane B. by Agnès V.*, where Varda casts Birkin as Ariadne
in a retelling of the myth of the Minotaur. I hope to look more
closely at Varda's engagement with antiquity in
future work.

22. Islands and beaches have a particular value in Varda's affective
world, seen in the valuation of the island of Noirmoutier, where
she had a house with Jacques Demy, which she films in *Jacquot*; in
the Belgian beaches of her childhood featured in *The Beaches of
Agnès*; and in the mother-and-son world of Venice Beach figured
in *Documenteur* (France/US, 1981).

23. Flitterman-Lewis, *To Desire Differently*, 346.

24. Colville, "Autoportraits d'une autre," 153.

25. Brody, "Family Affair," 8.

Emma Wilson is professor of French literature and the visual arts at the University of Cambridge and a fellow of Corpus Christi College. She has written on Varda in her two most recent books, *Love, Mortality, and the Moving Image* (2012), where she considers *Jacquot de Nantes* and *Les plages d'Agnès,* and *The Reclining Nude: Agnès Varda, Catherine Breillat, and Nan Goldin* (2019), where she looks at figures of reclining women across Varda's films.

Figure 2. Julien (Mathieu Demy) in *Kung-fu Master!* (*Le petit amour,* France, 1988)

Figure 1. Becoming-imperceptible: *Visages Villages* (*Faces Places*, dir. Agnès Varda and JR, France, 2017) and *Varda by Agnès* (*Varda par Agnès*, dir. Agnès Varda, France, 2019)

She Listened: Vardian Self-Portraiture and Auto-Refrains of Sea, Wind, and Sand

Nadine Boljkovac

We filmed . . . a sequence to show that the tomb is near the sea. . . . This small cat who was so important to our lives took on another dimension with the tomb. . . . Seen from further away, she was like any human. Minuscule in the universe.
—Agnès Varda, *Varda by Agnès*

What does *to be* listening, *to be* all ears, as one would say "to be in the world," mean?
—Jean-Luc Nancy, *Listening*

The wind is rising! . . . We must try to live!
—Paul Valéry, "The Graveyard by the Sea"

Camera Obscura 106, Volume 36, Number 1
DOI 10.1215/02705346-8838541   © 2021 by *Camera Obscura*
Published by Duke University Press

Backward at Low Tide. Right to Left . . .

At one hour, three minutes, and twenty-four seconds into Agnès Varda and JR's *Visages Villages* (*Faces Places*, France, 2017), the two directors face the sea amid swirling sand and wind. As a hand-held camera cuts closer, this landscape effects the film's most immersive image, offering new movement to a series of *tableaux vivants* that have hitherto shown the two directors seated in long and static shots with their backs to the camera, frequently facing bodies of water. As it newly repeats a Vardian trope of chairs on a beach, this moving image sequence—the last of Varda's filmic life when renewed in her final film, *Varda by Agnès* (*Varda par Agnès*, France, 2019)—serves as an exemplary sequence of her feminist, ethical, and ecological multimedia career.[1]

Eventually engulfed by this world of sea, wind, and sand, Varda and JR disappear in the blur. Decades earlier, Marguerite Duras's screenplay, realized in Alain Resnais's film *Hiroshima mon amour* (*Hiroshima My Love*, France/Japan, 1959), describes a meeting and brief love affair between an anonymous French woman, She, and an anonymous Japanese man, He: "In the beginning of the film we don't see this chance couple. Neither her nor him."[2] In place of any definable human body or coupling of bodies, *Hiroshima mon amour*'s sensual portrayal of a woman's becoming-imperceptible or opening to the world expresses a process that touches on questions of survival as actualized across and between bodies and surfaces of skin.[3] A lifelong commitment to realizing doublings—such as that between materiality and immateriality—pervades Varda's works and those of her close friends and collaborators, Resnais and Chris Marker. These extremes, which extend from the personal to universal, and back, manifest through Varda's oeuvre.

This "perpetual and reverberating dialectic," as Sandy Flitterman-Lewis writes, this "continual interchange between historical context and issues of the female self in society at every stage of Varda's work," corresponds with dyad relations articulated through her artistry.[4] Moments from its end, *The Beaches of Agnès* (*Les plages d'Agnès*, dir. Agnès Varda, France, 2008) cuts to shots of Varda seated outdoors at a table seen from medium- and long-shot distances, with sea beyond, work afore, and camcorder behind. While printed photos take flight in the wind and as she attempts to grasp fleeing pages, the film cuts as she closes her large book and eyeglasses case to the next frontal medium shot that finds Varda at her desk indoors with a seascape painting behind. Varda's voice-over reveals her far-reaching concerns: "Often I stop writing. The world's in bad shape and I'm overwhelmed."

The Beaches of Agnès cuts to a striking image of the painting: its bottom fourth, a golden shore, lies beneath a royal blue sea; its waves reach toward sky. "At this very moment, disasters, wars, earthquakes. I sit in safety and imagine those situations. People without shelter, entire families on the road. I sit motionless and think of my dear ones," Varda's voice-over persists. Moving images of her children with their children surface across the painting's blue yonder with sands beneath and against a score, the sounds of which Varda reserves for moments in her works that approach nearest the heart. "Family is a somewhat compact concept," Varda's voice continues. "We mentally group everyone together and imagine them as a peaceful island." A cut finds Varda in a medium-long shot at the same desk yet screen-left, her body and face inclined away from the camera toward the wall opening that sees beyond into her courtyard, where a superimposed close shot of Jacques Demy materializes as cello and piano play. In rhythm with the flows of Varda's memory, Demy's face fades as the next cut discovers Varda's frame passing through, at "low tide," the factory curtain of heavy plastic slats from her installation *Le Passage du Gois* (France, 2006, *L'île et elle* exhibition), which re-creates the passage from island to mainland. "Visitors had to go through a filter," Varda explains in conversation with Hervé Chandès, Fondation Cartier's director. "They had to wait for low tide to go into the exhibition," Chandès adjoins. "Then," Varda continues, "the barrier lifted. You entered the island and my world."

Varda strides silently toward an unseen handheld camera whose backward movement recalls Varda's own steps and handheld camera in *The Gleaners and I* (*Les glaneurs et la glaneuse*, France, 2000) and elsewhere. With another cut, she enters the first of various film shacks she created from celluloid film stock, *Ma cabane de l'Échec* (*My Shack of Failure*, 2006, *L'île et elle* exhibition, which was followed by variations showcased at the Lyon Biennale, 2009; Los Angeles County Museum of Art, 2013; and Galerie Nathalie Obadia, 2018), the walls of this cabin composed of footage reels from Varda's 1966 film, *The Creatures* (*Les créatures*, France). A hand-held camera yet watches. Located within this thoroughly self-made house of cinema, Varda poses with one foot atop a pile of film reel canisters. *The Beaches of Agnès* concludes here, with Varda in her filmic home, prior to the film's spirited and humorous epilogue with Varda at home on the rue Daguerre.

With works that celebrate the material world in its myriad forms and scales, from a beloved button to a bottomless sea, Varda developed a method of empathetic engagement premised on listening. Her encounters grasped relations extending from a person, family, or group, to a greater world-memory and duration comprising "us" all. As it heeds these layers of world, this article considers subjectification processes that fold into a self all elements of nature.

Building upon Dominique Bluher's perceptive remarks regarding Vardian self-portraiture vis-à-vis Jean-Luc Nancy's texts, "The Look of the Portrait" and *L'Autre Portrait* (*The Other Portrait*),[5] these pages shift toward Nancy's thoughts on listening and the "formation of a subject first of all as the rhythmic reployment/deployment of an enveloping between 'inside' and 'outside.'"[6] Beyond any "gap and tension,"[7] this intersubjective folding produces another doubling movement, as between processes of separation and creation, "division and participation, de-connection and contagion," all of which, as Anthony Gritten notes, simultaneously "drives the subject towards itself (referral) and divides or separates it from itself (resonance)."[8] When listening in this mode, as Nancy suggests, quoting from Wagner's *Parsifal*, "time becomes space."[9] This externalization of a subject's becoming-other—beyond what/who she was, toward a becoming-imperceptible—exists alongside an internalization of that subject. With regard to the subject's increasing awareness of its instantaneous interiority and existence within a larger network, we might speak of a coupling process that corresponds to the event of cinema that folds us within its folds.[10]

As processes of individuation, acts of looking and listening correspond to a subject's constitution as inextricably tied to the temporality of a (self-)portrait and Gilles Deleuze's thoughts on desert islands: the "élan that draws humans toward islands extends the double movement that produces islands in themselves."[11] Bluher, Cybelle H. McFadden, and others find the "figuration of the look" and the "gaze of the beholder" useful as they stress the reflexivity of Varda's works.[12] This article concurs with these significant reflections, particularly regarding an extended reflexivity that stresses Varda's relations with others, as it embraces this inward-outward dimension, a quality Varda refers to in this article's opening epigraph as she reflects on Zgougou's tomb: "Seen from further away, she [Varda's late cat] was like any human. Minuscule in the universe."

From farther away, Varda and Deleuze's early encounters with islands resonate with one another. Their cine-philosophies express "the relation of sensation and imagination to location,"[13] processes that pertain to intimate experiences of life and that can potentially open to sight a greater beyond. Through qualities of humility, grace, and, finally, an abandonment of self and set identities, a seismic shift in subjectification might be realized along with a fundamental change in how we live. At times overwhelmed by global conflicts, but always buttressed by instances of new life, Varda celebrates kindred spirit Pierre Soulages's *outrenoir* practice of painting primarily in black throughout his career during the fourth episode of her five-part miniseries, *Agnès de ci de là Varda* (*Agnès Varda: From Here to There*, France, 2011).

"A beached whale. Angry at the state of the world," Varda's voice-over explains approximately fifteen minutes into this fourth episode, as footage of her video installation, *La mer . . . etSETEra* (*The Sea . . . etSETEra*), at the tenth Lyon Biennial ("The Spectacle of the Everyday," 2009) appears. Her installation, composed of beach chairs on sand facing a screen, centers on the video of the seaside. Against its audible and visible waves, the video cuts to an image of a now deserted beach with sea beyond and a superimposed image of an Orcus mouth centered in the shot. A frame within a frame emerges, a *mise en abyme* as in countless Vardian works as her practice of layering one life—memory, moment, and image—within another abounds and repeats the folding, unfolding, and refolding processes of subjectification.

Surrounded by darkness and also the brightness of the chairs and screen's light, this shot in the fourth *Agnès de ci de là Varda* episode centers the installation's screen within "our" screen. In the earlier *The Beaches of Agnès*, at its thirty-six-minute mark, and later in *Varda by Agnès*, the installation's video cuts from a long shot of this fabricated whale on a beach—the same whale of a tent in whose "belly" Varda reclines in *The Beaches of Agnès* amid fabrics as vibrant as Varda's own—to a shot of an Orcus mouth. With its recurring shots of the whale across Varda's works, the camera routinely enters this "hell" that presages Varda's thoughts of global horrors.

A montage of suffering follows the Orcus and reveals glimpses of the plights of countless anonymous people: drowning and drowned migrants, mutilated corpses, murdered children. And yet, with every reiteration of this montage across Varda's works, she senses a reprieve inasmuch as she feels "safe in the belly of this whale. Sheltered from the world, sheltered from the coastal wind, inside my coastal shelter." As Varda asserts in another instance of the film, "Time has passed, and passes, except on the beaches, which are timeless." Despite all terrors, she insists that a sea and its beaches beckon toward an ethics of ecological, worldly engagement. For here lies a blank slate and canvas, an "empty horizon," as Soulages tells Varda, through which one might find discretion, vitality, energy, and, perhaps, peace to recommence anew.

A sea and its beach—or an island—are, as Varda repeatedly claims in *Varda by Agnès*, "a place of inspiration. A mental landscape." Through its reflective surface, a sea gives us ourselves; as blank canvases, we lose ourselves to become its pure consciousness. This process of frightening yet luminous perception offers greatest potential when we think, see, and listen beyond narcissistic reflections to selflessly, openly discern time and the planet itself. If humans were, as Deleuze writes, "sufficiently separate, sufficiently creative, they would give the island only a dynamic image of itself, a consciousness of the movement which produced the island, such that through them the island would in the end become conscious of itself as deserted and unpeopled. The island would be only the dream of humans, and humans, the pure consciousness of the island."[14]

These movements exceed a notion of mirroring or reflexivity alone. One might extend McFadden's persuasive insights, for instance, with respect to the "carefully layered reflexive elements of the opening sequence [of *The Beaches of Agnès* that] not only draw attention to ways of seeing but also highlight the *limits* of vision—the boundaries that are set by the filmmaker." "Varda demonstrates," McFadden continues, "that what we see is always already mediated in some way: the overabundance of picture frames on the beach is a playful way for Varda to draw attention to the frame of the film, that which demarcates what the spectator sees onscreen."[15] To open McFadden's observations further, the surface of a sea, its beaches and islands across Varda's art, correspond with nothing less than "the depth of bodies and the height of ideas":[16] the sorrows that haunt Varda as well as those promises of imagination she holds dear, of "inspiration, creation, sharing," the "words that guide me," as Varda declares in *Varda by Agnès*.

In keeping with the spirit of Varda's practice, the notion of a limit could also be reconceived, as might thoughts of any separation between the artist, screen, and spectator and their affective encounters. As she insists in *Varda by Agnès*, "The opposite of a wall is a beach." Of course, Varda not only joyfully re-created beaches; she also repurposed and recycled walls, frames, and conceptual limits, as well as all manner of treasured refuse between art and life. She frequently experimented with and between these forms and artifacts, as evidenced in her *Le triptyque de Noirmoutier* (*The Triptych of Noirmoutier*, three 35mm films on three folding wooden screens, 2004–5), a piece, among others, that defies fixed perspective and pure formalism. Among these works, her 2003 photographic installation, *La mer immense* (*The Immense Sea*), transitions in scale from a snapshot of the sea Varda took in Noirmoutier to an instance of image-becoming-environment. Through an experience of the installation, visitors were to feel "as if [they] could actually set foot in the sand," as Varda explains in a 2012 interview with Thomas Delamarre for Fondation Cartier.[17] With a much smaller reproduction of the same photo framed in gold and placed next to a large-scale image, *La petite mer immense* (*The Immense Small Sea*), Varda suggests not only means for contemporary photography's use or consumption but also the aforementioned sustained doubling, a duality which, as Yvette Bíró suggests, "characterises Varda's vision: the intimacy and the magnitude of the experience, the enframed boundlessness."[18]

A beach and its sea: their surfaces also embody, as James Williams writes with regard to a surface itself, the "limits or borders of things . . . where identity breaks down and becomes other."[19] Varda repeatedly multiplies perceptive surfaces as her works push fixed notions of identities to their limits. Her practice exposes restrictions of gender, race, and other "norms," and their power in/exclusions, as it challenges the notion of a self and urges us to listen and see further.

In line with Varda's lifelong commitment to new forms of making visible the invisible through fragmentation, montage, and collage, and her embrace of a sea as a groundless source of inter-subjective relations, limits transform via her works into reflective, dissolving surfaces. Varda's evocative, nonrepresentational means recall Jean-François Lyotard's thoughts on poetry that materializes absences and "brings the sensory into itself: no longer speaking only through its signification, it expresses through its blanks."[20] Soulages's empty horizon. Varda's mental landscape. From this view of Varda's personal yet vast vision, McFadden's remarks ring truer. Varda's strategy deliberately destabilizes conventional perspectival and perceptual relations, as McFadden delineates: the "reflections and the images within the mirrors' frames, coupled with movement, disorientate the spectator, since the image source seems to shift as its reflection does. Since the spectator is unable to see both the origin and the reflection simultaneously, it becomes challenging to distinguish between the two."[21] This effect seems, again, to be Varda's aim.

The notion of a sea as empty horizon gives way too, to the reflective "blank" surfaces of Soulages's black paintings: "When I started doing these paintings, I realized I wasn't working with black. I was working with light reflecting off different surfaces of black.

It's shiny in some places, muted in others. Muted, or rhythmic . . . depending. . . . I invented a word meaning 'beyond black,' 'beyond black light.' That word was *outrenoir*. *Outrenoir* designates, finally, a mental space not an optical phenomenon." During her interview and filming of Soulages, who faces Varda's camera in a close shot against the black of his paintings as he voices these words, Varda's unsurprising responses pertain to her foremost thoughts of survival and seas. She, who vitally embodies an energy of *outrefemme*, proposes the terms *outre-tombe* and *outre-mer*, a beyond of grave and sea.

With these waves, seas, sands, and winds of time, Varda's later works incessantly reflect on her own aging as they reveal a growing consciousness of self within world and universe, of life that precedes and persists beyond any single life. "The Desert Island," quoted above, one of Deleuze's earliest writings, found and published posthumously, "move[s] the center of subjectivity in the perceiver to the island itself as creative force," writes Tom Conley.[22] "Inhabitation, or a sense of being and becoming-in-the-world," he continues, "begins when the illusion of mastery of the island is renounced in favor of letting the space realize a consciousness of its own."[23] A self-portrait, a perception of oneself in time and space, offers more than a personal history and narrative, even one as remarkable as Varda's. Through her self-portraiture, and with sustained awareness of the "hundreds of thousands of people" she doesn't know, as she murmurs to us during *Agnès de ci de là Varda*, Varda attains an anonymity, an imperceptibility and oneness, with processes that exceed a narcissistic closed relation, or one merely between herself and another. Varda's invitation to listen extends even to whispers and murmurs of time, as embodied by a sea and revered by Varda and Paul Valéry. In Valéry's words, the sea is "the only intact and most ancient thing in the world," from whence life came and to which it will return.[24]

Of these murmurs and Varda's sonorous femininity, So Mayer ruminates:

How can one translate the bilingually punning title of [Varda's] 1981 documentary about murals, *Mur Murs*? Perhaps "whispers of walls," the way a mural calls out to the passerby the secrets of the community it lives in. To such whispers, Varda's ears attend and call the viewer to become fully an audience by doing the same. That associative, often punning logic shapes the voiceovers that frame both fiction features such as 1977's *One Sings, the Other Doesn't* (delivered by Varda herself) and 1981's *Documenteur* (delivered by her collaborator, actor and filmmaker Delphine Seyrig) and her late documentaries. It is still rare that a woman's voice takes up the space of the voiceover; when Varda made *Mur Murs* and *One Sings . . .* that was truer still.[25]

To global sorrows, and even the whispers of the elements themselves, Varda's ears attend. An image of Varda on a beach reveals this consciousness of herself within an oft troubled world. She so thoroughly inhabits the resonances of beaches that they have, as Varda famously claims in *The Beaches of Agnès*, informed her self-formation and universalization: "If one opened me up, one would find beaches."

With regard to Deleuze but with equal significance for Varda, Conley submits that the "island becomes an enchanted space where concept continually moves in all directions and reinvents itself."[26] A beach surfaces globally, as in Varda's installations, and locally, as Varda frequently faces a reflective sea. Her memories of "all the times I marched with others," as Varda recalls in *The Beaches of Agnès* and *Varda by Agnès*, exemplify these outer and inner folds of world and self. With characteristic humor and in homage to a drawing by Jean-Jacques Sempé, the accompanying high-angle shot of Varda at a street protest discovers her with a placard that reads "J'AI MAL PARTOUT" (I HURT EVERYWHERE).

Worldly dimensions of Varda's art also emerge through listening to the auto-refrains of sea, wind, and sand that she encounters and repeats. For Nancy, as for Varda and Deleuze, the point is "not just that listening is a matter of ethics, but that it is an ontological issue concerning the sense of the world" and its time.[27] This "sonorous time," as Nancy suggests, "takes place immediately according to a completely different dimension, which is not that of simple succession. . . . It is a present in waves on a swell, not in a point on a line; it is a time that . . . becomes or is turned into a loop, that stretches out or contracts."[28] Near the end of her life, and

Figure 2. "The island and my world," *The Beaches of Agnès*
(*Les plages d'Agnès*, France, 2008)

her final film, *Varda by Agnès*, Varda's voice-over echoes: "Things
are double. Even as I enjoy the gentle seascape, I know the world is
filled with war, violence, suffering, and wandering."

Through its openness to the world, her art seems a Möbius
movement from the familiar to the cosmic and back as it gleans
intimate experiences through a compassionate global embrace.
This perception turned outward, and hence inward, distinguishes
Varda's searching presence in her art as a central yet modest persona. Along this line, a Varda work often bears her name in its title
and inherently embodies aspects of her personal experiences, while
her omnipresence celebrates a greater awareness through which
she herself becomes "minuscule in the universe." Particularly in her
later works, Varda's now-famed identity seems a matter of course as
it also gestures to a future that finally witnessed the movement her
works so often foretell: that of a self's full dissolution into memory
and world and, in Varda's case, the becoming-imperceptible, or
becoming-minuscule, of a woman whose loving openness to life
became complete on 29 March 2019 in her ninetieth year.[29]

To follow backward movements with Varda, in its concluding minutes, *Varda by Agnès* recalls her monumental installation, *Hommage aux Justes de France* (2007), that honors those who, during France's Occupation, sought to protect Jewish lives, an installation crucially assessed by Flitterman-Lewis.[30] Varda's recognition of these countless people testifies to their selfless acts and embraces of life, and hers. Her thoughts extend to all vulnerable individuals and repeat throughout her works, as demonstrated in the twenty-sixth minute, third episode, of *Agnès de ci de là Varda*, which leads to an encounter with Christian Boltanski's plaintive works, and most notably his Grand Palais installation, *Personnes* (*People*, France, 2010).

Within this third episode of *Agnès de ci de là Varda*, her remembrances of children and beaches return. A black-and-white video image of Boltanski appears, and Varda explains: "This is a self-morphing video portrait." A wind blows across the portrait seen projected against a draped fabric that slowly ripples in a breeze. Against these tangible movements and Varda's voice-over, Boltanski's adult face transitions and, in moments, returns to his childhood face. As Boltanski speaks, the episode cuts from a long shot of this face as depicted across time to Varda's courtyard and home on the rue Daguerre. "My mind wanders," Varda's voice-over once more murmurs, "to the children behind veils in Malakoff." Grayscale projections of other children's faces fill the screen with an ephemerality accentuated by flowing gauzes. "The breeze gently makes them disappear and return," Varda continues. A rapid pan left skirts from one child's face to another: "Children in memory." With a jump cut and zoom closer, one child's portrait dissolves into another on the words, "Children almost lost." Varda's voice-over halts as the camera lingers on a child's indistinguishable face that morphs into another's. From here, the episode encounters the *Personnes* installation. This, too, is where Varda's last film, *Varda by Agnès*, grafts itself in as it repeats Varda's description: "Hundreds of anonymous people, gone and forgotten, inspired this Boltanski installation that I filmed."

At last, at one hour and fifty-three minutes into *Varda by Agnès*, the film stages a prophetic return to the stormy *Visages Vil-*

lages moments with which this article opened, and that became the final moments of her final film: "At one point, JR and I imagined ending the film this way. Disappearing in a sandstorm. I think this is how I'll end this chat. Disappearing in the blur. Leaving you." A doubling of the personal and cosmic, that quality that so singularizes Varda, emanates through this weave of her art and life. As a chiasmatic double herself who effected encounters that brought extremes into contact, Varda demonstrated a concern for the future of the world that persisted alongside an awareness of her own mortality.

Kelley Conway and others have noted that Varda "looks at the world around her with a rare intensity and empathy and then transforms her thoughts and emotions into new work."[31] With sensitivity, Varda listened, and seemingly still listens, to individual voices: to vagabonds, wanderers, outcasts—people whose presence and dignities Marker also long perceived. The second part of this article continues to explore the refrains of a sea and its beaches in relation to Varda's commitments as exemplary *outrefemme*. "Valéry, as much as Rilke [and Varda], is the poet of beginnings," Stephen Romer writes, a "relentlessly inquiring spirit."[32] Through polymorphous portraits of different people and places, whether famed or ordinary, Varda's acts of portraiture affirm life through an inherent feminism or, to reiterate Soulages's wave of thought, an *outreféminisme.*

Outrefemme, Outreportrait, Outre-tombe, Outre-mer (A Beyond of Woman, Portrait, Grave, and Sea)

So what is reflective writing? Montaigne writes reflectively, intending to speak of nothing but himself, and ending up not speaking of himself at all.
—Jean-François Lyotard, interview with Richard Beardsworth

Varda has found a way to insinuate the idea of a feminine consciousness, one based on a vision of relations of compassion that are at the base of all human interaction.
—Sandy Flitterman-Lewis, "Varda: *The Gleaner* and the Just"

But at the same time, it is being so small in a huge world that
gives it its value.
—Agnès Varda, *Varda by Agnès*

Photographer, writer, filmmaker, collage and installation artist:
in step with her skills across these forms, and championing of
all whom she encountered, Varda produced a series of still, moving, and literary portraits. These expose a series of endless folds
of artist, subject, and viewer and proffer far more than simply a
portrait of another, or of "Varda," or of stasis or movement alone.
In keeping with Varda's perception of a "desire for movement
linked to immobility," as she asserts in *Varda by Agnès*, a fundamental component of her oeuvre pertains to mediating moments
between stillness and movement. Varda frequently explores this
elusive temporal between through the diptychs and triptychs of
her installations. Comprising only static images, or moving and
still alike, these forms are also often covertly and rapidly inserted
into the bodies of her films. The effect of such seeming formalism
contributes not only to the celebrated playfulness of Varda's art,
with its layered series of ever-new repetitions, but also to the som-
ber undercurrent of all her works that derives from a humility and
an admission that reality and fantasy are interwoven elements of
life. Everything is double, and so too in art, if as questioning and
empathetic as Varda's.

The depth of Varda's temporal acuity, which emits a vulnerability so prevalent in her work, abides in her devotion to reac-
tivating the lives of loves lost. And so, beyond the faces seen in
Varda's art, including and perhaps especially her own, are reve-
lations of worlds and experiences that commence with and then
journey beyond any one portrait. These transitory, oft fragmented
portraits assume various forms. They exist in the extreme close-ups
of hands, feet, napes, limbs, breasts, and torsos; in aerial views of
landscapes and tombs near the sea; and across staged tableaux that
renew stunning moments of art history. These chance emergences
of (self-)portraiture in Varda arise from even a wrinkle or eyelash,
are dispersed across a milieu, and pass into the landscapes of her
installations and films. Varda indeed becomes imperceptible and

yet remarkably corporeal as her own body features in extreme self-close-ups, and her voice speaks through interviews and voice-overs. These works expose us to ourselves while always foregrounding the woman, and women, behind, before, and beyond the lens.

Varda's methodology for gleaning hearts among potatoes, and sensuality from the quotidian, seemingly derives, as she claims in *Varda by Agnès*, from "filming things we didn't understand" in a quest "to feel, to experience" the world at large. In the process of creating *Documenteur* (France, 1981), Varda continues, "Nurith Aviv [director of photography] and I would go out evenings to capture images." What they captured, as throughout Varda's career, are specifically feminine processes of self-creation, authorship, fragmentation, pain, motherhood, abortion, "silence or speech, pain or peace," as Varda recalls. As Mayer among others repeats, *Documenteur* coalesces *documentaire* (documentary) and *menteur* (liar), which stresses an osmosis, again, between reality and fantasy.[33] Along this line and with respect to Varda's *Jane B. by Agnès V.* (*Jane B. par Agnès V.*, France, 1988) and its companion, *Kung-fu Master!* (*Le petit amour*, France, 1988), Flitterman-Lewis has identified "two distinct strategies that Varda employs to elaborate and problematize issues of feminine identity" through the "imaginary portrait of a real person and the real portrait of an imaginary person."[34] What emerges, Flitterman-Lewis proposes, "is a notion of the portrait as a 'matrix of dreams and associations' in which fantasy and desire are as much a part of the person as are physical features and remembered events."[35]

"One image in particular struck me," Varda interjects. From a long shot in *Varda by Agnès* of Varda and Aviv, seen seated from behind facing an audience within a cinema of red plush chairs, the film cuts to a frontal close-up of Varda, which then cuts to an evocative sequence from *Documenteur* that observes a woman in a laundromat. The ephemeral allure, the ever-new sonorous beauty and "thisnesses" of an anonymous woman, immediately recalls moments from Marker's film *Chats perchés* (*The Case of the Grinning Cat*, France, 2004).[36] The camera, entranced, lingers upon the movements of her fingers in her hair. In *Varda by Agnès*, Varda recalls this *Documenteur* sequence, its discovery and filming from a car window into the laundromat's window that reveals only the seated woman's back, as an "extraordinary moment of solitary sensuality" enhanced by Georges Delerue's extradiegetic piano, a "score that is captivating, frail and subdued. Like a gentle ache." Composer also for Varda's *L'Opéra Mouffe* (*Diary of a Pregnant Woman*, France, 1958) and of the jukebox waltz in Resnais's *Hiroshima mon amour*, Delerue's scores invariably contribute to a work's haunting persistence.

Of the ravishing ways of Varda's camera, Emma Wilson writes of attention granted to "memory, virtuality and mourning on the one hand, and . . . the textures, shapes and surfaces of the material world on the other."[37] Along these thought waves concerning corporeal and incorporeal experiences, what of ache, pain, and other forms of bodily and affective living in Varda? Both Wilson and Rebecca J. DeRoo illuminate the immense influence of painting, sculpture, and photography on Varda's interwoven cinematic and moving image practices and stress the inseparability of realist and formalist approaches. As DeRoo writes, "Varda shows us how to pursue intermediality without losing sight of the rich distinctiveness of artistic media, traditions, and experience. Varda doesn't collapse film, photography, and objects; rather, she films them, restages them, and otherwise portrays one medium within another to underscore their differences. She puts diverse media and conventions into dialogue to comment on them, with an understanding of their various histories and properties."[38]

Even a beach via Varda can assume different resonances. The opposite of a wall is a beach, as Varda reminds us, "but it can become a wall, as in this installation." She makes this remark in *Varda by Agnès* following a sequence that witnesses her conversation with homeless people who have been evicted from their building where their belongings remain, the entrances blocked by newly built brick walls. From the close-up of a young woman's face the film cuts to two shots taken from alternative distances and angles of the building's wall, with its windows and door barricaded with bricks, to a close-up of one window-that-was and, finally, to an image of her installation. Varda's threefold audiovisual evocation includes a giant still image of a sea and its foam projected against a wall with clouds above, an equally large moving image projected on the ground with waves lapping against a shore, and real sand surrounding the waves to offer, as Varda explains, a bit of "tangible reality."

This reality recalls others. Corpses washed ashore. Fluorescent beach toys. These divergent associations resummon thoughts of children, their bliss yet also their vulnerabilities and sufferings, as well as thoughts of those forever young. In *Visages Villages*, on the Saint-Aubin-sur-Mer beach, Varda memorializes her late friend, Guy Bourdin, as she and JR affix a giant photo that Varda had taken of Bourdin as a young man onto a fallen German bunker. Although the sea washes the image away by the next day, its momentary, massive resurrection upon the beach brings Varda peace. By way of heartache, Varda discovers new means of comfort and expression. "I didn't know how to film my loss," she discloses with reference to another work, her self-restaging in *The Beaches of Agnès*, repeated in *Agnès de ci de là Varda*, of George Segal's installation *Alice [Notley] Listening to Her Poetry and Music* (1970). Across decades, Varda's renewal of Segal's work might be termed "Agnès [Varda] Listening to Her Poetry and Music."

Through this faceless embodiment of a self-portrait with her body and face wrapped in a white sheet, seated at a desk and with back, once more, to viewer/listener, Varda's reworking of Segal's installation recalls "how listening is paradigmatic of the subject and an essential constituent of subjectivity."[39] Relations between grief, unknowing, and the unmaking and remaking of a self might also provide new meaning to Nancy's thought: "To listen is to be straining toward a possible meaning, and consequently one that is not immediately accessible."[40] Between past and future, Varda and her art again embody that double movement of loss and joy, or separation and creation. While reflecting on the desert island with thoughts of "being already separate . . . of being lost and alone," Deleuze likewise sensed a conjoined beginning with its dream "of starting from scratch, recreating, beginning anew."[41]

With further relevance to Varda's subjectification and mourning processes through her art, Nancy continues: "To be listening will always . . . be straining toward or in an approach to the self (one should say, in a pathological manner, *a fit of self*: isn't [sonorous] sense first of all, every time, a *crisis of self*?)."[42] Although he admits his aim does not extend as far, Nancy finally concludes that

it is the . . . codification of affects themselves that we should be interested in (what do we label love, desire, passion, joy, chagrin, bravura, etc.?). . . . Even further, we would have to go so far as to touch a fundamental rhythmic of affect as such, namely—perhaps—the beat of a blending together and a pulling apart, of an accepting/rejecting or a swallowing/spitting: in fact, from movement (impulse?) from which there comes an outside and an inside and, thus, something or someone like a "subject." (38)

Could anything other than the beating rhythms of hearts, as in Boltanski and Marker's works, or waves, as against shores, rushing in and pulling away, seem more apt for thoughts of Varda's oeuvre and her life's explorations? The entirety of these, dreamt of together, seems to suggest a grand self-portrait marked equally by sadnesses, that may wash away, and joys that her art enduringly imparts.

And yet, despite all still and moving images of Varda that find her, and other women, seated with their backs to a viewer's gaze, there are several other mesmerizing moments across Varda's works when women's gazes directly return the camera's look, when listening invites touch. "To listen," to repeat Nancy,

is to enter that spatiality by which, *at the same time*, I am penetrated, for it opens up in me as well as around me, and from me as well as toward me: it opens me inside me as well as outside, and it is through such a double, quadruple, or sextuple opening that a "self" can take place. . . . Listening thus forms the perceptible singularity that bears in the most ostensive way the perceptible or sensitive . . . condition as such: the sharing of an inside/outside. (14)

Relations between pain and painting persist across Varda's works. In her recent book *The Reclining Nude*, Wilson considers Varda's participation with and "reflections on naked women reclining"[43] and notes associations in Varda's films between "pre-existing images and spontaneous everyday gestures" alongside notions of the survival of images and their "spectral resonance" (43). Wilson's discussion of *Jane B. by Agnès V.* extends these associations to thoughts of "evanescent loveliness," "sentience, liveliness, desire" (77). Wilson also asserts the vital multiplicity that Varda celebrates in her film with Jane Birkin. There are as many Birkins and Monas as there are Vardas.[44] Once more, everything is double, or more, and the montages, collages, and restagings are recycled anew through Varda's works. These processes, endowed with Varda's passion for things and people less seen and heard, illuminate the experiences of various people, and several women, even within one woman. Varda's exploratory method is "like doing a puzzle," she explains to Birkin in *Jane B. by Agnès V.*, a patchwork of particularly feminine voices that never denies Varda's abiding love for Demy, and respect for her male collaborators and accomplices.

But her means also stress a lifelong commitment to always, at every moment and opportunity, attune herself to the "other" stories of women, of any age, race, class. This is, as Homay King contends, a "feminist cinema: . . . once upon a time there were only female *glâneuses*, not male *glâneurs*, because gathering society's leftovers was considered women's labor—but this is a type of labor with which Varda proudly identifies her own filmmaking."[45] Through the decades, Varda's productions reveal and revel in a process-making among women: layers of media, cameras and their technicians, directors, assistants—all discovered in frequent behind-the-scenes shots that reinforce the artisanal qualities of her artworks, works made indelible by affective power and meticulous technique. Varda's "people," her relationships with her daughter and other family members, actresses, "unknown" women or colleagues who assume various roles, exist beyond conventional determinations of "woman." All contribute to a Vardian *outreféminisme*.

At twenty-three minutes and forty-nine seconds into *Varda by Agnès*, the film presents a playful sequence as Varda discusses her film *Vagabond* (*Sans toit ni loi*, France, 1985). "The film's structure was precise. I wanted the camera to walk the roads with her. To do that, I used tracking shots." At this point, a "present-day" camera commences a leftward track across a field resembling the barren landscapes of the 1985 film, and encounters Varda. "There are thirteen [tracking shots] in the film. The shots move right to left, which is jarring, because it's the opposite of how we read in the West. Each tracking shot lasts one minute. We accompany Mona and her backpack. We're in rural farm landscapes, not particularly charming." Varda is in top form, seen seated on a propelled tracking dolly that matches the filming camera's own tracking movement; also accompanying Varda is a fabricated image of a film camera propped upon a real tripod, the cardboard likes of which Varda and Marker favor in *Agnès de ci de là Varda* to include Marker's cartoon cat, Guillaume-en-Egypte, in their encounters.

Varda continues: "At the end of each tracking shot, the camera leaves Mona to film a local element or object." Slowly, and while Varda sits on the dolly that continues to track left, the filming camera zooms nearer to Varda. "Actually, the entire film is a portrait in the form of a discontinuous tracking shot." Here, on Varda's words that stress not only an aleatory move across time and memory but also a resistant feminist cinema as manifested by the layering of a formative 1985 work within the final work of a "relentlessly inquiring spirit," the filming camera continues its tracking motion left, leaving Varda, as Mona, on her track behind.[46]

The resonances with Resnais's tracking movements are strong, their ethical potentials clear. Yet Varda's art resists reductive comparison. Aware of a precarious balance between self and world, her works effect their own worlding that stares back at interstices between the seen and unseen: at childhood homes, family photos, and further backward into the depths of a world-memory that haunts us all, as evinced through thoughts of children, suffering, and corresponding affects that resonate through present and future. These are Varda's timeless beaches through which she listens with a fervent reverence.

I listened closely.
—Varda, *Varda by Agnès*

I don't know much about her myself.
But to me, she seemed to have come from the sea.
—Varda, *Vagabond*

The sea always has the last word. And the wind, and the sand.
—Varda, *Visages Villages* and *Varda by Agnès*

Notes

I am indebted to Rebecca DeRoo, Homay King, and Sarah Lerner. My thanks as well to Adrian Martin, Eugenie Brinkema, Abe Geil, and Lennard Davis for their thoughts on earlier drafts. With loving gratitude, this work is dedicated to Hanjo Berressem, Sandy Flitterman-Lewis, and all of our nonhuman loves, past, present, and future.

1. Claire Colebrook's discussion regarding a third connotation of the term *postfeminism* as akin to *postmodernism* or *poststructuralism* is useful to consider in this article's approach to Varda's works. See Colebrook, "Modernism without Women: The Refusal of Becoming-Woman (and Post-feminism)," *Deleuze Studies* 7, no. 4 (2013): 427–55.

2. Marguerite Duras, *Hiroshima mon amour*, trans. Richard Seaver (New York: Grove, 1961), 8.

3. For a fuller discussion of *Hiroshima mon amour* in this context, see Nadine Boljkovac, *Untimely Affects: Gilles Deleuze and an Ethics of Cinema* (Edinburgh: Edinburgh University Press, 2015).

4. Sandy Flitterman-Lewis, "Varda: *The Gleaner* and the Just," in *Situating the Feminist Gaze and Spectatorship in Postwar Cinema*, ed. Marcelline Block (Newcastle upon Tyne: Cambridge Scholars, 2010), 215.

5. Dominique Bluher, "The Other Portrait: Agnès Varda's Self-Portraiture," in *From Self-Portrait to Selfie: Representing the Self in Moving Images*, ed. Muriel Tinel-Temple, Laura Busetta, and Marlène Monteiro (Oxford: Peter Lang, 2019), 47–76.

6. Jean-Luc Nancy, *Listening*, trans. Charlotte Mandell (New York: Fordham University Press, 2007), 5.

7. Bluher, "Other Portrait," 49.

8. Anthony Gritten, "*Listening,* by Jean-Luc Nancy," trans. Charlotte Mandell, *Music and Letters* 91, no. 3 (2010): 468.

9. Nancy, *Listening,* 14.

10. See Nadine Boljkovac, "Screen Perception and Event: Beyond the Formalist/Realist Divide," in *The Anthem Handbook of Screen Theory,* ed. Hunter Vaughan and Tom Conley (London: Anthem, 2018), 318.

11. Gilles Deleuze, *Desert Islands and Other Texts, 1953–1974,* trans. Michael Taormina, ed. David Lapoujade (New York: Semiotext(e), 2004), 10.

12. Bluher, "Other Portrait," 49; Cybelle H. McFadden, *Gendered Frames, Embodied Cameras: Varda, Akerman, Cabrera, Calle, and Maïwenn* (Madison, NJ: Fairleigh Dickinson University Press, 2014), 41.

13. Tom Conley, "The Desert Island," in *Deleuze and Space,* ed. Ian Buchanan and Gregg Lambert (Edinburgh: Edinburgh University Press, 2005), 209.

14. Deleuze, *Desert Islands,* 10.

15. McFadden, *Gendered Frames, Embodied Cameras,* 41.

16. James Williams, *Gilles Deleuze's Logic of Sense* (Edinburgh: Edinburgh University Press, 2008), 107.

17. Agnès Varda, interview by Thomas Delamarre, Fondation Cartier pour l'Art Contemporain, 2012, YouTube, 5 March 2014, www.youtube.com/watch?v=yVEZXxEzYqw.

18. Yvette Bíró, "Agnès Varda's Open Harbour," *Rouge,* September 2006, www.rouge.com.au/9/varda.html.

19. Williams, *Gilles Deleuze's Logic of Sense,* 107.

20. Jean-François Lyotard, *Discourse, Figure,* trans. Antony Hudek and Mary Lydon (Minneapolis: University of Minnesota Press, 2011), 65.

21. McFadden, *Gendered Frames, Embodied Cameras,* 42.

22. Conley, "Desert Island," 213.

23. Conley, "Desert Island," 213.

24. "Paul Valéry," *UNESCO Courier* 10, no. 8 (1957): 5.

25. So Mayer, "Le chat d'une poete," *Sight and Sound*, 1 April 2019, bfi.org.uk/news-opinion/sight-sound-magazine/features/seven -facets-agnes-varda.

26. Conley, "Desert Island," 217.

27. Gritten, "*Listening*, by Jean-Luc Nancy," 468.

28. Nancy, *Listening*, 13.

29. With regard to the passage of perception from perceptibility to imperceptibility, see Colebrook, "Modernism without Women," 448.

30. See Flitterman-Lewis, "Varda"; and Flitterman-Lewis's article in this issue.

31. Kelley Conway, *Agnès Varda* (Urbana: University of Illinois Press, 2015), 7.

32. Stephen Romer, "'Esprit, Attente pure, éternel suspens . . . ': Valéry's Prose Poetry," in *Reading Paul Valéry: Universe in Mind*, ed. Paul Gifford and Brian Stimpson (Cambridge: Cambridge University Press, 1998), 122.

33. Mayer, "Le chat d'une poete."

34. Sandy Flitterman-Lewis, *To Desire Differently: Feminism and the French Cinema* (New York: Columbia University Press, 1996), 344.

35. Flitterman-Lewis, *To Desire Differently*, 344.

36. For a discussion of *Chats perchés* and its corresponding instance with *Documenteur*, see Boljkovac, *Untimely Affects*, 168.

37. Emma Wilson, *Alain Resnais* (Manchester: Manchester University Press, 2006), 195.

38. Rebecca J. DeRoo, *Agnès Varda between Film, Photography, and Art* (Oakland: University of California Press, 2018), 9.

39. Gritten, "*Listening*, by Jean-Luc Nancy," 468.

40. Nancy, *Listening*, 6.

41. Deleuze, *Desert Islands*, 10.

42. Nancy, *Listening*, 9.

43. Emma Wilson, *The Reclining Nude: Agnès Varda, Catherine Breillat, and Nan Goldin* (Liverpool: Liverpool University Press, 2019), 41.

44. The name Mona refers to the protagonist in *Vagabond* (*Sans toit ni loi*, France, 1985).

45. Homay King, *Virtual Memory: Time-Based Art and the Dream of Digitality* (Durham, NC: Duke University Press, 2015), 74.

46. "There is no identity of woman lying in wait to be described, but must be created in an encounter with the force of perception." Colebrook, "Modernism without Women," 453.

Nadine Boljkovac is author of *Untimely Affects: Gilles Deleuze and an Ethics of Cinema* (2015), which examines responses to suffering via Chris Marker and Alain Resnais, and the book in progress "Beyond Herself: Feminist Portraiture and the Moving Image," which explores works by international women artists. Recent peer-reviewed essays and chapters appear in *The Sustainable Legacy of Agnès Varda* (forthcoming), *Revisiting Style in Literary and Cultural Studies* (2019), *Studies in European Cinema* (2019), "Materialising Absence in Film and Media" (coedited with S. Walton for *Screening the Past*, 2018), and *The Anthem Handbook of Screen Theory* (2018).

Figure 3. Varda becoming-world, *Varda by Agnès* (*Varda par Agnès*, France, 2019)

Figure 1. Installation view of *Les Justes au Panthéon*
(*The Righteous at the Pantheon*, France, 2007)

Passion, Commitment, Compassion: *Les Justes au Panthéon* by Agnès Varda

Sandy Flitterman-Lewis

Somewhere in chapter 3 of *The Beaches of Agnès* (*Les plages d'Agnès*, France, 2008), Agnès Varda's autobiographical celebration of her eighty years, she discusses her childhood and early youth in the port town of Sète. The sequence is redolent with Varda's characteristic blend of personal revelation and social observation, something that defines her unique experimental voice. But this sequence is far from the typical nostalgic reverie that we encounter in so many autobiographical works. Embedded within the account of the family's move to Sète during the great exodus of World War II—a collection of sunny images of houseboat life and joyful games (plus the typical Vardian ironic shock shot of a man exposing himself)—is a sequence in which Varda describes in detail her 2007 installation at the Pantheon in the heart of Paris. Commissioned to commemorate the placement in the Pantheon's crypt of a plaque honoring the many "Righteous" who saved Jewish children during the war, it was part of the inaugural ceremonies attended by survivors and scholars of

Camera Obscura 106, Volume 36, Number 1
DOI 10.1215/02705346-8838553   © 2021 by *Camera Obscura*
Published by Duke University Press

the Shoah and dignitaries from around the world, as well as the general public. The honorees, by now mostly deceased, were the 2,600 French individuals, some known and many anonymous, who made it possible that three-fourths of the Jewish population survived the French variant of the Shoah, which saw the deportation of 76,000 Jews to Auschwitz and other extermination camps. For sixty years these rescuers remained invisible, until President Jacques Chirac made the decision to honor them in the marble crypt alongside martyred resistance leader Jean Moulin. He asked Agnès Varda—whose relation to the tragedy as a fourteen-year-old girl who didn't really know Jews was somewhat limited—to create an installation for the dedication ceremony. Her dazzling solution is a breathtaking combination of historical recognition and minutely detailed, intensely personal fictive vignettes, which inscribe a distinctive female voice and sensibility in this institutional hall celebrating great men.

While the installation was intended to last one weekend in January, the lines outside the Pantheon after the official opening led to an extension of two more weeks (Varda later reproduced a version of the installation for the Festival d'Avignon in July 2007). As all installations are fleeting, lacking extensive documentation and existing for a finite period of time, it is very difficult to grasp their process and reception. In fact, in the third phase of a career that spanned six and a half decades, Varda embraced this form for its spectatorial freedom, its liberated possibilities of invention, and its radical reformulation of the cinematic experience. For *Les Justes au Panthéon* (*The Righteous at the Pantheon*, France, 2007) Varda displayed photos of the rescuers and some of their fictional counterparts on the floor of the Pantheon. Surrounding them, a ten-minute film loop of fictive scenes of rescue was projected on four screens: two in color and two in the black-and-white newsreel style of the World War II era. As Varda describes it, she wanted to create an evocative, fragmented, historical, and subjective vision: "Memories, faces, landscapes, feelings. Yesterday, and today as well."[1] In the program for the ceremony, she adds, "While they are watching this double film on separate screens, I wanted [the visitors to the Pantheon] to experience many fragmented feelings, bits of emo-

tion linked both to History and to certain key images of our collective memories."[2]

For a long time, access to this short film was available only
through an internet search. Then it was finally collected as a bonus
to Varda's 2017 *Tout(e) Varda: L'intégrale Agnès Varda* box set, placed
among the surprise features, which included a recipe for chard au
gratin and a 35mm strip from one of her films, *One Hundred and
One Nights* (*Les cent et une nuits de Simon Cinéma*, UK/France, 1995),
a comprehensive and joyful survey of cinematic history. Whereas
the installation itself is elusive, Varda offers an ingenious solution
in *The Beaches of Agnès*: she embeds the installation and her creative process within an account of personal memory in her autobiographical film. By manipulating temporalities and making the
installation part of her own subjective and creative history, Varda
invents a way to personalize the historical and to immortalize the
ephemeral.

In keeping with Varda's taste for proliferating forms, *The
Beaches of Agnès* was soon accompanied by an illustrated text. This
book is in the collage mode that Varda loves: references and asso-

Figure 2. *Les Justes au Panthéon* (France, 2007)

ciations are encouraged since they go beyond the fixity of the cinematic form. The complete text of Varda's ubiquitous voice-over is reproduced along with a relatively random selection of images from the visual track, virtually detached from their predetermined and immutable relation to the soundtrack, in favor of what coeditors Freddy Denaës and Gaël Teicher call "narrative importance or visual force."[3] In suggesting readings that ebb and flow like the tides that are the central metaphor of *Beaches*, they aim to "respect the fluidity of the text, with no indication of the place or person who speaks [in conversation with Varda], leaving the spectator/reader the liberty to zigzag between the words and visual indices, in order to reconstruct one's own memory of the film, between the simple pleasure rendered by the text of a writer and that offered by the film by the same Agnès Varda, cineaste" (2). This perfect interaction of image and text with spectatorial pleasure and imagination is part of the Vardian *ars poetica* and, as such, profoundly illustrates the intention and practice of her installation in the Pantheon. The created environment of the installation, embedded in the film and mirrored in the book, thus reverberates with simultaneous visions and sensations, allowing the individual subjectivity of the viewer/reader to merge with a felt sense of history.

In this mode, Varda addresses her historic work, her work of history, from the standpoint of personal engagement. This section of the book and the film are titled "Plages de Sète." This section matches text with four photograms of Varda walking backward on the beach (and literalizing the cinematic effort to evoke her childhood). She begins with a precise memory: "In school we had two obligations: to wear the blue-checked Vichy pinafores and to sing praises for old Marshal Pétain." The girls sing, their song resonant with the spirit of the period, "Maréchal, nous voilà," evoking the triad "Travail, Famille, Patrie" that replaced "Liberté, Égalité, Fraternité" in Vichy France (14). More wartime memories lead to a short recollection of camping with the Girl Scouts and the realization, years later, that some of the girls were led to freedom in Switzerland because, unbeknownst to Varda at the time, they were Jewish (16). This then allows Varda to turn, appropriately, to the installation that she created in the Pantheon.

Fifty years later I made a short film on the horror that was inflicted on the Jews and also on those named the Righteous, because they saved thousands of children. They were peasants, pastors, and priests, school principals, and ordinary folks. . . . I placed their photographs and those of anonymous others on the Pantheon's floor below several screens. Viewers saw the vile spectacle of French gendarmes arresting Jewish children, forcing them toward the extermination camps. To speak of it and to film it, even in fiction, makes me shudder. (43)

The book's editors chose three images taken from the ten-minute loop to illustrate these words. Each medium close-up depicts a kepi-wearing gendarme arresting Jews. On the next page are photos of two of the actual "Righteous" selected from the many photos Varda had chosen from the Musée-Mémorial de la Shoah's archives and elsewhere—portraits of Jean Kroutz and Jeanne Vallat. Finally, a full-page image of the installation in its entirety (including one of the images of arrest on the giant screen) emphasizes the singularity of the armed state against the vast and populous throng of ordinary French rescuers (yesterday) and of viewers (today) (17–19). Still, the flow of the film itself is more comprehensive, for it is with the actual screening of *Beaches* that the historic impact of the installation is strongest. In the program for the Pantheon ceremony, Varda chooses her words with precision: "Three hundred archival photographs, posed on the floor like open books; two films on four screens, in the style of Occupation newsreels or fictional and fleeting vignettes, and a large tree projected on a screen at the back of the nave."[4] Varda's characteristic interest in dialectics creates what she calls a "double-récit":[5] the Righteous and the children, photo portraits and cinema, vibrant nature and solid marble. The same precision is shown in the images she chooses (from the abundance in the installation's film loops) to accompany her description in *Beaches*, where page numbers no longer pose a limit.

The transition from recollection to installation is achieved with the sudden and stunning appearance of the most recognized symbol of the Shoah in France: the yellow felt star inscribed with the word *Juif*. Offered in a close-up while a pair of tailor's scissors lies next to it and patient hands sew stitches, this symbol of the process of social exclusion, normalized isolation, and eventual deportation of Jews under the Occupation is our entry into the world of the Righteous and Varda's composition. The yellow star, imposed by the Decree of 29 May 1942, required all Jews over the age of six to visibly declare their difference from the so-called authentic French population. In Varda's cinematic artistry it signals both the world of personal memory that spans decades, from youthful insouciance to artistic intervention, and the imperative of public recognition that the installation represents. For *Les Justes au Pantheon*, the star appears early in the film loop, an abrupt and vivid transition from the familiar black-and-white newsreel footage of Nazis under the Arc de Triomphe, swastika-adorned buildings, and, significantly, a phone booth with the admonition *Accès interdit aux Juifs*. The Magen David belongs to a series of what Varda calls "key images," images whose iconic significance telegraphs a collective meaning: a tree whose burst of red leaves suggests the Burning Bush, a stamp on an identity card marking *Juif*, a false baptismal certificate, a suitcase, a basket of food, a child's blanket, and so forth. There is also a wordless sound collage of familiar noises, such as shouts, train whistles, typewriter clacking, farm animals, and in one scene, a Yiddish lullaby. After a brief discussion of the historical background, I return to a description of the installation itself.

Passion

Agnès Varda has always been one to explore and document the diverse lives and social realities of those whose experience differs from hers. With curiosity as her lodestar, she transforms the investigative gaze, and even the gendered gaze, into a compassionate engagement with the Other. Varda's interest in people (the fishermen of Sète, the merchants on her street), in politics (Black Panthers, Cuba, women's rights), in different social contracts (bourgeois marriage, popular muralist groups, scavengers), and always in children (and families of all kinds) has informed every part of her oeuvre, from photography to film to installation art. And although there is a constant sociological refrain, her films are far from the traditional inquiries of sociology. In fact, the perpetual movement from the publicly factual to the subjective and intimate, the border between them continually contested, is something that defines her art. In the Pantheon, this blending becomes the key to the power of the installation, for here, Varda's passion for a history that is in one way not her own becomes a shared passion for collective history and its contemporary ramifications.

That *Les Justes* focuses on Jewish children and their rescuers is not an arbitrary choice. What has come to be known as the "War against Children" in Occupied France literally began on 16–17 July 1942, a date that has been called the "hinge" of the Occupation for its status as a turning point in both the persecution and the rescue of Jews. The roundup of entire Jewish families—for the first time—led to the widespread phenomenon of "hidden children" and the many forms of heroic rescue that worked in the shadows and on the margins of the established lines of resistance. Their recognition was only gradual; it can be said to have culminated in the 2007 ceremony in the Pantheon where Varda's installation celebrated, in an unexpected and enduring way, those people hidden from history. The Vel' d'Hiv roundup is the name given by historians to the sudden but systematically prepared roundup of Jewish men, women, and children by French police. Vel' d'Hiv is shorthand for the Vélodrome d'Hiver, the glass-domed winter cycling stadium where over fourteen hundred Jews were held for a week without food or water before being deported to their deaths in the East. Previously only "suspect" foreign Jewish men were sought for deportation, so the unexpected arrest of women and children, two-thirds of the detainees, put Jewish children in particular in immediate danger.

Weeks passed while French and German officials discussed what to do with the children once the parents were deported. This "bartered brood" became the singular endangered population, such that when the arrested children finally followed their parents, from whom they had been separated in the holding camps, all Jewish children in the general French population were placed in danger. At the same time, networks for rescuing Jewish children were organized, clandestine safe houses were formed, and relays

Figures 3–4. *Les Justes au Panthéon* (France, 2007)

Figures 5–6. *Les Justes au Panthéon* (France, 2007)

Figures 7–8. *Les Justes au Panthéon* (France, 2007)

Figures 9–10. *Les Justes au Panthéon* (France, 2007)

Figures 11–12. *Les Justes au Panthéon* (France, 2007)

Figure 13. *Les Justes au Panthéon* (France, 2007)

of escape and underground flight were mapped out. Thus, given Varda's traditional concerns, it is no surprise that her installation honoring the thousands of French rescuers would also emphasize the relations between these heroes and their juvenile charges. In her hands, the celebration of the Righteous became the honoring of Jewish memory at the same time; while most of the rescuers are very old or no longer alive, the children that were saved are living memorials to the human capacity for goodness and ethical behavior.

Commitment

Varda's commitment to make the stories of the Righteous palpable, to combine the images of real people with those in her fictions, and to evoke the silences of the hidden children themselves materialized in a set of ingenious solutions to the problem of historic memory. To honor the rescuers in her installation, she populated the floor of the Pantheon with their portraits, some in black-and-white (real rescuers), some in color (their fictive counterparts), creating a sort of carpet of righteousness through which the viewer/participants could wander. She conceived of her installation as an invitation to meditate and to contemplate, along the lines of her praise of artist Christian Boltanski, whose installations Varda said made her feel like "walking through the work instead of standing before it like a picture."[6] In addition to the floor of portraits, as noted, Varda created four film loops (two in black-and-white, two in color) comprising vignettes of rescue capable of being perceived instantaneously by a casual, intermittent glance.

In thirteen momentary anecdotes we find (1) a little boy hidden under the protective sleeve of a nun as a Jewish tailor and his family are herded into a police van; (2) a young mother with a suitcase who leaves her two small children at a house in the countryside of the "Zone Libre"; (3) a baptismal certificate signed by a priest; (4) two young Jewish women chatting while a man registers as a Jew at City Hall; (5) two children shaking apples from a tree while they silently indicate *no* to some inquiring gendarmes; (6) the passage of baskets filled with food in the mountains, a detail in close-up; (7) a little girl given to the protective arms of a peasant woman; (8) children playing in a huge tree in the country as a Yiddish song wafts from their perch; (9) adults talking in front of a church while a man gets on his bicycle with a mission of warning; (10) the travel from village to farm by the man on his bicycle; (11) children on a playground being told in a whisper to hide; (12) children at an outside farm table being rushed into a hayloft to hide; and (13) the arrival of the Gestapo, the capture and deportation of two trapped children being marched to a waiting car, and the arrest of their protectors. Each episode ends with a photograph and name of one or two of the Righteous, as the color portrait of each fictional counterpart fades. And yet, it is undeniably the story of Jewish children that Varda tells, finding a way to create, within the prescribed ceremonial honoring the Righteous, a sense of the haunted reality of these children whose experience has been historically erased. The double register—fiction/actuality, French rescuers/Jewish children—a hallmark of Varda's artistic practice, is most evident in how she approaches the plight of the children, in an oblique movement that changes them from abstractions to living beings. These actors are no longer characters; they are attitudes, gestures, and ideas concretized in the space of an instant, telling the double story of the rescuers and the rescued. Varda explains: "I wanted to tell this story with a certain naturalness, making the viewer feel the childhood of these little ones, their loneliness, the omnipresent fear, but also the discovery of the countryside."[7]

Compassion

I have noted elsewhere that Varda's *Les Justes* conveys an overwhelming presence of "empathetic reciprocity," the recognition of a common network of caring relations that holds us all together.[8] The varied filmed vignettes are exquisite, emblematic gems of hiding and rescue, each radiating compassion in a different circumstance. Within the grandeur of the majestic hall, the installation celebrates intimate, individual acts of loving kindness.[9] In fact, all of Agnès Varda's work, in each of her self-identified phases as photographer, cineaste, and visual artist, foregrounds a relational aesthetic that embraces artist, viewer, and subject in a social bond born of a compassionate commitment to humanity. "Nothing is banal if you film with empathy and love," declares the cineaste in her final film, *Varda by Agnès* (*Varda par Agnès*, France, 2019), and in retrospect, this underlines the contemporary imperative for moral action evoked by her installation in the Pantheon.

Interestingly, our return to the very site of the dedication ceremony delivers an unexpected sisterhood, for among the attendees were two exact contemporaries of Agnès, Simone Veil and Marceline Loridan-Ivens, two Jewish women, each with a specific and moving story about her teenage experience of the war. These three French women of profound humanistic conviction, all age fourteen at the time, joined in honoring people of conscience who had been hidden from public recognition for decades. It could be said that an accident of fate dictated their reunion, ten years before Veil's death, eleven years before Marceline's, and seven and a half decades after the event that inevitably binds them: the Shoah. Feminist icon Simone Veil (neé Jacob), a Holocaust survivor, created the Fondation pour la Mémoire de la Shoah and was its first president. When she was minister of health, she agitated to legalize contraception and abortion in France; the final law was named "la loi Veil" in her honor. When she was ceremoniously buried in the Pantheon with her husband in 2018, thousands of people attended in the sweltering heat. Her Auschwitz number was prominently displayed in the ceremony and in the crypt.

Marceline Loridan-Ivens (neé Rozenberg), that diminutive ball of energy with a wild halo of red hair, is increasingly recognized as one of the most prolific witnesses of the Shoah, having been a prisoner in her teenage years and filming and writing about her experience of familial losses literally up until the day of her death. Her public life is framed, start (*Chronicle of a Summer* [*Chronique d'un été* (Paris 1960)*,* dir. Edgar Morin and Jean Rouch, France, 1961]) to finish (her 2018 novel *L'amour après*, cowritten with Judith Perrignon), by the intimate, searing memory of loss, a yearning to survive, and a commitment to remember. After her husband, documentarist Joris Ivens, died in 1989, Loridan made her first and only fiction feature at age seventy-five, *The Birch-Tree Meadow* (*La petite prairie aux bouleaux*, France/Germany/Poland, 2003). The film takes its name from the translation of Birkenau, the concentration camp where Loridan was imprisoned and where her father was murdered. At the time of Simone Veil's induction into the "hall of great men," Loridan said, "I felt like all the girls of Birkenau entered the Pantheon."[10]

Finally, it turns out that after Veil's death, a short video was circulated that had Simone and Marceline sitting on a bed, characteristically laughing and reminiscing about their time together as teenagers in Auschwitz-Birkenau. This is a visual reminder of Marceline's wild sense of humor that not only helped others survive but also survived the war itself. Agnès Varda documented and commemorated the reality that they, as Jewish children, lived. Each of them (Varda in the manner of Franco-German activist and journalist Beate Klarsfeld) has left us a legacy of feminine solidarity, social commitment, and boundless compassion.

The Red Kitchen, the Atelier, and the Courtyard

From the joyful solidarity of *One Sings, the Other Doesn't* (*L'une chant l'autre pas*, France/Soviet Union, 1977), with its celebration of female friendship and positive social action, to the mature recognition of the sanctity of memory and the profound understanding of women's historical power evoked by *Les Justes*, Agnès Varda's work has been the heartbeat of a dedicated feminism that transcends the particularity of specific films and situations. For her valedictory film she came up with her own triad of guiding principles: "inspiration," "création," "partage" (sharing). She speaks of the trio in detail in *Varda by Agnès*, where she outlines her artistic procedure for "exciting the creativity of each person . . . [her] privilege as a director."[11] First, there is the raw material, the starting point, images and ideas gleaned from an eclectic and varied life. Then, there is the artistic process, the making of the finished work, a construction molded out of knowledge and dreams. Finally, there is—most importantly—sharing, the ability to give that work to others and to start a conversation, the desire of the spectator and the artist's pleasure as well.[12] Thus it was with a particular sense of joy that I realized there was a correspondence between Varda's trio of watchwords and mine. Varda's inspiration matched my idea of passion; her creation evoked my idea of artistic commitment; and her sharing involved my idea of compassion. An invisible affinity, something I have felt about Agnès for years, materialized for me in the writing of this article. And so I invoke the rubric of this section. The Varda-Demy house on the rue Daguerre was filled with variety, color, and light; articles recognized from her films populate the space: a clock without hands, a heart-shaped potato, a photograph of her mother in the garden, even the cats. As she notes in the booklet accompanying *The Beaches of Agnès*, "The house in Paris. Workplace, lifespace, and homebase, for the whole family. The courtyard is its epicenter, with over fifty years of history to tell. To help tell it, the courtyard was rebuilt on a set, looking as it did in 1951, and after."[13]

I go even further with the creative triangulation: the kitchen is the scene of ideas, something's always cooking; the atelier is the scene of work, resembling a medieval workshop and reminding Varda of Demy; and the courtyard is a special scene of sharing, a place to exchange ideas in the casual setting of food and friendship. Anyone who's seen a picture of Varda or met her in person knows immediately that she has an exquisite sense of color: purple and mauve scarves, patterned ethnic tunics, unusual combinations of fabric and design. This extends to her surroundings: vibrant pink and Greek blue in the courtyard, bright red tile in the kitchen. This kitchen is something stunning to see, this defiance of established norms and a refusal to conform to the conventional feminine space. At the same time, Varda adapts this space of cultural givens to her own vision, one of unexpected vibrancy and joyful novelty. Varda has invited us into her atelier in many of her films, the clutter always reminding us that visual ideas often emerge in creative chaos. Most notably, in *The Gleaners and I* (*Les glaneurs et la glaneuse*, France, 2000) she lets this space create parallels with the wide variety of gleaners and environments that she has explored throughout the film.

But most important to me personally is that leafy courtyard where one sunny day in June 2007, Agnès and I had tea while she explained her installation in the Pantheon in January. She told me about the ordinary people who hid or saved Jews during the war and about the children who so intrigued her, and, leaping about in time from her youth to the present moment, she delighted in telling me about her experiences and her process. She even showed me the maquette, with a kind of anticipatory excitement because she was going to mount the installation in Avignon. Sometime after the conference in Rennes where I presented my paper, Varda made *The Beaches of Agnès* with the aforementioned inclusion of that very installation. When I saw her afterward I congratulated her on noting *Les Justes* in the film, and she responded, characteristically, "Et les juifs!" From my perspective today, I marvel at how *Les Justes* has moved from a footnote in the Varda canon (difficult to see and not necessarily noted in discussions of her installations) to a memorable position of prominence and visual power in one of her most personal masterworks.

And finally, for me, the most wonderful example of Varda's *partage* is her inscription in the book that contains the French version of my essay on *Les Justes. Agnès Varda: Le cinéma et au-delà,* is a collection of the papers presented at a conference in her honor in November 2007.[14] I asked Agnès to sign my copy when she was in New York, and without a moment's hesitation she invoked the empathetic relay that is so central to her work, the *I* of creation and the *you* of reception in a productive back-and-forth that reverberates with perpetual connection. She wrote: "Chère Sandy FL, Merci pour ta vision de mon travail. Agnès V."

Notes

This is a version of a paper presented at "Virtual Varda." I dedicate it to my twin sister, Sharon, and her husband, David, in gratitude for their help in its preparation. And thanks, as ever, to my husband, Joel, for his poetic insights.

1. Quoted in Armelle Héliot, "Les Justes au Panthéon," *Le Figaro,* 22 December 2007. Here I want to mention two corrective points, suggested to me by Nancy Lefenfeld, author of *The Fate of Others: Rescuing Jewish Children on the French-Swiss Border* (Clarksville, MD: Timbrel, 2013): "In France the term *les Justes* is basically synonymous with those designated by Yad Vashem as *Righteous Among the Nations* (formerly called *righteous gentiles*). It does not encompass Jews who were themselves engaged in the work of saving other Jews. Networks of Jews worked hand in hand with networks predominantly Catholic or Protestant or Quaker, etc. Also (in spite of my title) I have long argued that the word *rescue* is a poor one to use for talking about this subject. I advocate using the term *humanitarian resistance* instead." Phone conversation with Lefenfeld, 6 July 2020.

2. *Hommage de la Nation aux Justes de France,* program for the *Les Justes au Panthéon* installation at the Pantheon, 18 January 2007, 7.

3. Freddy Denaës and Gaël Teicher, eds., *Les plages d'Agnès: Texte illustré* (Montreuil, France: Les Editions de l'Oeil, 2010).

4. *Hommage de la Nation aux Justes de France,* 7.

5. This term is from a personal conversation, although Varda has said similar things in various interviews.

6. *Agnès de ci de là Varda* (*Agnès Varda: From Here to There,* France, 2011).

7. *Hommage aux Justes de France*, program for the *Les Justes au Panthéon* installation in Avignon, 7–27 July 2007.

8. Sandy Flitterman-Lewis, "Varda: The Gleaner and the Just," in *Situating the Feminist Gaze and Spectatorship in Postwar Cinema*, ed. Marcelline Block (Newcastle upon Tyne: Cambridge Scholars, 2008), 214–25.

9. The Book of Ruth, an ancient Hebrew text, is part of the Bible, as is the Book of Esther, the only two Books attributed to women. The Book of Ruth is included in the third division of the Writings of the Hebrew Bible. As I write in another essay on *Les Justes*: "The Book of Ruth has another title, *The Book of Chesed* (loving kindness, *caritas*, compassionate tenderness—there is no exact translation) because it is about relations of generosity and kindness among human beings, inspired in the Book of Ruth by women's caring for each other." Flitterman-Lewis, "Varda," 222.

10. Loridan says this in *Marceline. A Woman. A Century* (*Marceline, une femme, un siècle*, dir. Cordelia Dvorak, France/Netherlands, 2017).

11. Quoted on the display accompanying the Varda retrospective at Film at Lincoln Center, December 2019–January 2020.

12. This is a rough approximation taken from the same beautiful and engaging display.

13. Sleeve notes, *The Beaches of Agnès* (DVD, Criterion Collection, 2008).

14. Antony Fiat, Roxanne Hamery, and Éric Thouvenal, eds., *Agnès Varda: Le cinema et au-déla* (Rennes: Presses Universitaires de Rennes, 2009).

Sandy Flitterman-Lewis is an internationally recognized scholar on Agnès Varda. Her book *To Desire Differently: Feminism and French Cinema* (1st ed., 1990; 2nd ed., 1996) was the first sustained examination of Varda's career in English and has proved foundational for subsequent work on the filmmaker. She is one of four founding editors of *Camera Obscura* and is also a founding coeditor of the cultural studies journal *Discourse*. Her current work is on Jewish families in France during World War II, the subject of her conference "Hidden Voices: Childhood, the Family, and Antisemitism in Occupation France," Columbia University, 4–5 April 1998.

Figure 14. Sandy Flitterman-Lewis with Agnès Varda at the Université de Rennes, November 2007

Figure 1. *The Young Girls of Rochefort* (*Les demoiselles de Rochefort*, dir. Jacques Demy, France, 1966) pressbook created by Ciné-Tamaris on the occasion of the DCP restoration of the film in 2013. The booklet contains an explanation of the restoration process, excerpts of the photo comic based on the film and published in *Mon film* in 1967, excerpts of interviews with the cast and crew, reproductions of pages from Demy's original script, excerpts from reviews, and statements from the donors.

Agnès Varda, Producer

Kelley Conway

The accolades Agnès Varda received shortly before her passing in 2019 leave little doubt that her importance as a filmmaker is well established. The Honorary Palme d'Or at the 2015 Cannes Film Festival, the Honorary Oscar at the 2017 Academy Awards, and the Best Documentary Feature nomination for *Visages Villages* (*Faces Places*, France, 2017) attest to Varda's standing as a director at the end of her life. In the realm of film scholarship, too, Varda has received considerable attention for her work, most of it oriented toward her films' aesthetic and narrative innovation. But what would it mean to think of Varda as a producer? She was not only a film director but also the creator of a production company, first called Tamaris Films and then, in 1975, Ciné-Tamaris. At the helm of Ciné-Tamaris, Varda made some specific and surprising moves that resulted in the extension of her viability and visibility as a filmmaker. In this article, after looking at the establishment and evolution of Varda's production company, I examine closely Ciné-Tamaris's strategic use of its back catalog starting in the late 1990s. An examination of both ends of Varda's career reveals that her distinctiveness extended to the choices she made as a producer. Varda was an artist, but she was also a businesswoman.

Camera Obscura 106, Volume 36, Number 1
DOI 10.1215/02705346-8838565   © 2021 by *Camera Obscura*
Published by Duke University Press

Experimenting with Funding Strategies

From the very beginning of her career as a filmmaker, Varda employed a variety of strategies to fund her productions. Between 1954 and 1962 she engaged in no fewer than four financing mechanisms: the cooperative—*La Pointe Courte* (France, 1954); the commissioned film—*O saisons, ô chateaux* (France, 1957) and *Along the Coast* (*Du côté de la côte*, France, 1958); the self-produced experimental film—*L'Opéra Mouffe* (*Diary of a Pregnant Woman*, France, 1958); and New Wave–style independent production— *Cleo from 5 to 7* (*Cléo de 5 à 7*, France, 1962). *La Pointe Courte* was funded without the backing of a major studio such as Pathé or Gaumont or a bank loan from Crédit National, the traditional lender for French film productions.[1] A complete outsider to the film industry, Varda instead assembled a small sum comprising a gift from her mother and an inheritance from her father and used it to pay for film, equipment rental, and room and board for the crew.[2] Her cast consisted of local residents of the small Mediterranean port town of Sète, where the neighborhood of La Pointe Courte was located, and theater actors whom Varda knew from her work as a photographer at the Théâtre National Populaire. Varda also relied more broadly on the generosity of the inhabitants of Sète, where she and her family had sought shelter during the war. Film historian Bernard Bastide, who worked as Varda's archivist for many years, reported that the local press solicited residents' participation in Varda's dance and jousting scenes, the local police loaned uniforms, the bridges and roads department supplied a barge, and the army supplied a generator.[3] In lieu of paying her cast and crew during the shoot, Varda formed a cooperative and assigned shares to each participant proportional to their contribution to the production.[4] The goal was to pay her collaborators when the film had its commercial release. In the end, no one earned money from *La Pointe Courte*; the film's distribution was limited to the ciné-club circuit and a few art house screenings in Paris due to the administrative rules of the Centre National de la Cinématographie (CNC). Varda had registered her company as a producer of short films and so could not release *La Pointe Courte*, a feature film.[5] Varda registered the project with the CNC in September 1954 as a short film; she then decided she was going to make a feature, but she lacked the capital to pay the required registration fee to do so. As a result, the film was confined to the noncommercial circuit. The film nevertheless caught the attention of producer Pierre Braunberger and critics André Bazin and François Truffaut, among others.

What did it mean to use a cooperative as a mode of financing in 1954? Most obviously, it meant that Varda was able to make a film on a microbudget at a time when even low-budget films were exceptionally rare in France. In the mid-1950s, the French film industry did not favor low-budget productions featuring unknown actors. Instead, commercial filmmaking was characterized by a proliferation of international coproductions, an increase in budgets, and the use of stars, all of which aimed to secure an adequate return on investment.[6] Certainly, there were independent producers who embraced risk, such as Braunberger, who produced many of Jean Renoir's films in the 1930s; short films by Varda, Jacques Rivette, Chris Marker, and Maurice Pialat; and New Wave features, including *Shoot the Piano Player* (*Tirez sur le pianiste*, dir. François Truffaut, France, 1960), *My Life to Live* (*Vivre sa vie*, dir. Jean-Luc Godard, France, 1962), and *Muriel, or the Time of Return* (*Muriel ou le temps d'un retour*, dir. Alain Resnais, France, 1963). But most films in the 1950s were financed through a combination of bank loans, funds from distributors' and exhibitors' networks, credit from studios and laboratories, and some state aid.[7] Varda's budget was unusual even by the standards of the New Wave, which emerged in full force in 1959, four years after *La Pointe Courte* was made. Richard Neupert reported, "They eventually completed the production with the extremely low production cost of fourteen thousand dollars (7 million old francs), or roughly one-quarter of the budget of later New Wave films as *The 400 Blows* or *Breathless*."[8] After making *La Pointe Courte*, Varda never again used the cooperative as a mode of financing because she considered it "unsustainable."[9]

Following her experiment with a cooperative, Varda made two commissioned tourism films, one about the castles of the Loire Valley (*O saisons, ô chateaux*) and the other about the pleasures of the French Riveria (*Du côté de la côte*). This was not an anodyne assignment; the postwar period in France saw a proliferation of noteworthy short films, many of them made by future New Wave directors, and many of which resulted from governmental or corporate commissions. Varda's shorts were financed by the tourism board and produced by now-legendary New Wave producers: *O saisons, ô chateaux* was produced by Pierre Braunberger's Films de la Pléiade, and *Du côté de la côte* was produced by Anatole Dauman's Argos Films. The result was two highly inventive documentaries that conformed to the technical and administrative norms of the film industry. Varda's decision to accept these commissions was strategic. After producing *La Pointe Courte* outside the system of classical production, she was advised by Chris Marker and Alain Resnais to demonstrate that she was capable of "pouring herself into the mold of classical production. . . . and to prove that she could be trusted with the budget for feature length fiction film."[10] *O saisons, ô chateaux* was screened at the Cannes Film Festival and the Festival de Tours in 1958 and distributed with the feature film *Bourgeois gentilhomme* (*Would-Be Gentlemen*, dir. Jean Meyer, France 1958).[11] *Du côté de la côte* was screened at the Festival de Tours in 1958 and distributed with *Hiroshima mon amour* (dir. Alain Resnais, France, 1959).[12] The successful completion and circulation of the shorts paved the way for Varda's second feature, *Cleo from 5 to 7*.

With *Cleo from 5 to 7*, Varda once again aligned herself with a producer associated with the New Wave, Georges de Beauregard. Like Braunberger and Dauman, Beauregard produced small-scale films and generally eschewed corporate finance in favor of a mix of loans, inheritances, and state aid. Out of this low-budget model came many landmark films of the French New Wave, including *The 400 Blows* (*Les quatre cents coups*, dir. François Truffaut, France, 1959), *Hiroshima mon amour, Breathless* (*À bout de souffle*, dir. Jean-Luc Godard, France, 1960), *Lola* (dir. Jacques Demy, France, 1961), and *Cleo from 5 to 7*. Once again, Varda worked with a very low budget, constructing a narrative with a constrained time frame and location to save money. While the average cost of a French film in 1959 was $300,000,[13] the budget for *Cleo from 5 to 7* was only $64,000.[14] This time, her film enjoyed a traditional theatrical distribution, widespread critical acclaim, and inclusion in the official selection at the Cannes Film Festival in 1962. After working with Beauregard, Varda made *Le bonheur* (*Happiness*, France, 1965) and *The Creatures* (*Les créatures*, France, 1965) with another important New Wave producer, Mag Bodard, who produced *Umbrellas of Cherbourg* (*Les Parapluies de Cherbourg*, dir. Jacques Demy, France, 1964), *Young Girls of Rochefort* (*Les demoiselles de Rochefort*, dir. Jacques Demy, France, 1967), *Au Hasard Balthazar* (dir. Robert Bresson, France, 1966), *Two or Three Things I Know about Her* (*Deux ou trois choses que je sais d'elle*, dir. Jean-Luc Godard, France, 1967), and *La Chinoise* (dir. Jean-Luc Godard, France, 1967). The producers of the New Wave era were motivated not only by the prospect of working with young, exciting directors but also by the availability of state aid, a subject beyond the scope of this article, but an important part of any producer's strategy in the 1950s.[15]

Before returning to the making of feature-length fiction films, Varda launched a third type of production to which she would return periodically throughout her life: the self-produced experimental short. Between the making of the two commissioned shorts, Varda made *L'Opéra Mouffe* (*Diary of a Pregnant Woman*, France, 1958), a film that was even more modest in cost, cast, and crew than *La Pointe Courte*. More personal than her commissioned shorts, *L'Opéra Mouffe* is typically categorized as an essay film and linked with her later films *Uncle Yanco* (France, 1967), *Ulysse* (*Ulysses*, France, 1982), and *7p., cuis., s. de b., . . . à saisir* (*7rm., kitch., bath., . . . for sale*, France, 1984).

After *L'Opéra Mouffe*, Tamaris Films went dormant as a producing enterprise until the mid-1970s, when Varda resuscitated it, renamed it Ciné-Tamaris, and produced *Daguerreotypes* (*Daguerréotypes*, France, 1976) and *One Sings, the Other Doesn't* (*L'une chante, l'autre pas*, France, 1977).[16] Ciné-Tamaris is a type of company called *société à responsibilité limitée* (SARL), roughly equivalent to the American limited liability company. Varda established Ciné-Tamaris as a category of film production company that required only 100,000 francs of startup capital, rather than the more traditional 300,000 francs, which limited her activities to the production of her own films.[17] She became a producer not because she wanted to but because she had to.

Each of the films directed by Agnès Varda has its own specific history of funding. Each production is worth studying in depth for what it can reveal about the possibilities and constraints of auteur filmmaking from the mid-1950s to 2019. A close look at *One Sings, the Other Doesn't* reveals Varda at another pivotal point in her career, in which she began self-producing her feature films. No longer a rookie working on a microbudget outside the system, as she was with *La Pointe Courte*, nor the beneficiary of enthusiasm around the New Wave, as she was with *Cleo from 5 to 7*, Varda struggled to find the funds to make *One Sings, the Other Doesn't*.

Rebecca J. DeRoo details the challenges Varda faced leading up to her decision to self-produce the film, which Varda had initially titled *Mon corps est à moi* (*My Body Is Mine*):

When Varda submitted *Mon corps est à moi* to the Commission of the Centre National de la Cinématographie, it was denied an *avance sur recettes* (an interest-free loan) and no producer would agree to take on the film. Over the next two years Varda rewrote and redesigned the script as *L'une chante*, making the musical numbers less disjunctive and the feminist ideas less radically presented; the striking female factory workers were eliminated in favour of featuring the enduring friendship between two women.[18]

Varda resubmitted her script to the CNC and received a loan for 500,000 francs of her 3 million franc budget, yet still could not find a producer. And so she decided to have Ciné-Tamaris produce the film. Varda explained:

I had thought about it and there were only two solutions: either enter the "star system" and work with stars or produce the film myself. This second solution is obviously the sole possibility if I want to do what I love and do it freely. I saw several producers, none of them wanted to produce my film. I was thus forced to take on a different profession, to learn to do it on a different scale (a budget of three million) than that of the short films I had previously produced.[19]

When *One Sings, the Other Doesn't* was still in theatrical distribution, but not doing well financially, Varda gave an interview to the trade journal *Le Technicien du film*.[20] Citing the names of other directors who also produce their own work—René Allio, Gérard Blain, Jacques Rozier, Liliane de Kermadec—Varda emphasized the "heroic" nature of working under such conditions. She provided precise details about the funding of *One Sings, the Other Doesn't*, which included a modest advance from Gaumont, the film's distributor, for prints and publicity; "two or three contributions from French co-producers"; an unsuccessful attempt to get a Belgian *avance sur recette*; credits for postproduction services such as sound mixing and the creation of the credits; and presales to Germany, Quebec, Spain, and France's Antenne 2, the television channel. She reported that she collected an additional 200,000 francs from the CNC for her completed film, "justified by the withdrawal of certain producers" from the production. Ciné-Tamaris's office expenses were not covered by the film's budget, and most striking, Varda was "holding her salary as a screenwriter and director in reserve. . . . which is to say that [she was] not being paid." Producing one's own films is thus a considerable risk, a "veritable lottery." Seeking to differentiate her current mode of production from that of the beginning of her career, she stated, "I specify that I shot with a professional crew and that everyone was paid at union rates. I had made *La Pointe Courte* as a cooperative, but I did not want to do that again, because I believe that people who work should be paid." The interview emphasizes primarily the costs of self-producing, but also acknowledges the advantages:

I spent six months preparing and signing the contracts. . . . The negative aspect of this enterprise is the enormous loss of energy for the *auteur*, who must do the work of a producer and the creative activities simultaneously; it's an uncomfortable and really acrobatic situation for a director. The positive aspect is the freedom in the work and the wonderful team spirit, because there's no hierarchy, no separation between the capital and the work; it's a kind of self-management that links everyone in the same collective enterprise.[21]

Varda provided even more precise budget figures for *One Sings, the Other Doesn't* in an interview the following year. She ultimately received a total of 700,000 francs from the CNC's *avance sur recettes* program, 300,000 from the distributor Gaumont, 150,000 from the National Audiovisual Institute, the equivalent of 350,000 from the postproduction service provider SFT (French Production Society), "a Belgian co-producer [Paradise Films] that only gave me 50% of what they pledged"; and 350,000 from a Dutch-Antilles company (Population Film). Ciné-Tamaris contributed another 1 million to the budget, which, for a company that depended on government subvention, was "a lot."[22]

One Sings, the Other Doesn't was ultimately not commercially successful, but Varda learned how to produce a large-scale project as a result of it. As time went on, however, film financing did not become any easier. By the early 1980s she was weary. She explained, "In France I am a beloved filmmaker, relatively known as original, a pioneer, a kind of cultural gadget. I am invited to festivals, seen in cinematheques and by the press, but I am not put to work [*on ne me fait pas travailler*]."[23] In a poignant comparison between her situation and that of Jean-Luc Godard, she said in 1982,

I'm unstoppable. But I admit that I'm tired of chasing after money. There is a strange phenomenon going on: everyone likes me . . . I provoke affection. . . . I am entitled to their respect, not their money. Godard, who is prodigiously clever, succeeds in making them do what he wants. I seem to be condemned to the realm of craft [*artisanal*] and I would really like to get out of it. I'm not a pauper by choice.[24]

Relegated to the realm of "artisanal" filmmaking, Varda nevertheless continued to self-produce after the mixed experience of *One Sings, the Other Doesn't*. Ciné-Tamaris produced many of the films Varda directed in the 1980s, including *Mur Murs* (France, 1980), *Documenteur* (France, 1981), *Vagabond* (*Sans toit ni loi*, France, 1985), *Jane B. by Agnès V.* (*Jane B. par Agnès V.*, France, 1988), and *Kung-fu Master!* (*Le petit amour*, France, 1988). In the early 1990s, after the death of Jacques Demy, Ciné-Tamaris produced and directed three films devoted to his work and life. And then, demoralized after the box office failure of the star-studded yet critically lacerated *One Hundred and One Nights* (*Les cent et une nuits de Simon Cinéma*, France, 1995), Varda temporarily withdrew from filmmaking. She bought and renovated a hotel near the town of Bonnieux in Provence. Her life as a provincial innkeeper was short-lived, however; four years later she was traveling the globe, accepting awards for *The Gleaners and I* (*Les glaneurs et la glaneuse*, France, 2000), her first digital feature.

Constructing the Catalog

One of the most decisive moments in Varda's management of Ciné-Tamaris occurred in 1993. In the wake of the production of *Jacquot de Nantes* (France, 1991), which had required seeking rights to many clips from Demy's films, Varda decided to organize her own archive, track down the rights to her films and the films of Jacques Demy, and purchase those rights. The process took a long time, and she was very systematic about it. She hired a legal specialist to comb through the archives of Ciné-Tamaris and the CNC to gather the names of all rights holders, assuring that no one was overlooked so as to avoid future legal problems.[25] She also identified the countries for which the rights remained free and thus available to be purchased. Varda's one-time archivist Bastide noted, "To my knowledge, it's very rare that a company would be organized in such a military fashion, as if launching a battle plan."[26] Also at this time, Varda began a lengthy, laborious, and expensive process of restoring Demy's films, which required extensive communication with archives and consultation with labs. Interviewed on the occasion of winning an award from the International Federation of Film Archives in 2013 for this work, she explained her motivation: "I found myself doing restorations, conducting inquiries, going to see people, out of love for Jacques and respect for his work, because I think he really is a great film-maker, so the effort was worth it."[27] Respect for the memory of her late husband and his work was a key reason for gathering together all film rights and restoring the work, but it was not the only motivation.

The purchase and subsequent distribution of *Donkey Skin* (*Peau d'âne*, dir. Jacques Demy, France, 1970) reveal an additional reason that Varda would want to engage in this laborious and expensive process of acquiring and restoring films: it was profitable. It is possible to chart the history of ownership transfers and broadcast rights via the public registry of the CNC's Cinema and Audiovisual Register (Registres du Cinéma et de l'Audiovisuel).[28] One learns, for example, that on 22 November 1990, shortly after the death of Demy, Bodard authorized Ciné-Tamaris to include excerpts of *Donkey Skin* in *Jacquot de Nantes*, Varda's film about Demy's childhood. On 5 May 2003, "Cinémag," as Bodard's company was known, sold its 45 percent share of *Donkey Skin* to Varda's children, Mathieu Demy and Rosalie Varda-Demy.[29] One can assume that Ciné-Tamaris purchased the remaining 55 percent of the rights owned by Paramount. Five months later, on 1 October 2003, Ciné-Tamaris sold the French broadcasting rights of *Donkey Skin* to Canal+ for the period 1 October 2003–31 August 2004 for €137,000. Later that same year, Ciné-Tamaris sold the broadcasting rights of *Donkey Skin* to ARTE France for one year at a cost of €110,000. Even the noncommercial uses of films generate income; on 7 October 2011, Ciné-Tamaris sold the noncommercial rights of six films to the CNC for distribution in French cultural centers abroad. For €42,000, the CNC had the right to screen the six films for a period of three years. The strategy is clear: bring a title into the Ciné-Tamaris catalog, use television funds to finance both the film's purchase and its restoration, and then, over time, launch additional production and restoration projects.

Digital Restoration, DVDs, and Exhibitions

Another decisive moment in the history of Ciné-Tamaris concerns yet another kind of production: the use of public and private monies to fund the digital restoration of the catalog. Although the photochemical restoration of the works of Demy in the late 1990s had been exhausting and time-consuming, Ciné-Tamaris launched the digital restoration of the catalog in 2011 so that the films could continue to be screened as digital cinema packages (DCPs). This wave of restorations required both public and private contributions. Rosalie Varda, charged with locating funds for the restorations, needed to seek private funding because Ciné-Tamaris did not qualify for a loan through the *grand emprunt* (big loan), the €35 billion program launched in 2009 by the French government to support educational institutions, sustainable development, and digitization projects. "We had to invent ways of funding our restorations," she said.[30]

Ciné-Tamaris was able to attract funds for film restoration from a variety of sources, including government subventions, private foundations, for-profit companies, and individuals. The digital restoration of *Umbrellas of Cherbourg* was funded in part by the Cannes Film Festival because the film won the Palme d'Or in 1964. Additional contributions emerged to cover the €110,000 cost of restoration from the luxury conglomerate LVMH, the city of Cherbourg, and the region of Basse Normandie. Ciné-Tamaris also launched a crowdfunding campaign—the first ever conducted for a film restoration—on the platform KissKissBankBank.[31] The goal was to raise €25,000 through KissKissBankBank, but more than €50,000 were contributed. The timing of the digital restoration of *Umbrellas of Cherbourg* and Demy's other films was not casual. The restorations were made possible in large part because of the planned Cinémathèque Française exhibition *Le Monde enchanté de Jacques Demy*, which took place 10 April–4 August 2013. The exhibition attracted sponsors like the luxury conglomerate LVMH because it presented significant promotional opportunities to them.[32] Once the project of restoring *Umbrellas of Cherbourg* was launched, it was easy to convince others to come on board. Sony, owner of the Columbia-produced *Model Shop* (dir. Jacques Demy, France/US, 1970) agreed to restore that film upon learning that all of Demy's films were being restored for the Cinémathèque Française exhibition and retrospective.[33] The exhibition was a success; more than one hundred thousand people visited the exhibition over four months.[34]

Ciné-Tamaris embarked on another restoration, this time of one of Varda's films, for reasons that underscore the familial nature of the company. Mathieu Demy, the son of Agnès Varda and Jacques Demy, directed *Americano* (France, 2011). The film's protagonist, played by Mathieu Demy, travels to Los Angeles after the death of his mother to organize her affairs. For the film's flashbacks, Demy wanted to use extracts from *Documenteur*, the film Varda had made in Los Angeles and in which he played a boy living with his single mother. As a result, Rosalie Varda, charged with raising funds for the digital restoration of the Ciné-Tamaris catalog, launched her effort to raise funds for the restoration of Varda's films, beginning with *Documenteur*. Two foundations, Gan and Technicolor, covered the cost of digitization and restoration of *Documenteur*.[35] Martin Scorcese's film preservation arm, Film Foundation, then stepped up to cover the cost of restoring the rest of the films Varda made in the US, including *Uncle Yanco, Black Panthers* (France/US, 1968), *Lions Love (. . . and Lies)* (France/US, 1969), and *Mur Murs*.

Ciné-Tamaris's restorations were rarely isolated projects; they were nearly always linked to other initiatives, such as museum exhibitions, theatrical rerelease, film retrospectives, festival screenings, and DVD distribution. Budgeted into each digital restoration was the striking of a new 35mm print, even if the work was initially shot digitally, which in turn sometimes led to sales of newly struck prints to museums and archives. With each restoration came the production of a glossy pressbook produced in house, as well as a short video explaining the restoration process that serves as a supplement to the DVD or content for a streaming platform. As Cecilia Rose of the Ciné-Tamaris team explained, "It's not just [a question of] the technical process [required] to make it possible to show the films. It's also the idea of creating the desire to watch the films. . . . We need to offer something new every time for these films that are sixty years old, fifty years old . . . exhibitions, books, DVD distribution."[36] Production, distribution, restoration, exhibition, the creation of ancillary materials such as catalogs, posters, and buttons; everything is linked at Ciné-Tamaris.

Near the end of Varda's life, several elements of her mode of production shifted once again. When she decided to make *Visages Villages* with JR, she agreed, for the first time, to codirect a film.[37] The funding of *Visages Villages* also constituted a departure. Ciné-Tamaris agreed to work with a broader range of investors, moving away from the traditional mix of state and television funding. Whereas *The Beaches of Agnès* (*Les plages d'Agnès*, dir. Agnès Varda,

France, 2008) was funded primarily by Canal+ and the CNC, *Visages Villages* was coproduced with a number of production companies and distributors, including Social Animals (JR's company), Rouge, Arches, and Pacte. Cecilia Rose explained, "Times are changing and we cannot finance a film with public funding only, not anymore. It used to be the case, but it's not the case any longer." Rose continued:

Agnès was very, very reluctant to give away any parts of her negatives. . . .
Rosalie said, "Okay. We can't manage it by ourselves. And we won't have
enough money from the CNC and from TV, so we need to open up,
even if it means giving away parts of the negative." Agnès considered it a
bit of a threat to Ciné-Tamaris, but it worked out really well. . . . No one
tried to overrule Agnès [on aesthetic decisions], and it's actually all that
matters.[38]

After decades of maintaining control over her own negatives, Varda shifted away from this strategy in order to make *Visages Villages*, all the while managing to maintain aesthetic control over the film.

Varda deftly managed the financing and the scale of her filmmaking activities through the decades. She also managed her persona very carefully, as do all public figures. In the early 1990s Varda bought a bicycle shop across the street from her home on rue Daguerre. She turned it into a work space as well as a display window for Ciné-Tamaris. Anyone could walk in the front door of the shop, buy a DVD or a poster, and have a chat with Agnès while she sat at her editing station working on her latest project. This charming storefront operation, one that would not have been out of place in her documentary portrait of her neighborhood *Daguerréotypes*, belies the larger sphere of Ciné-Tamaris's reach and ambition. Over time, Ciné-Tamaris used a wide variety of funding mechanisms, launched projects both modest and large in scale, and worked in conditions of both hard-fought independence and collaboration with others. Gathering the rights to Varda's negatives and to those of Jacques Demy allowed Ciné-Tamaris to monetize its back catalog, engage in both photochemical and digital restoration, survive the changes wrought by a digital media environment, and preserve both filmmakers' work for future generations. Few independent filmmakers have been so intentional and organized in these realms, which explains in large part the longevity and vitality of Ciné-Tamaris.

Notes

I am grateful to Rosalie Varda, Cecilia Rose, Bernard Bastide, David Gardner, and Sullivan Sweet for their assistance in the research of this article.

1. Laurent Creton, *Histoire économique du cinéma français: Production et financement 1940–1959* (Paris: CNRS, 2004).

2. Claude-Marie Trémois, "La Pointe Courte," *Le Cinéma chez soi*, no. 5 (February–March 1956): 28–29.

3. Bernard Bastide, "*La Pointe Courte* ou comment réaliser un film à Sète (Hérault) en 1954," *Cahiers de la Cinémathèque*, no. 61 (September 1994): 32.

4. Trémois, "La Pointe Courte."

5. Bastide, "*La Pointe Courte*," 32.

6. Creton, *Histoire économique du cinéma français*, 220–21.

7. Colin Crisp, *The Classic French Cinema, 1930–1960* (Bloomington: Indiana University Press, 1997), 272.

8. Richard Neupert, *A History of the French New Wave Cinema*, 2nd ed. (Madison: University of Wisconsin Press, 2007), 57.

9. Agnès Varda, interview by Jacques Ledoux, Cinémathèque de Belgique/Radio Télévision Belge, 1961–62, transcript, Ciné-Tamaris archive.

10. Bernard Bastide, email correspondence with the author, 1 May 2020.

11. Agnès Varda, *Varda par Agnès* (Paris: Editions Cahiers du cinéma, 1994), 229.

12. Varda, *Varda par Agnès*, 232.

13. Michel Marie, *The French New Wave*, trans. Richard Neupert (Malden, MA: Blackwell, 2003), 49.

14. Neupert, *History of the French New Wave Cinema*, 333.

15. Neupert suggests that the 1959 revamping of the aid program had a decisive impact on the New Wave, strengthening aid for lower-budget, riskier films and encouraging new producers to enter the industry. Neupert, *History of the French New Wave Cinema*, 36–38. For a detailed discussion of aid programs in the first half of the 1960s, see Frédérique Gimello-Mesplomb, "Le prix de la qualité: L'État et le cinéma français (1960–1965)," *Politix* 16, no. 61 (2003): 95–122.

16. Marcel Martin, "Agnès Varda: Le cinéma d'auteur est une entreprise héroique," *Le Technicien du film*, no. 247 (15 April–15 May 1977).

17. Martin, "Agnès Varda."

18. Rebecca J. DeRoo, "Confronting Contradictions: Genre Subversion and Feminist Politics in Agnès Varda's *L'une chante, l'autre pas*," *Modern and Contemporary France* 17, no. 3 (2009): 258.

19. Quoted in Martin, "Agnès Varda."

20. Martin, "Agnès Varda."

21. Martin, "Agnès Varda."

22. Michel Boujut, "Si le cinéma ne meurt: Entretien avec Agnès Varda," *Les Nouvelles littéraires*, no. 2636 (18–25 May 1978).

23. Jacques Siclier, "Portrait de l'exil," *Le Monde*, 21 January 1982.

24. Jean-Jacques Bauby, "Agnès Varda: Le cinéma en exil," *Le Matin magazine*, 13 February 1982.

25. Bastide, email correspondence.

26. Bastide, email correspondence.

27. Esteve Riambau, "Cinéaste et restauratice: Entretien avec Agnès Varda," *Journal of Film Preservation*, no. 89 (2013): 18.

28. Registres du cinéma et de l'audiovisuel, CNC, www.cnc.fr /cinema/registres-du-cinema-et-de-laudiovisuel-rca_777234.

29. Bernard Bastide, email correspondence with the author, 30 April 2020. Bastide recalled that the purchase price for 45 percent

of the rights from Bodard's company was €23,000. The other 55 percent of *Donkey Skin* was owned by Paramount, so one can assume the total price was significantly higher.

30. Rosalie Varda, interview by the author, Paris, France, 14 January 2020.

31. Cecilia Rose, interview by the author, Paris, France, 14 January 2020.

32. Rose interview.

33. Rosalie Varda interview.

34. Jean-Pierre Berthomé, "Un héritage confisqué? Jacques Demy et Ciné-Tamaris," *1895*, no. 72 (2014): 147.

35. Riambau, "Cinéaste et restauratice," 18.

36. Rose interview.

37. Varda had considered codirecting *The Beaches of Agnès* with assistant director Didier Rouget but rejected that idea after the shooting of the film's first scene.

38. Rose interview.

Kelley Conway is professor in the Department of Communication Arts at University of Wisconsin–Madison. She is the author of *Chanteuse in the City* (2004), *Agnès Varda* (2015), and articles on Chantal Akerman, Jean-Luc Godard, Jean Renoir, Agnès Varda, popular music in films, and multimedia installations.

Figure 2. *Cleo from 5 to 7* (*Cléo de 5 à 7*, France, 1962) pressbook created by Ciné-Tamaris on the occasion of the 2K restoration of the film and its official selection in the Festival de Cannes's 2012 "Cannes Classics" program. The booklet contains a synopsis of the film, a brief history of the film's initial screening at Cannes and its restoration, excerpts from press reviews, and a series of ten still images from the film, the location where they were shot, and the time of day the scene was meant to take place.

Figure 1. Agnès Varda presents speech with Cate Blanchett at the 12 May 2018 Cannes Film Festival demonstration. She stands beside director Céline Sciamma and with members of the French 50/50 en 2020 collective. Clarence Tsui, "French Film Legend Agnès Varda on *Faces Places*, Her Feminist Vision, and Visits to Hong Kong and China," *South China Morning Post*, 5 June 2018

Agnès Varda and Le Collectif 50/50 en 2020: Power and Protest at the Cannes Film Festival

Rebecca J. DeRoo

Agnès Varda created cinematic work for more than six decades, from her first film, *La Pointe Courte* (France, 1954), to her final film, *Varda by Agnès* (*Varda par Agnès*, France, 2019). She is regarded as one of the most prolific female and feminist filmmakers worldwide. She first forged her directorial career by forming a cooperative, and she later formed her own production company, Ciné-Tamaris, which she often called "artisanal." Working with a small team of collaborators, modest budgets, and regularly seeking out subsidies and coproductions, Varda maintained great creative control in writing screenplays, directing, and editing films. While the feminist thematics of her films have been interpreted in generations of excellent scholarship, and her involvement in the 1970s French women's liberation movement is well-known, her late-career activism in the field of cinema has not been the subject of sustained scholarly study.[1] Varda, I argue, used speeches, symbolic actions, and activism at the Cannes Film Festival in recent years to reveal and contest the dynamics of power and the chal-

Camera Obscura 106, Volume 36, Number 1
DOI 10.1215/02705346-8838577   © 2021 by *Camera Obscura*
Published by Duke University Press

lenges faced by female directors in French cinema. She evoked these challenges in her speech and interviews upon receiving the honorary Palme at the 2015 Cannes Film Festival. At the 2018 festival she protested the underrepresentation of women's work with activists of the French 50/50 en 2020 collective, a gender equity campaign comprising writers, directors, producers, actresses, cinematographers, talent agents, editors, distributors, sales agents, and other members of the film industry (fig. 1). The 2019 Cannes festival tribute to Varda following her death in March of that year further reveals relations of socioeconomic power and perceptions of cultural worth.

Varda has sent films to the Cannes festival throughout her career. For example, her French New Wave film *Cleo from 5 to 7* (*Cléo de 5 à 7*, 1961) was screened in competition in 1962 (and was re-presented in 2012 under the "Cannes Classics" rubric). Films such as *Jacquot* (*Jacquot de Nantes*, France, 1990) and *The Gleaners and I* (*Les glaneurs et la glaneuse*, France, 2000) were screened outside competition, and others such as *Mur Murs* (France, 1980), *Ulysse* (*Ulysses*, France, 1982), and *The Young Girls Turn Twenty-Five* (*Les Demoiselles ont eu 25 ans*, 1993), were screened in the category "Un Certain Regard," which runs parallel to the main competition and suggests original vision.[2] Varda was a member of the Cannes jury in 2005 and president of the Caméra d'Or (the Golden Camera) jury in 2013. In 2017 she won a documentary award, L'Oeil d'Or (the Golden Eye), for her film *Visages Villages* (*Faces Places*, France), codirected with the French muralist JR, and she received a rousing standing ovation.[3]

Yet Varda's recent actions at the Cannes Film Festival allow us to see the challenges that she and other female directors have faced. In particular, Varda and 50/50 en 2020 examine how institutions of power in creative fields may affect women's access to the highest honors and levels of success. Cannes is, of course, a central institution of power. At the festival, held on the French Riviera each May, movie deals are made and funding and distribution are often negotiated. Indeed, it is considered one of the largest international film marketplaces for industry professionals, and it attracts investors, producers, and distributors, who meet throughout the festival.[4] Juries and screenings are set by the festival. Most visible are the approximately twenty films selected for the main competition, which vie for prizes, the most prestigious of which is the Palme d'Or. These are awarded by a jury composed of directors, actors, and other prominent members of the film industry. Additional films are selected for screening outside the main competition in other categories, tributes, or special events. The festival is famous for its glamorous invitation-only black tie and gown screenings, where directors and stars appear on the red carpet and at festivities. Having a film in competition at Cannes and winning an award have a tremendous impact on a film's international distribution and on a director's ability to receive support for new work. So although Varda was active at Cannes throughout her career, it is significant that she never won the Palme d'Or in competition or achieved access to the immense budgets that such acclaim can bring.

Varda's and 50/50 en 2020's examination of Cannes as a cultural institution brings to mind the methodology of the feminist art historian Linda Nochlin. In revealing the social and institutional factors that were needed for success (and limitations to them), Nochlin demystified the notion that artists or their works were acclaimed solely due to notions of innate talent or personal genius, concepts that she argued often remained ambiguous.[5] Varda and 50/50 en 2020 articulate a continuing need for this type of gendered critique of cultural institutions and the relations of power they represent, albeit focusing on concerns particular to the festival and the film industry: exploring the differences between awards and support for creating new work, challenging customary social roles on the red carpet, and pursuing how and by whom films are selected to screen in competition at the festival. In other words, they have sought to make visible economic, social, and institutional factors involved in success. Furthermore, Nochlin advocated not only for investigating women's artistic accomplishments but also for examining the tensions and contradictions in the careers of "exceptional women" as revelatory of larger cultural institutions and the unspoken assumptions of the field. We can see Varda late in her career making a similar critique through her actions at Cannes. Varda, I argue, used the successes and opportunities of her late career both to celebrate recognition of women's work and to underscore gendered obstacles, the work yet to be done.

Honors as Platform for Commentary

Critics referred to the 2015 Cannes Film Festival as the year of "women in the spotlight."[6] The festival planned to highlight women's accomplishments as a response to concerns about the underrepresentation of women at the festival and in the field of cinema.[7] Within this context, Varda received a Palme d'Honneur, a lifetime achievement award.[8] This award recognizes the work and career of important filmmakers and is granted outside competition. Festival publicity explained the decision to honor Varda: "Her work and life are infused with the spirit of freedom, the art of driving back boundaries, a fierce determination that brooks no obstacles. Simply put, Varda seems capable of accomplishing everything she wants."[9] However, at Cannes Varda worked to make those obstacles visible. In an unusual acceptance speech, Varda expressed thanks for this award of what she termed a Palme of "resistance and endurance," which she dedicated to creative and courageous directors not yet in the spotlight.[10] Her comments imply that official attempts at retrospective honor obscure such omissions without interrogating the structural reasons for them or increasing the number of women's films in contemporary competition. Given that the festival was promoted as putting "women in the spotlight," her word choice suggests that that goal had not in fact been achieved. Furthermore, in interviews at Cannes Varda commented that she received prizes but not large sums of money to fund her films, underscoring the difference between symbolic gesture and material support for continuing her projects.[11]

That year Varda was part of a series of dialogues called "Women in Motion," which was organized in conjunction with the Cannes festival to highlight the accomplishments of women in cinema, as well as the challenges they encountered. Thierry Frémaux, the general delegate of the festival, explained that the dialogues provided "additional prominence to the talented women of film and their outlook on cinema" but didn't offer specific plans for change.[12]

The issue of film funding was a pressing one for Varda. Upon returning from Cannes, she launched what would become the film *Visages Villages*, a collaboration with artist JR. Both traveled across France to create work about the people they encountered, JR making large-scale photographs and murals and Varda filming and interviewing individuals, making "local documentary." The project was partially crowd-sourced in June and July 2015 via a thirty-day online campaign on KissKissBankBank (a French vehicle for funding creative projects using a participatory model, loosely based on Kickstarter). The website requested individual dona-tions beginning at €10, accompanied by a promotional video, in which the two artists presented the project and reached out for support. When JR proclaimed, "We wish no brands or other types of financiers to be behind it, but that the people support it," Varda interjected, insisting, "We need financiers! But we haven't found them."[13] The film would eventually be distributed by the Cohen Media Group and receive international acclaim. But at that time, Varda and JR explained they had partial funding and were appeal-ing for resources necessary for realizing the project; they received crowdsourcing of €58,106.[14]

During the 2015 Cannes festival and in the days follow-ing, Varda was working to launch the *Visages Villages* campaign on KissKissBankBank. I was conducting research in her archives and wanted to discuss with her what was happening, so we set up a for-mal, recorded interview. I asked Varda about the greatest challenge she faced in creating new work. As at Cannes, she underscored the contradiction between receiving prizes but not large budgets. She explained:

We have to find money. . . . At Cannes, Frances McDormand was giving a speech about the situation of women in the cinema business. . . . She said, "We don't want help, we want money." And that's the point. As long as women are not given enough money to make films, we cannot do them. I spent I think three-quarters of my life looking for money. And I did some films and I enjoyed what I did. But I could have made more if I was not always looking for money. . . .

The investors don't like to invest in my films. They say "Bravo!" with awards and a lot of thanks. But they don't come with a blank check and

Figure 2. Kristin Stewart, Léa Seydoux, Khadja Nin,
Ava DuVernay, Cate Blanchett, Agnès Varda, and Céline
Sciamma at the 12 May 2018 Cannes Film Festival red carpet
demonstration. "Female Stars Call for Equal Pay in Cannes
Protest," *AFP Relax News*, 12 May 2018

say "OK, do whatever you want." Never. I'm blessed to be loved and to
be admired . . . [and receive] lifetime achievement awards . . . but that
doesn't help me find money. Still the struggle is there.[15]

Collective Action at the 2018 Cannes Film Festival

In 2018 Varda moved from using awards and individual honors as
platforms for commentary to another kind of critique. On 12 May
she helped announce a collective action at the 2018 Cannes Film
Festival, organized in conjunction with the 50/50 en 2020 collective (fig. 1). With Cate Blanchett (the 2018 jury president) halfway
up the steps of the red carpet, Varda announced a gender equity
campaign. Joining them were eighty women in the international
film industry—directors, actresses, producers, crew members,
screenwriters, sales agents, distributors, talent agents, and editors—
totaling eighty-two, equal to the number of women who had
climbed the steps with films in the official competition during the
festival's seventy-one-year history. The movement compared this
figure with more than sixteen hundred male directors in official
competition over the same time period. They noted that there

Figure 3. The eighty-two women standing on the red carpet stairs, representing the eighty-two female directors with films in the official selection competition across the seventy-one-year history of the Cannes festival, 12 May 2018. Amancay Tapia, "If We Want Better Films, We Need More Female Directors and More Diversity in General," *Metro*, 17 May 2018

had been only twelve female jury heads of the main competition in the festival's seventy-one-year history.[16] The women walked arm in arm in rows on the red carpet; Varda is pictured with Céline Sciamma and the female jury members Kristen Stewart, Léa Seydoux, Khadja Nin, Ava DuVernay, and Cate Blanchett (fig. 2).[17] The women stopped and stood halfway up the red carpet steps to the Palais des Festivals building, where the main competition screenings are held (fig. 3). They called for "50/50 by 2020," or gender equity at the Cannes festival and in the film industry more broadly in two years. They underscored the limited number of women directors' work in competition across the festival's history and announced specific demands for institutional change.[18]

Blanchett, in English, and Varda, in French, read a collective statement, declaring:

Women are not a minority in the world, yet the current state of our industry says otherwise. As women, we all face our own unique challenges, but we stand together on these stairs today as a symbol of our determination and commitment to progress. We are writers, producers, actresses, cinematographers, talent agents, editors, distributors, sales agents, and all involved in the cinematic arts.

We stand in solidarity with women of all industries.

We will expect our institutions to actively provide parity and transparency in their executive bodies and safe environments in which to work.

We will expect our governments to make sure that the laws of equal pay for equal work are upheld.

We will demand that our workplaces are diverse and equitable so that they best reflect the world in which we actually live. A world that allows all of us behind and in front of the camera to thrive shoulder to shoulder with our male colleagues.

We acknowledge all of the women and men who are standing for change.

The stairs of our industry must be accessible to all.[19]

They ended the speech with "*on monte*" (let's climb), naming their climb up the ladder of the film industry and also up the red carpet steps, where women have conventionally been treated as fashionable and silent objects, to enter the festival making powerful declarations.

While the event made global news, its complex institutional critique merits further investigation. For example, it is often assumed that Blanchett and Varda read the same statement, one in English and one in French, but there are subtle and important differences in their words. Blanchett noted that in the history of the festival only two female directors had won the prestigious Palme d'Or, whereas Varda noted that when Jane Campion won, it was *ex æquo* (two Palmes d'Or, the top prizes, were given that year) and that her own Palme d'Or was *honoraire* (honorary), not awarded in the festival's competition.[20]

The 50/50 en 2020 collective set out to use the protest's critique for broader institutional change. It underscored that the number of women's films in competition at Cannes remained low in 2018 (three of twenty-one films).[21] The fact that in 2017 Varda and JR's film *Visages Villages* was screened outside competition and won a special documentary award, L'Oeil d'Or, of €5,000, a modest sum, bears out their critique (and her own earlier critique) that these limited and symbolic honors do not win substantial financial and institutional support for creating new work. Activist and author Melissa Silverstein described the concerns:

The issue of the lack of female directors is dominating this year's Cannes Film Festival. Part of this conversation is how movies get selected and who selects them. Is there a clear submission process? Is it mostly curated? Is it all about who Thierry Frémaux, the head of the festival, knows and likes and wants to see on his red carpet? The only way to figure out why year after year more women can't get programmed here is to understand the process, which until now has remained hidden. The women who organized the march of the 82 women were very savvy to tie a pledge for gender parity to the march to push Frémaux towards answering some of [these] fundamental questions.[22]

The protest led to some change. The general delegate of the Cannes festival, Thierry Frémaux, signed a pledge to study wom-

Figure 4. Members of the 2018 Cannes jury—Ava DuVernay, Robert Guédiguian, Chang Chen, Cate Blanchett, and Khadja Nin—with Thierry Frémaux, the general delegate of the Cannes festival, who presents the signed 50/50 en 2020 Pledge. Gwilym Mumford, "Cannes Film Festival Unveils Equality Charter in Push for Gender Parity," *Guardian*, 14 May 2018

en's representation at the festival and in the film industry. The French minister of culture, Françoise Nyssen, and president of the Centre National du Cinéma et de l'Image Animée, Frédérique Bredin, attended the signing, along with representatives from the Cannes jury and film activist groups, including the French 50/50 en 2020, American and UK chapters of Time's Up, Italian Dissenso Commune, Spanish CIMA, and Greek Women's Wave (fig. 4).[23] The Cannes festival was the first to sign a pledge with 50/50 en 2020, but over one hundred international film festivals have since signed pledges.[24]

The pledge at Cannes signed by Frémaux and his colleagues Edouard Waintrop and Charles Tesson, artistic directors of the Director's Fortnight and Critics' Week,[25] agreed to disclose gender statistics regarding the directors and crews of films submitted to the festival, identify the members of selection and programming committees, and make a commitment to achieve gender parity on the executive board.[26] Silverstein summed up the significance of the agreement: "There is clearly very strong momentum to increase opportunities for women, to get a sense of the numbers in places where there have been no statistics previously, and to work together across borders to continue the push for change."[27]

Frémaux, however, did not commit to screening a certain number of films by women at Cannes, insisting that films be simply judged by "artistic merit."[28] Nochlin's points resonate here: artistic merit is ambiguously defined, and it is also the product of various institutional and social forces. Critic Gwilym Mumford described the decision: "The festival stopped short of promising to introduce gender parity in terms of directors of films selected, confirming festival director Thierry Frémaux's long-held position that the selections should be based on 'artistic merit' alone." She continued: "Frémaux said that by being transparent Cannes would respond to issues of diversity and parity while still using 'its own editorial and strategic judgment' in selecting films."[29] Members of the Cannes festival gave another familiar reason for the underrepresentation of women: that there weren't enough women-directed films to enter into competition.[30]

Others pointed out that there were equal numbers of women

in film school and countered the festival's insistence on pure artistic merit; the problem, they said, echoing Varda's 2015 critique and many others, is that women were not getting enough funding to make work.[31] And journalists insisted that women's film festivals internationally have for decades featured women directors' work, so in fact many women's films are available for Cannes to screen.[32] Similarly, the 50/50 en 2020 protestors actively work to make these forces of selection visible, building on the Cannes protest by researching and publicizing statistics about women's underrepresentation at Cannes and in the French film industry.

50/50 en 2020: Statistics and Study of Cannes

The French 50/50 en 2020 collective is part of larger 50/50 by 2020 international movements advocating for gender equality in the film industry. The French collective was launched on 1 March 2018 with more than six hundred signatories, including filmmakers Rebecca Zlotowski, Justine Triet, Bertrand Bonello, and Tonie Marshall; producers Marie-Ange Luciani and Caroline Benjo; and actors Adèle Haenel, Léa Seydoux, and Pierre Deladonchamps; as well as other scriptwriters, distributors, and film industry professionals.[33] It describes itself as an "action tank" advocating for equality. The 50/50 en 2020 website explains its central principles:

We believe that the distribution of power needs to be questioned.
　We believe that equality restores the balance of power.
　We believe that diversity deeply changes representations.
　We believe that the opportunity to work in an egalitarian and inclusive environment must be seized because we are certain that the equal sharing of power will promote profound creative renewal.[34]

The movement also defines its objectives:

1) Challenge our cultural institutions

With the aim of equal directorial boards by 2020. This concerns our public institutions, but also private entities, professional unions, festivals, juries, and film schools. We expect the decision makers at

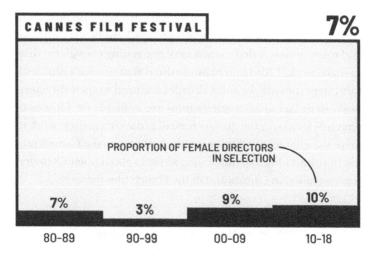

CANNES FILM FESTIVAL | **7%**

PROPORTION OF FEMALE DIRECTORS IN SELECTION

7% 3% 9% 10%

80–89 90–99 00–09 10–18

Figure 5. 50/50 en 2020, "Comparison of the Last Thirty-Nine Editions—1980–2018" (detail), in "The Role of Women in the Cannes Festival's Competition—A Comparative Study," collectif5050.com/en/study/cannes

FEMALE DIRECTORS SELECTED IN COMPETITION

The share of female directors in competition in Cannes has never been above 20%, even though it has been increasing in recent years.

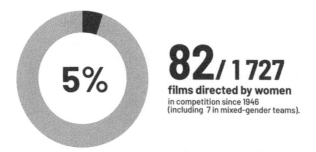

5%

82/ 1 727
films directed by women
in competition since 1946
(including 7 in mixed-gender teams).

Figure 6. 50/50 en 2020, "Female Directors Selected in Competition," 1946–2018, in "The Role of Women in the Cannes Festival's Competition—A Comparative Study," collectif5050.com/en/study/cannes

the head of these entities to cultivate awareness with the intent of encouraging equality, inclusion, and younger generations. The true diversity of our country needs to be duly represented.

2) Create an observatory to monitor equality in our industry

It will produce new statistics with the ambition of covering the full spectrum of our field: salary disparity between male and female crew members, between actors and actresses, the budget differences between films by male and female directors, and the lack of diversity throughout the industry.[35]

50/50 en 2020 works with the data collection agency Datcha to produce and analyze statistics on the French film industry, which 50/50 en 2020 makes public on its website, "using the power of numbers to raise awareness [and] increase the visibility of these issues."[36] The graph "A Very Unequal Distribution of Jobs: Portion of Women in Film Production" illustrates gender imbalance in jobs in the film industry (for example, women comprising 96 percent of script supervisors, but 24 percent of directors).[37] Other statistics specifically focus on the Cannes Film Festival.[38] 50/50 en 2020's graph on women's films in selection at Cannes since 1980 shows that an average of about 7 percent of selected films were directed by women (fig. 5). The protests underscored the small number of women directors in competition; another graphic demonstrates that the percentage has not been above 20 percent in one year and averages 5 percent over the history of the festival (fig. 6).

50/50 en 2020's 2018 graphic titled "Festival Heads" describes "100% masculine leadership" at major European film festivals, demonstrating that Thierry Frémaux has been the artistic delegate and then the general delegate at Cannes for over seventeen years (fig. 7). The graphic also includes the head of the Venice Film Festival, the Berlin International Film Festival, and the Cannes Critics' Week and Directors' Fortnight.[39]

50/50 en 2020's graphic on female jury presidents explains that "on average, only 17% of the Cannes Festival's jury presidents were women. This proportion hasn't seen any major evolution in

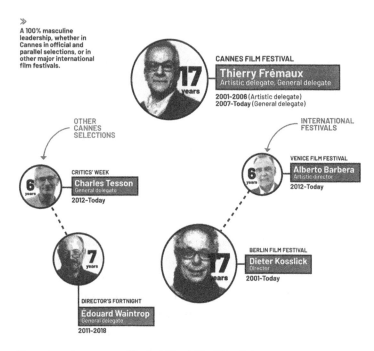

Figure 7. 50/50 en 2020, "Festival Heads," in "The Role
of Women in the Cannes Festival's Competition—A
Comparative Study," collectif5050.com/en/study/cannes

the last thirty years." It lists the twelve female presidents out of
seventy-one total jury presidents (fig. 8). It is evident that the female
presidents are overwhelmingly actresses, with only one writer/
screenwriter (Françoise Sagan) and two directors (Liv Ullmann
and Jane Campion) listed. Male film directors serving as jury presidents are much more common.

Another image indicates the Cannes Film Festival board of
directors comprised 25 percent women among its elected members
(fig. 9). 50/50 en 2020 notes, "The identity of 12 members 'ex offi-
cio' is not communicated," suggesting that more than the official
board affects the selection process. These graphics support 50/50

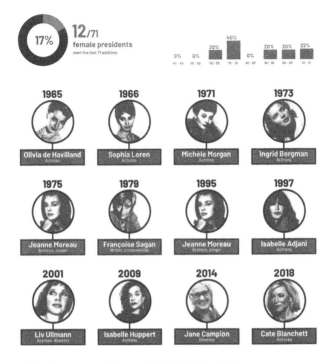

CANNES FILM FESTIVAL - 1946-2018

Figure 8. 50/50 en 2020, Cannes Film Festival female jury presidents, 1946–2018 (detail), in "The Role of Women in the Cannes Festival's Competition—A Comparative Study," collectif5050.com/en/study/cannes

en 2020's institutional critique about where power lies and how films are selected to screen in competition.

There has been some change. In 2019 four women's films were among the nineteen in competition for the Palme d'Or at Cannes (one more than in 2018), and three won prizes (though not the Palme d'Or).[40] Cannes honored its commitment and revealed the full selection committee, which in 2019 was composed of four women and four men.[41] The Cannes Film Festival was the first to sign the pledge for more transparency around the composition of festival boards and the selection process, and there has been a con-

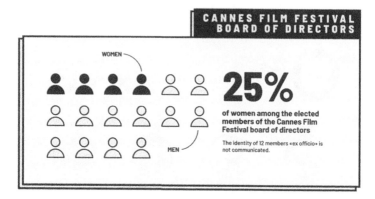

Figure 9. 50/50 en 2020, "Cannes Film Festival Board of Directors," in "The Role of Women in the Cannes Festival's Competition—A Comparative Study," collectif5050.com/en /study/cannes

tinuing wave of impact, with other festivals signing the pledge.[42] And 50/50 en 2020 continues to call for action and institutional change.

Tributes and Commemoration

In May 2019 Varda was featured on the posters for the Cannes Film Festival, the first female director to be so honored.[43] For comparison, I have included the historical photograph on which it is based (fig. 10). The poster celebrates Varda, but its rhetoric conceals obstacles and institutional and economic factors shaping perceptions of merit. The image shows Varda filming improvisationally, by standing on the back of cinematographer Louis Stein while making her first film, *La Pointe Courte*. She perched on his shoulders for additional height to get a shot, given the limited equipment she had for filming. The festival's press release praised Varda's "creativity and experimentation."[44] Festival president Pierre Lescure stated, "You can feel the strength of her engagement: she would do everything to create, everything to overcome hurdles."[45] Varda certainly was creative in overcoming hurdles and made it part of her work process: she made the film by creating a cooperative, and she filmed on location with a small cast and crew over two months with a very limited budget.[46] But the festival's triumphant rhetoric obscures the challenges she faced: filming improvisationally was necessary due to minimal resources. The poster also omits the part of the original photograph that shows a woman working in the foreground, thus promoting an image of independence and downplaying collaboration. Furthermore, *La Pointe Courte* was filmed on location in an impoverished Mediterranean fishing village and portrays a workers' struggle (the water is the site of the conflict), but the poster replaces its gritty beach with glitz and a vibrant color palette of purple, red, orange, and yellow that evokes the sunshine sparkling on the water of the Côte d'Azur and the bright lights of Cannes (with the glamour of Cannes replacing political struggle).

Moreover, this edited image suggests a historical association between Varda and the Cannes festival. Furthering this suggestion, journalists reported that the film screened at Cannes in 1955.[47] But the festival itself did not screen *La Pointe Courte*. Varda has recounted how she took a third-class train to Cannes with her film in canisters and rented a projection room to screen it in the city during the festival to try to interest distributors, without success.[48] In other words, this tribute suggests a relationship and level of institutional or economic support that she did not enjoy at the time.

It is notable that Varda was the first female director honored on the Cannes festival poster. Yet the festival's narrative of directorial intensity that overcomes hurdles suggests a notion of individual talent that obscures socioeconomic factors contributing to the absence of other women in this role. And this narrative does not fully respond to Varda's and 50/50 en 2020's critique: that challenges remain and need to be addressed in far-reaching and systematic ways. Varda and 50/50 en 2020 call for larger examinations of institutions and industry, rather than including an individual artist in an established canon, which may leave its values largely intact. This work is not an easy corrective, but revealing institutional, social, and economic dynamics is an important step toward changing them.

Varda helps us examine relations of power at the Cannes festival, first more subtly in her individual speech and then in joining with 50/50 en 2020 to more directly push for change. Both efforts seek to understand the processes of selection and the unspoken factors that may shape access and success.[49] This work is making an impact, as Cannes and other festivals sign the pledge and increasingly make their processes public. As we pay tribute to Varda, let us not obscure but remember the challenges she faced across her career and continually worked to address, both alone and with others. Her legacy is a call to action.

Notes

I thank the *Camera Obscura* reviewers and Jill Carrick for their helpful reading of this article.

1. For example, her engagement with concerns raised in the French *mouvement de libération des femmes* is conveyed in such films as *One Sings, the Other Doesn't* (*L'une chante, l'autre pas*, France/Belgium, 1976) and referenced in her autobiographical *The Beaches of Agnès* (*Les plages d'Agnès*, France, 2008) and *Varda by Agnès* (*Varda par Agnès*, France, 2019).

2. Moreover, Varda's *O saisons, ô châteaux* (France, 1957) screened in a competition for short films; her recent 2018 rerelease of *One Sings, the Other Doesn't* was presented at Cinéma de la Plage. See the Festival de Cannes, "Agnès Varda," www.festival-cannes.com /en/artist/agnes-varda.

3. As Peter Debruge describes: "Varda was a regular at Cannes, whether or not she had a film to screen there." Debruge, "Cannes: Official Poster Pays Tribute to Agnès Varda," *Variety*, 15 April 2019, variety.com/2019/film/festivals/cannes-official -poster-agnes-varda-1203181525/.

4. See the Festival de Cannes website "Marché du Film," www .marchedufilm.com.

5. Nochlin's groundbreaking early essay "Why Have There Been No Great Women Artists?" continues to be widely taught due to its contemporary potential as a feminist methodological model. Nochlin's essay was originally published in 1971, when female artists were largely underrepresented in cultural institutions and

college curricula. Nochlin called for examining the unspoken assumptions and institutions of the field. As a historian of nineteenth-century art, Nochlin identified various historical and institutional obstacles that women often faced in that century: not being admitted into art academies, not being allowed to paint the nude (one of the highest genres in the artistic hierarchy), and being expected to perform feminine social roles and domestic labor. She famously challenged the notion that artists or their works were acclaimed simply due to innate talent by underscoring the social, economic, and institutional factors that were needed for success. Nochlin, "Why Have There Been No Great Women Artists?," repr. in *Women, Art, and Power and Other Essays* (New York: Harper and Row, 1988), 145–76. Recently reflecting on Nochlin's essay, critic Eleanor Heartney wrote: "In an era in which young women are encouraged to aspire to the same career goals as men" but find they are unable to attain "the highest leadership positions . . . Nochlin's approach to questions about success continues to resonate." Heartney, "Linda Nochlin," *Brooklyn Rail,* July–August 2015, brooklynrail .org/2015/07/criticspage/linda-nochlin-heartney. This article uses the terms *women* and *female* to maintain consistency with the French sources quoted in my discussion. I have used the sources' own English translations when available.

6. Emma Jones, "Women in the Spotlight at Cannes Film Festival," *BBC News,* 16 May 2015, www.bbc.com/news/av/entertainment -arts-32763053.

7. For example, Emmanuelle Bercot's *La tête haute* (*Standing Tall,* France, 2015) was selected to open the festival; the festival also hosted a conference on gender equality supported by the United Nations and *Variety.*

8. For an extended analysis of the award ceremony at Cannes, see Rebecca J. DeRoo, *Agnès Varda between Film, Photography, and Art* (Oakland: University of California Press, 2018), 1–6, 157–59.

9. Quoted in "Cannes 2015: La 4ème Palme d'Or d'Honneur de l'Histoire remise à une cinéaste," *L'actualité cinéma sur Canal+,* 11 May 2015.

10. Quoted in Anne-Laure Deparis, "Cannes 2015—L'émouvant discours d'Agnès Varda, Palme d'or d'honneur," *Télé 2 semaines,* 25 May 2015, www.programme.tv/news/cinema/141009-cannes

-2015-l-emouvant-discours-d-agnes-varda-palme-d-or-d-honneur
-videos/.

11. "Women in Motion Talk with Agnès Varda—Cannes Film
     Festival 2015," *Le Figaro TV*, 23 May 2015.

12. Quoted in Elsa Keslassy, "Cannes Film Fest, Kering Launch
     Women in Motion," *Variety*, 24 June 2015, variety.com/2015
     /film/festivals/cannes-film-fest-kering-launch-women-in
     -motion-1201462413/. "Women in Motion" was organized with
     support from Frémaux and François-Henri Pinault, the chair
     and CEO of Kering, the fashion and luxury goods conglomerate
     that owns Gucci and Yves Saint Laurent, among other brands.

13. Ciné-Tamaris and Social Animals, "AV et JR deux artistes en
     goguette—lancement de la campagne KissKissBankBank," 10
     June 2015, www.kisskissbankbank.com/av-et-jr-deux-artistes-en
     -goguette, www.youtube.com/watch?v=1CDxElREXPE.

14. Ciné-Tamaris and Social Animals, "AV et JR deux artistes en
     goguette."

15. Agnès Varda, interview by the author, Paris, 8 June 2015.

16. For the full text, see Le Collectif 50/50, "12 mai 2018, La montée
     des 82, Le Texte," collectif5050.com/cannes (accessed 10 May
     2020).

17. The event preceded the screening of Eva Husson's *Les filles du
     soleil* (*Girls of the Sun*, France, 2018). Participants wore the 50/50
     by 2020 pin. Some wore black in solidarity with Time's Up.

18. The French 50/50 en 2020 website uses the terms *women* and
     men and has focused primarily on achieving gender parity. The
     American 50/50 by 2020 website provides statistics regarding
     representation of gender, race, ability/disability, and sexuality in
     Hollywood. Since the 2018 protests discussed in this article, the
     French movement has shifted its name to "Le Collectif 50/50"
     and has also used "50/50×2020." See the websites for French
     50/50 en 2020 (Le Collectif 50/50, collectif5050.com) and
     American 50/50 by 2020 (5050by2020.com).

19. Le Collectif 50/50, "12 mai 2018."

20. For reporting of the event, see Festival de Cannes, "82 femmes
     pour la parité, Cannes 2018," 15 May 2018, YouTube, www

.youtube.com/watch?v=Bkp_Yikd-Zs. For a list of the eighty-two participants, see Le Collectif 50/50, "5050×2020-Cannes-Press," collectif5050.com/cannes (accessed 10 May 2020). For a list of signatories supporting the French collective's work, see Le Collectif 50/50, "The Signatories," collectif5050.com/en/the -petitioners (accessed 10 May 2020). On how Varda's work has been marginalized historically in cinema studies scholarship, see, e.g., René Prédal, "Agnès Varda: Une oeuvre en marge du cinéma français," *Études cinématographiques*, nos. 179–86 (1991): 13–39; Genevieve Sellier, *Masculine Singular, French New Wave Cinema* (Durham, NC: Duke University Press, 2008); and Nick James, ed., "The Irrepressible Agnès Varda," special issue, *Sight and Sound* 28, no. 7 (2018).

21. Gwilym Mumford, "Cannes Film Festival Unveils Equality Charter in Push for Gender Parity," *Guardian*, 14 May 2018, www.theguardian.com/film/2018/may/14/cannes-film-festival -unveils-equality-charter-in-push-for-gender-parity.

22. Melissa Silverstein, "Cannes Film Festival Signs Pledge in Push for Gender Parity," *Women and Hollywood*, 15 May 2018, womenandhollywood.com/cannes-film-festival-signs-pledge/. Silverstein is the founder of the Women and Hollywood website, which promotes gender diversity and equity in the film industry.

23. Maha Dakhil represented the American Time's Up; Audrey Gagneux and Kate Kinninmont represented Time's Up UK; Sarah Calderon represented the Spanish Association of Women Filmmakers and Audiovisual Media Artists (CIMA); Jasmine Trinca and Ginevra Elkann represented the Italian Dissenso Commune; Memi Koupa and Daphné Patakia represented the Greek Women's Wave; and Céline Sciamma and Rebecca Zlotowski represented the French 50/50 en 2020 (5050×2020). The French minister of culture, Françoise Nyssen, launched the "Conference for Equality in the Film Industry." See the press release, Le Collectif 50/50, "Déroulé de la Table Ronde," 14 May 2018, and Le Collectif 50/50, "Communiqué de Presse," 12 May 2018, collectif5050.com/cannes (accessed 10 May 2020).

24. Examples include the Berlin Film Festival, Venice Film Festival, and Toronto Film Festival. See Le Collectif 50/50, "Festivals That Have Signed the Pledge," collectif5050.com/en/the-festivals (accessed 10 May 2020).

25. Paolo Moretti, incoming director of the Director's Fortnight, also attended.

26. See Rhonda Richford, "Cannes: Cate Blanchett, Kristen Stewart Join Thierry Fremaux as He Signs Gender Parity Pledge," *Hollywood Reporter*, 14 May 2018, www.hollywoodreporter.com /news/cannes-cate-blanchett-kristen-stewart-join-thierry -fremaux-as-he-signs-gender-parity-pledge-1111531.

27. Silverstein, "Cannes Film Festival Signs Pledge."

28. Mumford, "Cannes Film Festival Unveils Equality Charter."

29. Mumford, "Cannes Film Festival Unveils Equality Charter."

30. Rebecca Keegan quoted Frémaux: "Cannes and any festival, we are the last stage of that journey. . . . The journey of having more female directors starts in cinema school and university." Keegan, "Cannes' 50–50 Gender Parity Pledge, One Year Later: Has the Festival Delivered?," *Hollywood Reporter*, 10 May 2019, www.hollywoodreporter.com/news/cannes-50–50-gender-parity -pledge-one-year-has-festival-delivered-1208187.

31. For example, Agnès Poirier, author and critic who contributes to the Cannes Festival's informal preselection network, argued: "We have reached gender parity in film schools, but there is still a problem with funding. It's still more difficult for women to make a first feature, and even more difficult to make the second. All the directors I know say that financiers are reluctant to entrust women with a bigger budget." Quoted in Andrew Pulver, "Cannes in Crisis: Has the Festival Learned the Lessons of Weinstein?" *Guardian*, 4 May 2018, www.theguardian.com /film/2018/may/04/cannes-crisis-lessons-weinstein-scandal. See also Farah Nayeri, "Women Rally on the Red Carpet to Highlight Gender Inequality," *New York Times*, 12 May 2018.

32. For example, Corrina Antrobus (founder of the Bechdel Test Fest, which features women's films), explained: "I never buy the answer that there aren't enough films out there made by women. The problem does lie with the gatekeepers—of which Cannes is one—that are just not recognizing they have to make more of an effort. The talent is there. If you are at the absolute top of the pile, as Cannes is, it's easy to neglect the power you have to make a healthier film culture." Quoted in Pulver, "Cannes in Crisis." As Silverstein noted, "On the forefront of this issue across the

globe are women's film festivals, which have been programming women directors for decades." Silverstein, "Cannes Film Festival Signs Pledge."

33. Mathieu Champalaune, "300 personnalités du cinéma lancent le collectif '5050 pour 2020' pour l'égalité dans le cinéma," *Les Inrockuptibles*, 28 February 2018, www.lesinrocks.com/2018/02 /28/cinema/actualite-cinema/300-personnalites-du-cinema -lancent-le-collectif-5050-pour-2020-pour-legalite-dans-le -cinema/. The 50/50 en 2020 collective was an offshoot of the group Le Deuxième Regard and was launched following the Weinstein allegations and organization of the #MeToo and Time's Up movements. 50/50 en 2020 explained it wanted to go beyond the issue of sexual abuse alone and create a broad analysis of the industry. In March 2020, Le Collectif 50/50's Facebook page listed Delphyne Besse, Julie Billy, and Laurence Lascary as copresidents; Isabel Mercier as treasurer; Mikaël Gluschankof as general secretary; and the following board members: Cécile Aubert, Priscilla Bertin, Béatrice Boursier, Sandrine Brauer, Anna Ciennik, Tonie Marshall, Judith Nora, Céline Sciamma, Marion Tharaud, Agathe Valentin, Harold Valentin, Bérénice Vincent, and Rebecca Zlotowski. See Le Collectif 50/50, "Our Story," 2 March 2020, www.facebook.com /Collectif5050/.

34. See the Le Collectif 50/50 website, collectif5050.com/en (accessed 10 May 2020).

35. Le Collectif 50/50, "Actions," collectif5050.com/en (accessed 10 May 2020).

36. The 50/50 en 2020 website describes the collective's work and mission: "As an action tank, we are committed to conducting a thorough discussion and a struggle for equality and inclusion in our industry by 2020. The movement discusses and proposes incentives to public institutions and to key players of the industry by producing specific figures and monitoring transparency. In association with Datcha agency [data collection and visualization], specialized in the collection and analysis of statistics, 5050×2020 produces comparative studies with the aim of covering the full spectrum of our field: salary disparity between male and female crew members, between male and female actors, the budget differences between films by male and female directors, the release of these films, and the lack of

diversity throughout the industry. We are committed to using the power of numbers to raise awareness, increase the visibility of these issues, and fuel the workshops that we will be leading to produce ideas, solutions, and opportunities." See Le Collectif 50/50, collectif5050.com/en (accessed 10 May 2020).

37. "A Very Unequal Distribution of Jobs: Portion of Women in Film Production," collectif5050.com/ (accessed 10 May 2020). 50/50 en 2020 cites its source as CNC, "The Place of Women in the Film and Audiovisual Industries," 2017.

38. These charts and statistics are drawn from Le Collectif 50/50 en 2020, "1946–2018: Cannes Film Festival. The Role of Women in the Cannes Festival's Competition: A Comparative Study," collectif5050.com/en/study/cannes (accessed 10 May 2020).

39. Since then, Stéphanie Lamome was appointed the artistic adviser of the film department at the Cannes Film Festival. See Rachel Montpelier, "Upholding Gender Parity Pledge, Cannes Unveils Selection Committee for the First Time," *Women and Hollywood*, 16 January 2019, womenandhollywood.com /upholding-gender-parity-pledge-cannes-unveils-selection -committee-for-the-first-time/.

40. Andreas Wiseman, "Cannes: Record-Tying Four Films by Women Directors in Competition Signals Slow Progress," *Deadline*, 18 April 2019, deadline.com/2019/04/cannes-festival-competition -women-directors-record-1202598180/.

41. Delphyne Besse speaking for 50/50 en 2020: "Cannes has respected all the commitments relating to the pledge so far. . . . We are waiting for them to share the data of the submitted films during the time of the festival and we will analyze the figures with them." Quoted in Keegan, "Cannes' 50–50 Gender Parity Pledge." The 2020 selection committee included five women. However, the in-person Cannes festival planned for May 2020 was canceled due to the pandemic, with these events unfolding after submission of this article.

42. Le Collectif 50/50, "Festivals That Have Signed the Pledge."

43. Fleur Burlet explained, "For its 72nd edition, running from May 14 to 25, Cannes Film Festival has chosen to pay homage to French filmmaker Agnès Varda, who died on March 29, making her the first female director to be immortalized on a Cannes

Film Festival poster." Burlet, "Cannes Festival Pays Homage to Agnès Varda," *WWD*, 18 April 2019, wwd.com/fashion-news/fashion-scoops/cannes-festival-pays-homage-to-agnes-varda-1203111758/.

44. Andreas Wisemann, "Cannes: Festival Pays Tribute to the Late Agnès Varda with New Poster," *Deadline*, 15 April 2019, deadline.com/2019/04/cannes-film-festival-poster-agnes-varda-1202595848/.

45. Quoted in Burlet, "Cannes Festival Pays Homage to Agnès Varda."

46. In a 2008 interview, Varda recollected that the film would come to cost about 10 million old francs, which Richard Neupert converted to $14,000. See the filmed interview Agnès Varda and Alexandre Mabilon, *Souvenirs et propos sur le film (La Pointe Courte): Entretien d'Alexandre Mabilon avec Agnès Varda* (New York: Criterion Collection, 2008), DVD; Neupert, *A History of the French New Wave Cinema* (Madison: University of Wisconsin Press, 2007), 57. In the cooperative, actors and technicians worked for shares of the film. Varda explained, "No one would be paid during filming. It was thirteen years before they were repaid for their work." Agnès Varda, undated radio interview on *La Pointe Courte*, quoted in Agnès Varda, *Varda par Agnès* (Paris: Cahiers du cinéma, 1994), 227. See also Kelley Conway, *Agnès Varda* (Urbana: University of Illinois Press, 2015), 22–23.

47. For example, Orlando Parfitt asserted that after *La Pointe Courte* was filmed in 1954, "the film would screen at the Cannes Festival the following year." Parfitt, "Cannes Film Festival 2019 Poster Pays Tribute to the Late Agnès Varda," *Screen Daily*, 15 April 2019.

48. Quoted in Deparis, "Cannes 2015."

49. Women's efforts for recognition in the arts have, of course, spanned centuries and geographies; the activism at Cannes is an important example in our present.

Rebecca J. DeRoo is associate professor in the School of
Communication at the Rochester Institute of Technology. She
cocurated the 2016 retrospective *Agnès Varda: (Self-)Portraits, Facts and
Fiction* at the Dryden Theatre, George Eastman Museum. Her book
Agnès Varda between Film, Photography, and Art (2018) was a finalist
for the Kraszna-Krausz Book Award. This research was supported
by grants from the American Association of University Women, the
American Philosophical Society, and the National Endowment for the
Humanities. Her first book, *The Museum Establishment and Contemporary
Art* (2006, 2014), received the Laurence Wylie Prize in French
Cultural Studies.

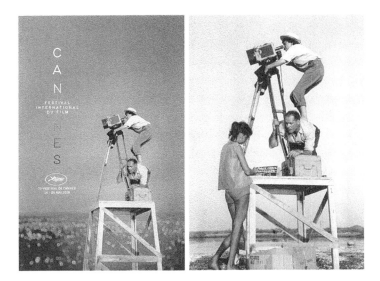

Figure 10. The 2019 Cannes Film Festival Poster featuring
Agnès Varda (left); it draws on the historical photograph
of Varda filming *La Pointe Courte* (1954) (right). Courtesy of
Rosalie Varda

Figure 1. Still from Instagram video of JR traveling with
Varda cutouts. The video caption begins, "Agnes couldn't
travel so . . . We took her on a ride 🖤 [red heart emoji]
@facesplacesfilm! Nominated for an academy award for best
documentary" (JR, 2018)

From Cannes to Cardboard: The Circulation and Promotion of *Visages Villages* and the Auteur on Instagram

Matt St. John

A Cardboard Nominee

On 5 February 2018 the Academy of Motion Picture Arts and Sciences hosted its annual luncheon for Academy Award nominees. As always, the nominated actors, directors, writers, cinematographers, and other professionals gathered around a giant-sized Oscar statuette for a group photo, with awards veterans like Meryl Streep from *The Post* (dir. Steven Spielberg, US, 2017) joining new nominees like Mary J. Blige from *Mudbound* (dir. Dee Rees, US, 2017) and Timothée Chalamet from *Call Me by Your Name* (dir. Luca Guadagnino, Italy/France, 2017). In the group of over 150 people, many were broadly recognizable American celebrities, but one person stood out for another reason: she was not actually present. Agnès Varda, who directed *Visages Villages* (*Faces Places*, France, 2017) with artist JR and received a Best Documentary Feature nomination, did not attend the luncheon but appeared in

Camera Obscura 106, Volume 36, Number 1
DOI 10.1215/02705346-8838589   © 2021 by *Camera Obscura*
Published by Duke University Press

the back row of the group as a cardboard cutout. JR held the cardboard Varda slightly above his head, the light reflecting brightly off the paper to make her stand out in the large crowd. JR posted an Instagram photo showing part of the group with a caption beginning, "(Almost) all the Oscars Nominee . . . incredible."[1] Varda's unconventional luncheon appearance garnered much attention from the American press, as did JR's multiday trip to the luncheon accompanied by a few cutouts of the legendary French New Wave auteur, which he documented on his Instagram feed before taking the group photo that includes the cardboard Varda. The cutouts showed Varda in a variety of poses, often placed in comical situations or carried by JR, like the cardboard Varda with an outstretched hand that he held on a bicycle ride (fig. 1).[2] While the cutouts were likely the most discussed awards-season moment for the *Visages Villages* team, this playful use of social media and Varda's image in particular characterize much of the film's promotional cycle, which helped maintain attention as it circulated at festivals and other screenings throughout the eight months between its Cannes premiere in May 2017 and the announcement of Oscar nominations in January 2018.

While film festival scholars have discussed the importance of the festival circuit for auteurs like Agnès Varda and have also identified the promotional function of festivals for the films that screen at them, very few have analyzed in detail how a film travels through the festival and art house circuits. The importance of other promotional tools that intersect with these screenings and events, like the use of social media for *Visages Villages*, has not received sufficient attention. As reported in *Variety*'s coverage of the Seventy-First Cannes Film Festival, filmmakers and consultants have questioned the viability of an early summer Cannes premiere for a film's Oscar prospects in the following March, so the success of *Visages Villages*—a relatively small film—in maintaining its position in the critical and industrial discourse long enough for an Academy Award nomination is noteworthy, offering a useful case for investigating how a film's circulation and promotion operate.[3] As a low-budget documentary about a European filmmaker—even a renowned one like Varda—and her new artist friend traveling the

French countryside to create large-scale photographic portraits of ordinary people, *Visages Villages* does not seem to have guaranteed appeal for the American industry that almost entirely determines Oscar outcomes. While the film ultimately did not win the Oscar, the nomination was Varda's first and a significant achievement for a foreign documentary, raising questions about its release. How did the distributors and filmmakers promote *Visages Villages* and maintain interest in the film through its release strategy? How were Varda and JR's social media involved in these processes, with a cardboard cutout becoming a key promotional element in the film's awards campaign?

To address these questions, this article examines the film's screening strategies, the social media presence of its directors, and the media coverage of the film and Varda, especially in online spaces. I argue that *Visages Villages* merges more traditional methods of achieving visibility, such as festival premieres and expanding theatrical distribution, with an atypical use of online presence and social media, especially for an established auteur who made films for more than sixty years. The film's trajectory suggests the value of different types of premieres and special screenings, beyond the world premiere at Cannes. The filmmakers employed festivals as a promotional opportunity, with appearances by Varda and JR at many of the screenings, and both directors used social media to emphasize her persona and the journey of the film, finding a new avenue for gaining attention from sources that might not usually highlight foreign films or documentaries. Through their presence at events and their social media, the distinctive looks of the filmmakers—with Varda's trademark purple hair topped with a white crown and JR's ever-present sunglasses and fedora—became closely associated with the film.

Varda's social media presence, in her own posts and in JR's, both documents and extends the film's promotional campaign, and her use of Instagram recycles and recontextualizes the strategies of self-representation and formal play seen in her documentaries. That she would be interested in a new platform like Instagram that focuses primarily on photography, with some video capabilities, is not surprising given her extensive history shifting between and mixing film, photography, and other visual arts, especially her installations, which Rebecca J. DeRoo and Kelley Conway have discussed in their studies of Varda.[4] But the extension of Varda's diverse media practice to a new online platform, known more for its use by young "influencers" and corporate brands than for artists with decades of experience, warrants attention. In this instance, the conventional release strategy of a documentary with potential of winning awards intersected with new online practices in the cardboard cutout's viral moment, bringing attention to the film from an unusual angle. I first discuss the film's release, involving festival premieres, special screenings, and theatrical distribution, before turning to the online presence of the filmmakers that became a key example and record of the film's promotional processes, resulting in Varda's treatment as a meme-worthy figure by outlets ranging from film publications to fashion websites.

The Circulation of *Visages Villages*

The release process of *Visages Villages* mirrors the release strategies of most non-Hollywood films with awards aspirations, such as art cinema and documentaries, but there have been few detailed analyses of this system of film circulation and the importance of certain types of screenings.[5] For this analysis of *Visages Villages*, I considered festival and American theatrical screenings that took place before the Academy Awards on 4 March 2018. The French César Awards and the Independent Spirit Awards in Los Angeles were also presented that weekend, marking a clear culmination of the awards campaign for *Visages Villages*, which had been nominated for awards by all three organizations. Because my focus is limited to the film's maintenance of its status as an awards frontrunner, I highlight a few of these screenings in particular to suggest ways that the *Visages Villages* team maintained the film's visibility and viability as an awards contender.

Agnès Varda fits into the category of filmmakers described by Cindy Hing-Yuk Wong and other festival scholars as a filmmaker whose auteur status has been developed and maintained by major festivals throughout her career.[6] While many of Varda's films screened at notable festivals around the world, *Visages Villages* experienced an especially impressive trajectory, beginning at Cannes in May 2017 and lasting well into 2018, screening at small festivals even months after the Oscars in March. The film was distributed by Cohen Media Group in North America, which managed its special screenings for festivals and art house theaters, as well as its theatrical run that began in October 2017.[7] Varda's own company, Ciné-Tamaris, typically handles European distribution for her films, but the filmmakers partnered with Le Pacte for the distribution of *Visages Villages*.[8] As Conway notes, the exhibition of Varda's films has always been an important part of her process, and she has spent significant time traveling with her films to festivals and other screenings.[9] Varda's presence at some screenings of *Visages Villages*, often accompanied by JR, continued this notable feature of her career, and her image and its circulation in turn helped promote the film, beginning with the world premiere at Cannes.

The Cannes Film Festival has long been part of Varda's career, with many of her films presented at the festival. Varda also received the Palme d'Honneur award in 2015, described in the festival's press release as an award "given to renowned directors whose works have achieved a global impact but who have nevertheless never won the Palme d'Or."[10] The Cannes board of directors selected Varda as only the fourth winner of the Palme d'Honneur in the festival's history. When *Visages Villages* had its world premiere at Cannes two years later, on 19 May 2017, Varda was once again denied the opportunity to win the actual Palme d'Or, as the film screened out of competition. Despite its noncompetition status, *Visages Villages* still received substantial acclaim and international press as an official selection of the festival. Manohla Dargis noted that the film was "for some reason playing out of competition" in her Cannes coverage for the *New York Times*, calling it "an exquisite, achingly moving nonfiction ramble on memory and history, cats and goats."[11] *Visages Villages* also received rave reviews from major outlets, including *Variety*, *Hollywood Reporter*, and *IndieWire*, after the Cannes screening.[12] Controversy about the inclusion of Netflix films, like Bong Joon-ho's *Okja* (South Korea/US, 2017), in the Cannes competition dominated coverage of the festival, but the reception of *Visages Villages* cemented it as one of the Cannes selections most acclaimed by the American press. The film also received the top documentary prize from Cannes, the Golden Eye, making it an award winner despite being ineligible for the Palme d'Or.[13] The Cannes premiere introduced the film as a new accomplishment by its auteur, with positive reception from both critics and the documentary award's jury, but subsequent festival screenings would confirm its position as an awards contender.

Although *Visages Villages* screened at a few festivals on other continents, its first North American screenings were reserved for the fall festivals that help establish the annual batch of films with awards potential. This schedule allowed the film to screen at the Telluride Film Festival, the Toronto International Film Festival, and the New York Film Festival before its theatrical opening in the United States, when Cohen Media opened the film in New York on 6 October 2017. Along with the Venice Film Festival, Telluride and Toronto are widely considered important "points of passage," in festival scholar Marijke De Valck's terms, to Oscar success, and the coverage of *Visages Villages* from these screenings confirms that function.[14] At the Toronto International Film Festival, which began on 6 September, *Visages Villages* won the audience award for best documentary, and critics like *IndieWire*'s Anne Thompson identified the film as a possible awards season frontrunner.[15]

Apart from the acclaim generated by the festival screenings, another key moment in the film's continued promotion occurred on the first day of the Toronto International Film Festival. On 6 September, the Academy of Motion Pictures Arts and Sciences announced that Agnès Varda was the recipient of a 2017 Governors Award, the honorary Oscar category presented each year.[16] Like most coverage of this award, a *New York Times* article about the Governors Awards noted that Varda had never been nominated for an Oscar and that she had a new film released that year.[17] In discussing her honorary award, Varda did not seem especially enthused. In multiple interviews, such as her discussion with the *Los Angeles Times*, she called it "a side Oscar" and compared it to her honorary Cèsar Award and her honorary Palme from Cannes, suggesting, "So it's like the academy is saying, 'That old lady has been working so continuously for cinema, at some point we should recognize that she worked.' I feel like it's recognition of my decent work."[18] The repeated "side Oscar" comment was often cited by journalists, like *Vulture*'s Jade Yuan, with seeming amusement over Varda's surprising attitude toward the situation.[19] The attention to these remarks highlighted the fact that Varda had never been nominated for a regular Academy Award at age eighty-nine and after sixty years of filmmaking, in turn adding momentum to the campaign for *Visages Villages* during its ongoing circulation.

After the fall festivals in North America, October screenings in New York and Los Angeles continued to promote the film as an awards season contender while expanding the type of coverage it received leading up to its theatrical release. In New York City, *Visages Villages* screened at the New York Film Festival and the Museum of Modern Art, a notable moment because of both the museum's status as a film institution and its role as one of the film's funders.[20] In Los Angeles, Cohen Media Group hosted a premiere screening at the Pacific Design Center. Jennifer Lawrence and Angelina Jolie attended the screening, causing celebrity news outlets to cover the event. In an image gallery that includes Selma Blair walking her dog in West Hollywood and Sienna Miller eating a bagel in New York, *Page Six* published photos of Lawrence patting Varda on the head and Jolie leaning down next to the director in front of the film's posters.[21] This interaction with major American stars at the Los Angeles premiere allowed Varda's image to appear in a new type of press, in addition to the film outlets and newspaper arts sections previously covering the film. Images from these events, especially photographs of Varda, became central to the film's promotion and awards campaign, and red carpet events and related social media posts received attention from various publications, including celebrity news websites. During this trip to the United States, Varda and JR were interviewed by numerous outlets, including *Variety*, *Slant Magazine*, *Vulture*, RogerEbert.com, *IndieWire*, and NPR's *All Things Considered*. With their varied audiences, the interviews underscore the broad promotional push for the film during this trip in October, with screenings and press coverage in major markets. The film opened theatrically in New York on 6 October and in Los Angeles one week later, and Cohen Media Group then began releasing the film in many smaller markets, through regional film festivals or art house theaters, with screenings taking place even after the Oscars in spring 2018.

The circulation of *Visages Villages* involved a strategic selection of festival screenings, with many of them playing important roles in the positive coverage of the film and its directors, eventually leading to the Oscar nomination on 23 January 2018. While this analysis has focused on the American circulation, *Visages Villages* also screened at international film festivals and smaller events to promote the film around the world during this period, especially in Europe. *Visages Villages* illustrates the value of different types of premieres, not just the world premiere, as well as the importance of the festival and art house circuit as complementary to the limited theatrical distribution of art films. These strategies for promoting the film coincided with the activity of its directors, especially Varda, on social media, which helped generate and maintain attention to the film from atypical sources and even after its widest distribution in October 2017.

The Directors of *Visages Villages* on Instagram

Before the release of *Visages Villages*, the film's two directors used social media in different ways and to varied degrees. JR had substantial experience with social media, often showcasing his art projects on Instagram. These projects are typically large-scale photographic prints temporarily pasted as murals in public spaces, frequently attending to political subjects such as violence against women or the experiences of refugees.[22] Before *Visages Villages*, Varda had less social media experience than her collaborator, especially on Instagram. While she first posted on Instagram a few days before the film's premiere at Cannes, Varda's official Facebook page existed before *Visages Villages*. In an approach that is common for social media accounts managed by an organization, the Varda Facebook page tended to prioritize posts about her company, Ciné-Tamaris, rather than any personal material. Her Instagram feed instead gave the appearance of being managed by Varda herself, at least in part. The director frequently appeared briefly in her account's Stories feature, which allows a user to run a temporary post, with posts often focusing on her travels and observations. JR often appears in Varda's images and videos on Instagram, and she in his, but she did not simply adopt the strategies established by JR on social media. Varda's Instagram instead demonstrates consistent investment in past experiences from her career, a strategy that was later adopted by JR with the popular cardboard cutouts project around the Oscars luncheon.

While both Varda and JR have other social media accounts, I focus on their Instagram accounts, which were their most popular accounts during this period. In May 2018, when the film was still being released in some markets, JR had 1.2 million followers on Instagram, compared to 472,400 Facebook likes and 87,400 Twitter followers, and Varda had 92,900 Instagram followers, almost four times her 25,300 Facebook likes.[23] As a platform that allows both photography and video in combination with text captions, Instagram also allowed the artists the greatest continuity with their other work.[24] Instagram's emphasis on visual material rather than text or audio, and the platform's assumed attention to faces, which Stefanie Duguay has identified in her analysis of queer celebrity social media, are appropriate for the *Visages Villages* directors.[25] On Instagram, JR and Varda emphasize their distinctive appearances, especially hers, making Varda herself a frequent visual element in the film's circulation and promotion. This deployment of her image succeeded, with many American users and outlets learning of Varda before even hearing about the film, as Instagram posts and social media strategies by the two directors were recycled by press. My analysis first addresses Varda's use of Instagram, and then JR's, before considering how these images and videos contributed to the press and other online attention to the film as its release and awards campaign progressed.

Varda first posted on Instagram thirteen days before the premiere of *Visages Villages*, and she posted forty-six other photos or videos by the time she attended the Oscars ceremony. Her Instagram offers one partial way to observe the film's journey through festivals and the awards season. Despite the frequency of posts related to *Visages Villages* and the industry events related to the film, two other topics regularly appear: references to Varda's life, both professional and personal, and political posts. In some cases, these three general topics merge, but most of the posts can be categorized in one of the three areas. Within all of the subjects, the posts tend to emphasize Varda's distinctive image. This quality demonstrates her willingness to be centrally present, identified by Conway as an intensified element in her work since 2000.[26] I suggest that even when these posts do not directly address *Visages Villages*, their timing and context connect them to the promotion of the film, as Varda's image was increasingly recognized and discussed during the film's circulation and awards campaign. These strategies are also at play in JR's posts using the Varda cutouts, likely the most widely discussed moment in the film's promotional cycle.

Varda's posts about *Visages Villages* typically refer to or are captioned with text about the film's screenings and other promotional events. She is often joined by JR in these images. The visual content and captions capture her style of self-referential, playful presentation, a trait seen in past documentaries like *The Gleaners and I* (*Les glaneurs et la glaneuse*, France, 2000) and *The Beaches of Agnès* (*Les plages d'Agnès*, France, 2008). One of her earliest posts demonstrates this style. Presumably on the way to Cannes on 18 May Varda posted a short video with a caption about JR hitting her in the eye once again.[27] The video shows the aisle of a train car, with Varda walking toward the camera holding a balloon that looks like a giant eyeball. As she nears the camera, she pulls the balloon down in front of her face, and JR's hand bumps the balloon, causing it to hit her in the face.

In a widely cited moment from Varda's first digital film, *The Gleaners and I*, she discusses her affection for the small, transportable digital camera, and this short video shows a similar enjoyment of the cellphone camera's simplicity and a platform that encourages such use. The rough handheld video shows her slow approach with the balloon, before JR's hand suddenly appears from behind the camera to push the balloon toward her, a simple surprise from the camera's point of view that would not be easily accomplished with larger equipment. Although the film had not yet premiered, this

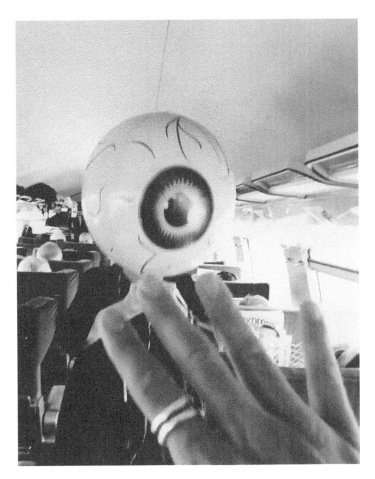

Figure 2. Still from Instagram video of eyeball balloon
with translated caption, "Once again JR hit me in the eye"
(Agnès Varda, 2017)

post seems to humorously reference the motif of eyes in *Visages Vil-lages*, developed through Varda's failing eyesight and her desire to see JR's eyes that are obscured by his sunglasses, a hope that is not fulfilled until the end of the film. Varda's posts often reference the film in this way, with images or videos that recall topics or moments in the film. In another post, Varda and JR, both wearing sunglasses, peer out of a pool with only the tops of their heads and their hands

Figure 3. Instagram of Varda and JR peeking out from a pool,
with the caption "👓😎 [emoji of eyeglasses and sunglasses]"
(Agnès Varda, 2017)

visible, captioned by emoji of glasses and sunglasses.[28] This image
and its caption offer another indirect reference to one of the film's
central motifs, eyes and sunglasses specifically, which become tied
to the directors' growing friendship. These posts about *Visages Villages* typically do not appear promotional in the traditional manner of providing details about the film's screenings or encouraging
people to see it directly. They instead showcase the relationship and
humor of the directors, always emphasizing their visual distinctiveness through the attention to faces. The more personal, playfully

Figure 4. Varda posing with a *Visages Villages* poster on
Instagram (Agnès Varda, 2017)

styled approach to her Instagram account differs from the overtly
promotional elements of Varda's Facebook page.

Even Varda's most clearly promotional posts feature playful framing or captions. In one image, the film's poster is visible
in the background, with JR and Varda walking in profile toward
the right side of the poster. In the Instagram post, a foregrounded
Varda looks to the left of the frame, seemingly eye to eye with her
miniature self, walking on the poster.[29]

Her outstretched hand mimics the gesture made by the
miniature Varda on the poster, with her thumb touching her chin
in the Instagram post and her palm facing the poster. This amusing composition of a large Varda in the foreground facing a small
Varda in the background is accompanied by a caption that trans-

lates, "Face to face with the fine team of #cinetamaris #lepacte #rougeinternational #cohenmediagroup #arte #VisagesVillages #Cannes2017."[30] While this post functions to promote the film and her production and distribution partners, the image demonstrates her dedication to visual composition and play, even in her Instagram posts. Between the Cannes premiere and the Oscars, these images often highlight major moments in the film's appearances around the world and Varda's career, but the posts offer a staged spin on the industrially significant events from Varda's perspective. Throughout the awards campaign for *Visages Villages*, Varda approached the Oscars with a pleasant, gently satirical tone, sharply contrasting with other art cinema directors like her French New Wave counterpart Jean-Luc Godard, who spurned the Governors Awards when he received an honorary Oscar in 2010. Varda participated in the awards even after her comments about a "side Oscar," and she presented her experience in a playful manner on Instagram. In one image, Varda pretends to sleep with her honorary Oscar speech under her pillow, indicating her excitement for the ceremony, as well as her humor about a formal industry event.[31]

Other posts about the film's screening and awards trajectory feature Varda at a Tintin mural for the film's Belgian premiere and her standing outside a McDonald's at the end of the October trip to New York and Los Angeles, drawing attention to amusing locations and frivolous sights. Many of the posts about the film refer to specific scenes or thematic material, like the eyeball balloon video, but even direct promotion is merged with Varda's unique sense of humor and composition in her Instagram posts.

After *Visages Villages* and the special events involved in its awards campaign, the second notable topic in her Instagram posts is Varda as the subject of self-portraits, including allusions to her past films and installations and her personal life. This subject offers a notable continuity with recent developments in her art. Conway has identified the recycling of previous characters, themes, and objects in her installations, writing, "Varda's installations both echo her films' narrative and stylistic preoccupations and extend her work into new subjects, forms, and techniques."[32] DeRoo has described this incorporation of personal material in *The Beaches*

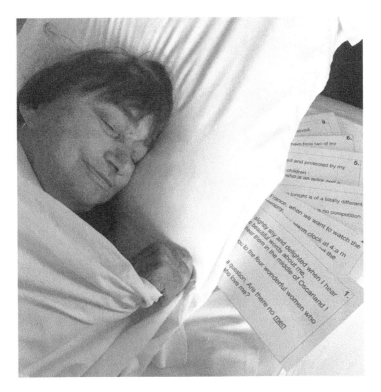

Figure 5. Instagram photo of Varda pretending to sleep with her honorary Oscar speech under her pillow. The caption partially reads, "Under my pillow to remind my speech. See you tomorrow!" (Agnès Varda, 2017)

of Agnès as Varda asserting "control over her legacy."[33] Autobiographical elements are a narrative and stylistic preoccupation in her work, from her marriage and motherhood to her friendships and career, and her Instagram maintains this interest. Videos from 5 and 6 June 2017 reference the birthday of her husband, filmmaker Jacques Demy, who passed away in 1990.[34] The first video shows workers laying pavement outside her front door, shot from inside the house through the doorway, with the translated caption, "Be careful before entering! . . . Jacques was born on June 5th. Today I have a heart in tar." The second video is framed slightly to the right of the first video, revealing a set of photos of Demy. It is

Figure 6. Still from one of Varda's Instagram videos, with
photographs of Jacques Demy near the door to her home
(Agnès Varda, 2017)

captioned, "Now we can enter! This time we see Jacques, born on
June 5 . . . and my heart calms down."

Apart from the biographical context, this video also includes
another tendency of Varda's work that DeRoo has identified: her
practice of portraying one artistic medium within another to highlight their distinctiveness, here with the framed photos of Demy
refigured within an Instagram video format.[35] Like her films, such
as *The Beaches of Agnès* and *Visages Villages*, these Instagram videos
assume some familiarity with her life and career, as users must
know about Varda's relationship with Demy and his death to fully
understand the posts and the events they reference.

Another example shows Varda holding up a poster that
advertises her role as the special guest at the August 2017 water

jousts in the port of Sète.[36] A cartoon version of Varda, with her trademark hair and notable short stature, sits on the end of a boat with one jouster and four other men, her legs dangling off the raised edge. The jouster holds a sign that says, "Agnes Varda," and all of the men share her distinctive short haircut with a white crown. One of them also holds a cat, an animal that appears in many of her films and other artworks. The caption notes that Chrisophe Vallaux created the poster. His cartoon Varda appears familiar to fans of the auteur, as it is the same style used in Vallaux's poster for *The Beaches of Agnès* and his DVD cover for her documentary miniseries *Agnès de ci de là Varda* (*Agnès Varda: From Here to There*, Arte France, 2011).[37] The water jousts also recall the famous water jousting scene from her first feature film, *La Pointe Courte*, exemplifying the oblique citations of past work that she sometimes employs, like the potato motif in some posts that recall *The Gleaners and I*. Her Instagram posts include many such allusions to her past films, and even their promotional materials, almost always calling attention to her familiar appearance and style.

The final category of posts from Varda's Instagram account is images and videos with political content and references, especially related to women's rights. Varda's feminist beliefs are the most obvious political thread throughout her work, and the expression of this identity on Instagram offers another line of continuity with her films and other art. On 25 November the International Day for the Elimination of Violence against Women, Varda posted a screenshot from *The Beaches of Agnès* with the captioned beginning of a quotation from the film, "I tried to be a joyful feminist."[38] The end of the quotation from the film is, "but I was angry," a fitting moment for her Instagram caption noting that "1 in 3 girls and women worldwide experience violence!" This post exemplifies the merging of categories in her Instagram feed, as a political post that also references her past work, and the image offers another example of media recycled and presented in another format. She has also posted about other political issues, including the refugee crisis, but overall these posts are less common than those about the circulation of *Visages Villages* or her career and personal life.

The promotional function of Varda's posts tends to be deliv-

Figure 7. Instagram photo with Varda posing next to joust
posters that feature her cartoon counterpart and other
references to her work, with the caption referencing the
poster by Christophe Vallaux (Agnès Varda, 2017)

ered through her familiar visual style and narrative tone in her
captions, whereas JR's posts are often blatantly promotional, with
less emphasis on his persona. JR posts more frequently on Instagram than Agnès Varda did, with 293 posts in the year after the
Visages Villages premiere, compared to Varda's 54. Most of his posts
show his art projects, especially his large-scale photography, like
his *Giants, Kikito* installation, which depicts a young Mexican child
climbing over the border wall into the United States.[39] These posts
often include information about the projects and their availability.
The Kikito post, for example, notes that 8 October is the last day
to see the installation. JR still expresses a playful persona in some

of his Instagram posts about *Visages Villages*, as he does in the film, but their primary function is often providing information. While Varda's photos relate to specific events in the film's circulation, highlighting her presence, like the selfie with the film poster, JR has posted marketing and promotional materials without any transformation for Instagram. For example, JR posted Cohen Media Group's "For Your Consideration" poster for the Best Documentary Feature category, with the film's accolades and positive quotes from reviews around an image of the two directors looking at a camera in a field.[40]

Many of JR's posts still feature Varda and himself in amusing poses and environments, even when they have promotional purposes that draw attention to the film's awards campaign, like the "Oscar Nominated Documentary" post.[41] This text lays over an image of JR sitting on Varda's shoulders, with his hands over his mouth in shock. Some outlets, like *Vulture*, used this Instagram post in stories about the film, drawing attention to both the film and JR's Instagram, where he often promoted his other work.[42] While most of his posts about *Visages Villages* are primarily promotional, his social media promotion of the film merged with some of the qualities of Varda's social media use when he brought her cardboard cutouts to the Academy Awards luncheon.

In the days leading up to the luncheon on 5 February, JR traveled with the cardboard Varda cutouts, documenting the adventures on his Instagram stories and posts. The three full-size cutouts show Varda reaching up with one hand toward the sky, Varda with one hand raised to her chest (which held a cardboard cat at the Oscars luncheon), and Varda with one arm extended out to her side. Life-size cutouts of film characters and actors are, in a way, a form of "old media": they were commonly used as forms of advertisement in movie theater lobbies well before the advent of social media. They also recall Chris Marker's use of Guillaume the cartoon cat as a surrogate for himself. When used by JR and Varda as Instagram props or opportunities for "selfies," they are brought into the contemporary digital era, as part of their social media documentation of the film's awards campaign. While Instagram posts published using the Stories function disappear after twenty-

Figure 8. JR's reaction to the film's Oscar nomination on Instagram, with the caption, "When our film @ facesplacesfilm is nominated at the Oscar for Best Documentary feature . . ." (JR, 2018)

four hours, JR reposted some of these video clips and photos in a compilation Instagram post that chronicles his whole journey with the cutout figures, even after the luncheon.[43] The caption for the post underscores the promotional function of the figures, reminding users that the film was nominated for an Academy Award for Best Documentary. The video begins with JR on a motorbike

Figure 9. Still from JR's Instagram video of the cardboard
Varda's travels, showing a cardboard Varda cutout going
through a TSA X-ray machine (JR, 2018)

holding the reaching Varda. He tells "Agnès" he will take her for a
ride, before airport security agents pose with a cutout and send it
through an X-ray machine, highlighting the surreal and humorous
nature of the whole promotional stunt.

    The promotional quality of the cutouts is also emphasized
by the many celebrities appearing in the video. Steven Spielberg
records a selfie video with the cat-holding Varda at the luncheon,

Figure 10. Still from JR's Instagram video of the cardboard Varda's travels, showing a cardboard Varda that appears mostly buried in sand at the beach (JR, 2018)

Alejandro Iñárritu dances with the outstretched-arm Varda, and Pharrell Williams welcomes a cardboard Varda to a recording studio. The cutouts also ski, direct traffic in a crosswalk, and watch fireworks, and a smaller cutout of Varda's head and hands visits the beach, peeking over the edge of the sand as a seal passes by in the background. The video ends with the sky-reaching Varda floating up, tied to a bouquet of balloons, as JR asks, "Agnès, where are you going?"44 With the cardboard cutouts, JR employs the light absurdity of Varda's posts for his promotional efforts on social media, and Varda returns the favor by taking a JR cutout to a *Visages Villages* screening in Milan.45

JR's widely discussed compilation video and the original posts created a new degree of awareness about the film, even though the film's release in the United States had slowed to infrequent screenings at small festivals by this point. The cutouts' appearance at the Oscar luncheon generated stories from the *Guardian, Hollywood Reporter, Vulture, New Yorker, Daily Mail,* and many other publications. Clearly extending the reach of the film's promotion beyond film publications, some of this coverage assumed that the audience would need a full primer on Agnès Varda, with *Daily Mail* including a "Who Is Agnès Varda?" inset in its article about the Oscars luncheon.46 The *Guardian* article structured its story around explaining who Varda is and why she sent a cardboard cutout to the luncheon.47 Many of these stories, like Chris Gardner's "Why a Cardboard Cutout Is the Star of Awards Season" in the *Hollywood Reporter* and Alexandra Schwartz's "Agnès Varda Is Still Going Places" in the *New Yorker,* note that the cutouts are featured on JR's Instagram, underlining the platform's importance for this promotion before it was recycled by conventional news sources.48

The cutouts combined the centrality of Varda's iconic image and her playful approach to promotion, as seen in her Instagram activity, with JR's promotional experience on social media. They garnered significant attention for the film and its directors, contributing to her status as a staple of red-carpet press for the remainder of the season. Her appearances at the Independent Spirit Awards and the Oscars received meme-like coverage. *New York Magazine* and *Vulture*'s Kyle Buchanan tweeted two photos of Varda, with the message "Agnes Varda at the Indie Spirits in an emblazoned hoodie sipping mineral water through a straw is IT."49 This was Buchanan's most popular tweet during the Independent Spirits and Oscars by a significant margin, with 438 retweets and 1,700 likes as of 10 May. Varda's silk, rose-print Gucci outfit for the Oscars also received coverage from fashion outlets. The celebrity style section of *Vogue*'s website featured an article about Varda's look, "The Oscars' Oldest

Ever Nominee Also Wears Gucci like a Boss."[50] Fashion and lifestyle website *The Cut* published an article titled "This Eighty-Nine-Year-Old Director Is Our New Style Icon." The author, Emilia Petrarca, noted, "The world knows Varda for her directorial abilities, but her style has made headlines only recently."[51] Both articles mention the cardboard cutouts at the Oscars luncheon, with *The Cut* concluding its article with a photo of JR and cardboard Varda at that event's red carpet. During the final days of the awards cycle for *Visages Villages*, the circulation of Varda's unique image resulted in her recognition as a style icon by mainstream American press, bringing attention to the film from new outlets and building awareness in potential new audiences. Like Varda's lighthearted treatment of awards season and the Oscars, her time as a viral fashion sensation, albeit brief, is a rare development for a long-standing auteur within international film culture. Apart from brief references to her identity as an important female filmmaker, this turn in her status as a celebrity and a meme did not often engage with the political content of her art, like her interest in feminist politics. But this shift remains in sync with her decades of playful self-presentation through her cartoon counterpart and her signature purple hair and white crown, and these qualities uniquely positioned her for attention in digital culture that prizes humor and distinctive visual characteristics.

Although *Visages Villages* did not win the Academy Award for Best Documentary Feature, which went to *Icarus* (dir. Bryan Fogel and Dan Cogan, US, 2017), Varda still returned to France with a statue to post on Instagram: *Visages Villages* won the Independent Spirit Award for Best Documentary Feature (fig. 11). Part of the caption for this post reads, "@jr and I did not receive one Oscar for #facesplaces, but two Independent Spirit Awards: one for each! Actually it suits us ;)."[52] The two awards are certainly fitting for the film, Varda's first and only directorial collaboration. Even after the two directors completed the film's American awards campaign, Varda and JR continued to accompany the film to festivals and special screenings in new markets, and they often documented these moments on their Instagram accounts, sometimes calling back to earlier moments in the film's release. This interplay between a traditional release pattern and a new method of documenting the experience lasted throughout 2018, as new countries showed the film for the first time.

The Auteur on Instagram

While the release strategy of *Visages Villages* demonstrates a fairly typical model for a foreign-language documentary aiming for awards success in the United States, the social media activities of its directors—especially Varda's Instagram and the cardboard Varda that received widespread attention on JR's Instagram— signal a new extension of aesthetic practice that warrants consideration. Varda's use of social media adapts many of her existing preoccupations, especially the incorporation of biographical material and the recycling of her past work, but it also complemented the film's traditional promotion through screenings and press coverage by documenting these processes from her perspective. The *Visages Villages* team strategically employed festival screenings to generate coverage at appropriate times in different regions after its premiere at Cannes. Cohen Media Group withheld the North American theatrical release until the fall, so the film would be eligible to screen at all the influential North American festivals mentioned above. Throughout this time, Varda's Instagram offered a unique, real-time documentary record of her travels and the film's promotion.

These screenings produced important positive coverage for the film, but the continued social media use of its directors ultimately helped at another significant point in its promotion, even after the major screenings and theatrical release were complete. The cardboard Varda cutouts at the Oscars luncheon in February introduced the filmmaker and the film to new media outlets and their audiences, renewing interest in an innovative way that maintained the style and collaborative approach of the auteur's online presence. Not all filmmakers have an immediately recognizable image like Varda's, or her playful, inquisitive way of viewing the world, and both of these qualities surface throughout Varda's and JR's Instagram documentation of the film's release and promotion. Even without these traits, the extension of film promotion into online spaces, particularly for films and filmmakers outside Hollywood's mode of production, provides greater understanding of how films circulate and succeed or fail in their goals, from building awareness and finding an audience to gaining a wider audience and recognition for an established auteur. As an artist who perpetually experimented with new practices and tools, Varda never stopped innovating, and her adoption of Instagram at eighty-eight years old marks one of her final enthusiastic experiments with a new art form.

Notes

1. JR (@jr), "(Almost) all the Oscars Nominee . . . ," 5 February 2018, www.instagram.com/p/Be1a5AtjOKY.

2. JR (@jr), "Agnes couldn't travel so . . . We took her on a ride," 25 February 2018, www.instagram.com/p/BfoR6dMjxR1/.

3. Ramin Setoodeh and Brent Lang, "With Netflix Out and Stars Absent, Will Cannes Remain Influential?," *Variety*, 3 May 2018, variety.com/2018/film/news/cannes-film-festival-relevance-influence-netflix-1202795621/.

4. Kelley Conway, *Agnès Varda* (Urbana: University of Illinois Press, 2015); Rebecca J. DeRoo, *Agnès Varda between Film, Photography, and Art* (Oakland: University of California Press, 2018).

5. Skadi Loist provides one example of this approach in her study of queer film circulation at festivals, although her study does not address the parallel awards campaigns. Loist, "Crossover Dreams: Global Circulation of Queer Film on the Film Festival Circuits," *Diogenes* 62, no. 1 (2015): 1–17.

6. Cindy Hing-Yuk Wong, *Film Festivals: Culture, People, and Power on the Global Screen* (New Brunswick, NJ: Rutgers University Press, 2011), 2.

7. Cohen Media Group, "Faces Places," cohenmedia.net/films/faces-places (accessed 1 June 2020).

8. "Visages Villages," *Le Pacte*, www.le-pacte.com/france/prochainement/detail/visages-villages/ (accessed 1 June 2020).

9. Conway, *Agnès Varda*, 121.

10. Cannes Film Festival, "A Palme d'Honneur to Agnès Varda," 9 May 2015, www.festival-cannes.com/en/infos-communiques /communique/articles/a-palme-d-honneur-to-agnes-varda.

11. Manohla Dargis, "A Lackluster Cannes and Not Just for the Extra Security," *New York Times*, 24 May 2017, www.nytimes.com /2017/05/24/movies/cannes-film-festival-the-florida-project-hit .html.

12. Owen Gleiberman, "Cannes Film Review: 'Faces Places' ('Visages Villages')," *Variety*, 26 May 2017, variety.com/2017/film/reviews /visages-villages-review-agnes-varda-1202444461/; Todd McCarthy, "'Visages Villages' ('Faces Places'): Film Review Cannes 2017," *Hollywood Reporter*, 21 May 2017, www.hollywood reporter.com/review/visages-villages-faces-places-review -1005799; David Ehrlich, "'Faces Places' Review," *IndieWire*, 22 May 2017, www.indiewire.com/2017/05/faces-places-review -agnes-varda-jr-documentary-cannes-2017-1201830084/.

13. Rhonda Richford, "Cannes: Agnes Varda's 'Faces Places' Takes Golden Eye Documentary Prize," *Hollywood Reporter*, 27 May 2017, www.hollywoodreporter.com/news/cannes-agnes-vardas-faces -places-takes-golden-eye-documentary-prize-1008246.

14. Marijke De Valck, *Film Festivals: From European Geopolitics to Global Cinephilia* (Amsterdam: Amsterdam University Press, 2007), 16.

15. Anne Thompson, "TIFF 2017: Here's the Winners and Losers of the Festival," *IndieWire*, 15 September 2017, www.indiewire.com /2017/09/toronto-2017-winners-losers-oscars-1201876327/.

16. Brooke Barnes, "Charles Burnett and Donald Sutherland among Four to Receive Honorary Oscars," *New York Times*, 6 September 2017, www.nytimes.com/2017/09/06/business/media/burnett -sutherland-honorary-oscars.html.

17. Barnes, "Charles Burnett and Donald Sutherland."

18. Justin Chang, "Agnès Varda on Making Films, Admiring Angelina Jolie and Winning a 'Side Oscar,'" *Los Angeles Times*, 8 November 2017, www.latimes.com/entertainment/movies/la-et -mn-agnes-varda-honorary-oscar-20171108-story.html.

19. Jada Yuan, "Agnès Varda and JR Talk Aging, *Faces Places*, and Road Trips over Afternoon Tea," *Vulture*, 11 October 2017, www .vulture.com/2017/10/agnes-varda-and-jr-interview-faces-places .html.

20. Rajendra Roy, "MoMA Year in Review 2016–17," www.moma.org /interactives/annualreportFY17/ (accessed 5 May 2018).

21. "J. Law, Angelina Take Director's Friendship to New Heights and More Star Snaps," *Page Six*, 12 October 2017, pagesix.com /2017/10/12/j-law-angelina-take-directors-friendship-to-new -heights-and-more-star-snaps/slide-1/.

22. "Rio de Janeiro, Brazil," JR—Artist, www.jr-art.net/projects /rio-de-janeiro (accessed 1 June 2020); Casey Lesser, "JR Mounts a Towering Monument to Refugees at The Armory Show," *Artsy*, 6 March 2018, www.artsy.net/article/artsy-editorial-jr -mounts-towering-monument-refugees-armory.

23. JR (@jr), www.instagram.com/jr/ (accessed 10 May 2018); JR (@JRartiste), www.facebook.com/JRartiste/ (accessed 10 May 2018); JR (@JRart), twitter.com/jrart (accessed 10 May 2018); Agnès Varda (@agnes.varda), www.instagram.com/agnes.varda/ (accessed 10 May 2018); Agnès Varda (@agnesvardaofficiel), www.facebook.com/agnesvardaofficiel/ (accessed 10 May 2018).

24. There is also an official Instagram account for the film's distribution, @facesplacesfilm, but I analyzed the filmmakers' accounts instead. The official account was started in August 2017, after the Cannes premiere and summer screenings in Europe, and it almost exclusively features promotional posters and official event photos, without the personal perspective shown in many of Varda's or JR's Instagram posts that seem to have made them successful. It also has only eight thousand followers, making it substantially less popular than the filmmakers' Instagram feeds.

25. Stefanie Duguay, "LGBTQ Visibility through Selfies: Comparing Platform Mediators across Ruby Rose's Instagram and Vine Presence," *Social Media + Society* 2, no. 2 (2016): 1–12.

26. Conway, *Agnès Varda*, 123.

27. Agnes Varda (@agnes.varda), "Encore une fois JR m'a tapé dans l'œil," 18 May 2017, www.instagram.com/p/BUOqHc7Fe75.

28. Agnes Varda (@agnes.varda), "👓🕶 [emoji of eyeglasses and sunglasses]," 22 May 2017, www.instagram.com/p/BUZskfIFTtK/.

29. Agnes Varda (@agnes.varda), "Pied de nez à nez avec la fine équipe de #cinetamaris #lepacte #rougeinternational

#cohenmediagroup #arte #VisagesVillages #Cannes2017," 20 May 2017, www.instagram.com/p/BUUEuEPl3D1.

30. Caption translations produced using Google Translate and other sources sometimes used for clarity.

31. Agnes Varda (@agnes.varda), "Hollywood . . . 🌴 [palm tree emoji] Sous mon oreiller pour retenir mon speech en dormant . . . ," 11 November 2017, www.instagram.com/p/BbXIM32FRqX/.

32. Conway, *Agnès Varda*, 92.

33. DeRoo, *Agnès Varda between Film, Photography, and Art*, 148.

34. Agnes Varda (@agnes.varda), "Attention avant d'entrer ! . . . Jacques était né le 5 juin. Aujourd'hui j'ai le cœur 💜 [purple heart emoji] en goudron," 5 June 2017, www.instagram.com/p /BU9HDhxlAfn; Agnes Varda (@agnes.varda), "Maintenant on peut entrer! Cette fois-ci on voit Jacques né le 5 juin . . . et mon cœur s'apaise," 6 June 2017, www.instagram.com/p/BU _ugFClMC9.

35. DeRoo, *Agnès Varda between Film, Photography, and Art*, 9.

36. Agnes Varda (@agnes.varda), "Invitée d'amitié pour les grandes joutes de #Sete (Affiche de Christophe Vallaux)," 18 August 2017, www.instagram.com/p/BX8oB3KFu8-.

37. Craig Caron, "The Affiches of Agnès," Toronto International Film Festival, 27 March 2018, www.tiff.net/the-review/the -affiches-of-agnes/; DVD distribution information for *Agnès Varda: From Here to There* (*Agnès de ci de là Varda*, France, 2011), DVD released by Arte Editions and Ciné-Tamaris Vidéo in 2011, www.cine-tamaris.fr/produit/dvd-agnes-de-ci-de-la-varda/.

38. Agnes Varda (@agnes.varda), "International Day for the Elimination of Violence against WOMEN," 25 November 2017, www.instagram.com/p/Bb7BDKRlz9N.

39. JR (@jr), "Sunday October 8 is the last day of Kikito installation!," 7 October 2017, www.instagram.com/p/BZ96K_Nj43G.

40. JR (@jr), "🙏 [praying hands emoji] @facesplacesfilm," 20 December 2017, www.instagram.com/p/Bc7oD4RDi37.

41. JR (@jr), "When our film @facesplacesfilm is nominated at the Oscar for Best Documentary feature," 23 January 2018, www .instagram.com/p/BeTI8_wDmNI.

42. Yuan, "Agnès Varda and JR Talk Aging."

43. JR (@JR), "Agnes couldn't travel."

44. JR (@JR), "Agnes couldn't travel."

45. Agnès Varda (@agnes.varda), "Revenge of all my cut boards that JR played with !," 19 March 2018, www.instagram.com/p/Bgg 8cPiDJxz.

46. Lizzie Smith, "And the Oscar for Best No-Show Goes To," *Daily Mail*, 6 February 2018, www.dailymail.co.uk/tvshowbiz/article -5355873/Meryl-Streep-amused-Agnes-Varda-cutout-Oscars -lunch.html.

47. *Guardian*, "Flat Screen Legend: Agnès Varda Sends Cardboard Cutout to Oscar Nominees Lunch," 6 February 2018, www .theguardian.com/film/shortcuts/2018/feb/06/agnes-varda-cut -out-oscars-french-film-maker.

48. Chris Gardner, "Why a Cardboard Cutout Is the Star of Awards Season," *Hollywood Reporter*, 14 February 2018, www.hollywood reporter.com/rambling-reporter/why-a-cardboard-cutout-is-star -awards-season-1084333; Alexandra Schwartz, "Agnès Varda Is Still Going Places," *New Yorker*, 4 March 2018, www.newyorker .com/culture/persons-of-interest/agnes-varda-is-still-going -places.

49. Kyle Buchanan (@kylebuchanan), "Agnes Varda at the Indie Spirits in an emblazoned hoodie sipping mineral water through a straw is IT," 3 March 2018, 1:12 p.m., twitter.com /kylebuchanan/status/970044310979624961.

50. Brooke Bobb, "The Oscars' Oldest Ever Nominee Also Wears Gucci like a Boss," *Vogue*, 4 March 2018, www.vogue.com/article /agnes-varda-director-oscars-academy-awards-2018.

51. Emilia Petrarca, "An Ode to Agnès Varda's Radical Style," *The Cut*, 29 March 2019, www.thecut.com/2019/03/agnes-varda -style-icon-gucci-oscars.html.

52. Agnès Varda (@agnes.varda), "@jr et moi, on a pas reçu un Oscar pour #facesplaces," 9 March 2018, www.instagram.com/p /BgGfkQehEec/.

Matt St. John is a PhD candidate in the Department of Communication Arts at the University of Wisconsin–Madison, where he is working on a dissertation about the history of film festivals in the United States and their shifting relationships with the media industries. His other research interests include digital humanities and contemporary documentary film and media.

Figure 11. Instagram photo of Varda's Independent Spirit Award for *Visages Villages* (*Faces Places*, France, 2018)

Figure 1. Exhibition view of *Photographs get moving (potatoes and shells too)*, Logan Center Gallery, Chicago, 2015

Varda's Third Life

Dominique Bluher

Agnès Varda never missed an opportunity to mention that she owes her "third life as a young visual artist" (as she liked to say) to Hans Ulrich Obrist. In 2003 Obrist invited her to participate in the fiftieth Venice Biennale as a part of the *Utopia Station* exhibition that he was curating with the art critic and historian Molly Nesbit and the artist Rirkrit Tiravanija. They asked artists from all sorts of disciplines to interrogate and revive the seemingly obsolete concept of utopia.[1] In retrospect it is not surprising that Varda seized the opportunity. Her love for painting and the visual arts had been a source of inspiration from the very beginning of her career. One might even consider some of her earlier films or parts of films, such as *7rm., kitch., bath., . . . for sale* (*7p., cuis., s. de b., . . . à saisir*, France, 1984) or *Jane B. by Agnès V.* (*Jane B. par Agnès V.*, France, 1985), as "installed films," to take up Raymond Bellour's expression in his text on *The Beaches of Agnès* (*Les plages d'Agnès*, France, 2008).[2]

Surprising, though, is that she started a new career as a visual artist at the age of seventy-five. Varda created over twenty large-scale video installations, not to mention the smaller ones and her numerous new photographic works. This was also possible only

Camera Obscura 106, Volume 36, Number 1
DOI 10.1215/02705346-8838601   © 2021 by *Camera Obscura*
Published by Duke University Press

thanks to the support of visual and video artist Julia Fabry, who from 2007 on collaborated with Varda and curated her visual artwork. Varda had over twenty solo exhibitions and countless group exhibitions in museums, galleries, and art biennials all over the world.[3] I had the chance not only to see several of these exhibitions but also to work with her closely on two exhibitions and retrospectives, at Harvard in 2009 and at the University of Chicago in 2015. I am currently preparing a monographic exhibition of nearly all of her multimedia installations. It is obviously impossible to discuss all of her video installations in a single article. I therefore limit my discussion to some major works and consider more closely how Varda took up and expanded on subjects that mattered to her throughout her cinematic career by means proper to this new medium.

As Claire Bishop has pointed out, installation art "differs from traditional media (sculpture, painting, photography, video) in that it addresses the viewer directly as a literal presence in the space. . . . This insistence on the literal presence of the viewer is arguably the key characteristic of installation art."[4] Varda didn't create any site-specific installations, but her installations are nevertheless ephemeral works of art since they have to be experienced in the context of an exhibition.[5] Like all installation art, they require a mobile, walking viewer who engages with the work, sometimes when the visitor is literally invited to interact with the installation. At its best, installation art does not deliver a content-based meaning or message but, rather, solicits an affective experience and personal emotional responses and questions. Sandy Flitterman-Lewis has noted in regard to her films that, as "a director, Varda is interested in questions, not answers."[6] This is even more true of her installation work. The impact of the encounter depends entirely on the state of mind of the viewers and the time they allow themselves for feelings and reflections. Even if the viewing of her installations is a personal experience, I share a certain understanding with critics and scholars who have described observations and responses similar to my own. Thus, I feel encouraged to prolong certain interrogations and to offer some context for considering works Varda made in her third life as a young visual artist.

Triptychs and Polyptychs

Varda's first multiscreen installation, *Patatutopia* (2003), is a three-channel video installation with seven hundred kilograms of potatoes on the ground, a triptych in celebration of the most modest vegetable. As is well-known, she discovered her passion for heart-shaped potatoes, dumped because they do not have the right shape and caliber to be sold to consumers, while shooting *The Gleaners and I* (*Les glaneurs et la glaneuse*, France, 1999), her essay film on gleaning, salvaging, and recycling in our consumer society, which throws out so many objects supposedly expired or considered useless. Fascinated by these heart-shaped potatoes, she took them home, photographing and filming the aging, shriveling, and sprouting potatoes over and over again. The installation *Patatutopia* is an outgrowth of this fascination—stemmed from it, so to speak. The title is a wordplay à la Varda that could be approximately translated to "potat-utopia" or "spud-utopia," since *patate* is a colloquial French word for potato.

Patatutopia also bears the mark of her love of painting. As a triptych, *Patatutopia* evokes an altarpiece, but there is nothing religious in this work. The subjects of traditional worship of Christian art have vanished. Instead of saints we see potatoes. Addressing as it does spectators' sight, hearing, and smell, *Patatutopia* is Varda's most immersive video installation. On the center screen the heart-shaped potatoes seem to be breathing, while the side panels display variations of rootlets, sprouts, and offshoots. A complex, disquieting sound design—composed of inhalations and exhalations, high-heeled footsteps, squeaks, whispers, grumbles, bursts of dissonant music, and many other sounds that are hard to identify—creates a disturbing soundscape with a few soothing moments, such as when birds start singing. Varda also hoped that *Patatutopia* would acquire an olfactory dimension over time when the potatoes dumped in front of the screens would start to decompose and emit a sweet scent of decay (though not every exhibition space welcomed the idea of having decomposing potatoes in the showroom). The three screens are imposing but not overwhelming. They are of human size, but to look at potatoes at a human scale makes them appear monumental. As an homage to potatoes, Varda wished "that those

Figure 2. *Patatutopia* poster (2003) and potato costume (2003). © succession varda

who enter this installation [would] be overcome with emotion and joy in front of this most banal and modest vegetable of all."[7] There was also a performative element to the initial installation, since Varda wandered through the exhibition hallways dressed up as an enormous potato, hailing and calling for visitors. Later iterations had a mannequin dressed in the potato costume with a photograph of Varda's face that emitted an audio recording of Varda reciting an endless list of varieties of potatoes with exotic and poetic-sounding names, most of which are completely unfamiliar to the contemporary consumer.[8]

In her next show, two years later, Varda exhibited *Patatutopia* and created two new video installations: *Le triptyque de Noirmoutier* (*The Triptych of Noirmoutier*, 2005) and one of her (by now most famous) video installations, the polyptych *Les veuves de Noirmoutier* (*The Widows of Noirmoutier*, 2005). She also added a series of photographs, the *Série patates coeur* (*Heart Potatoes Series*, 2002), taken of the heart-shaped potatoes collected during the shoot of *The Gleaners and I.* In my view, this series of eleven photographs of aging and resprouting potatoes puts the "utopian" project *Patatutopia* even more in perspective. *Série patates coeur* features heart-shaped potatoes lovingly pictured on makeshift pedestals, well lit in front of backgrounds chosen in accordance with the "personality" of the potato. These "portraits" do not anthropomorphize the vegetables but, rather, give the viewer the leisure to contemplate the unusual beauty and singularity of an aging, decomposing potato. Varda always had the gift to give us the opportunity to reframe our perception of overlooked objects and populations. One might remember the sequence in *The Gleaners and I* when Varda, at her return from a trip to Japan, inspects the water and mildew stains on her ceiling. She views landscapes or abstract paintings in them and presents these spots in golden frames, comparing them to paintings by Antoni Tàpies, Cai Guo-Qiang, and Clément Borderie. Her imaginative gaze transforms a domestic encumbrance into a work of art inseparable from those of renowned artists.

Her triptych pays tribute to the centuries-old practice of veneration, but at the same time she subverts it by appropriating these means of display, replacing the traditional figures of religious adoration with the "most banal and modest vegetable of all." This is her proposition for an antidote to the current state of the world, as the artists were invited to imagine for the *Utopia Station* project.[9] If we follow her invitation, we might direct or reorient our attention away from the spectacular and extraordinary toward what Georges Perec called the *infra-ordinaire* (infraordinary); that is to say, we might "take account of, question, describe what happens every day and recurs every day: the banal, the quotidian, the obvious, the common, the ordinary, the infraordinary, the background noise, the habitual."[10] Varda's work breathes new life into things that we fail to notice, just as Perec called for: "What we need to question is bricks, concrete, glass, our table manners, our utensils, our tools, the way we spend our time, our rhythms. To question that which seems to have ceased forever to astonish us."[11] *Patatutopia* represents, in Varda's words, her "utopian thought that the beauty of the world concentrated in these old potatoes can help us live with the chaos."[12]

Le triptyque de Noirmoutier displays a mundane scene: a kitchen with a man and two women, whom Varda identifies as his wife and his mother. With this triptych Varda transforms another aspect of the altarpiece: the fact that the side panels can be folded shut or displayed open. In her installation, this device permits a spatial and interactive play with the cinematic off-screen where the viewer is invited to manipulate the side screens. When the visitor opens the side panel, the center screen expands into a contiguous space, such as a beach landscape, or into another room. Here Varda transposes the time-based editing of cinema into a spatial interactive display.[13] It is up to the visitor to reveal or to hide the off-screen space. The spatial *next* of the images side by side in a triptych also presents the potential of a temporal before and/or after. In later installations, *La terrasse le Corbusier* (*Corbusier's Terrace*, 2011) and *Les gens de la terrasse* (*The People on the Terrace*, 2011), Varda returns to this questioning of the possible "before" of an image.

Her third video installation, *Les veuves de Noirmoutier*, is undoubtedly one of her most impressive and touching multimedia works; it is also the installation that has received the most commentary.[14] According to Varda, she first thought of *Les veuves de Noirmoutier* when, while she was working on the *Le triptyque de Noirmoutier*, a neighbor in Noirmoutier lost her husband only one year after their marriage. "It was probably at that moment," Varda wrote, that "I became aware that there are more widows than widowers in the world, and there are a tremendous number of them on the island, if my neighbors are any indication."[15] *Les veuves de Noirmoutier* is dedicated to these widows who opened up their hearts to her. Varda recorded their conversations in which they share with her their feelings about being widowed and their strategies for coping with the loss and the absence of their spouses. Each woman talks to Varda about the solitude, the silence, the void, but also about the presence of their lost husband in their homes and lives. In return for their candor, Varda included herself as one of them. Varda lost Jacques Demy in 1990. It was Demy who introduced her to the island Noirmoutier off the Atlantic coast of France, near the

Figure 3. Preparatory sketch for *Les veuves de Noirmoutier* (*The Widows of Noirmoutier*, 2005). © succession varda

city of Nantes, where he was born. They bought an old mill and spent much of their time there working or vacationing. Ever since his passing, her work bears witness to the enduring presence and his sharply felt absence in her life.[16]

Les veuves de Noirmoutier is a video installation in the fullest sense. It proposes a radically different viewing experience than a projection of moving images in a movie theater or a black box. The defining elements of cinema are present but rethought and reworked. We are not sitting immobile in the dark in front of a single bright screen, and we are not watching the same movie together at the same time. We are not removed from reality, trying to ignore the presence of the other spectators in the room, but we are also not responding emotionally at the same time to the same images and sounds on the screen. A polyptych composed of fifteen screens awaits us when we enter the dim room: one big central screen surrounded by fourteen little monitors. Similar to *Patatutopia*, the work is at the same time an homage to and a *détournement* of a traditional altarpiece. Of the work, Varda wrote, "I had certainly thought of early paintings with a predella composed of narrative scenes. (Fra Angelico painted seventeen portraits of saints on the bottom of his large *Crucifixion,* and even added eleven smaller portraits on the upper half-moon shaped frame.)"[17] Here, instead of looking at saints, we are invited to watch the portraits of the women on the monitors who are visibly addressing us. They are talking, but we don't hear them. "These portraits are silent," explained Varda, "because society does not hear these widows. This was the motivation behind this work. Lacking, missing is a subject of great importance in our society."[18] If we want to hear what the widows are saying, we have to take a seat on one of the chairs positioned in the room and put on the headphones attached to the chair. However, each headset links us to only one voice and one monitor; if we want to listen to the account of another widow, we have to change chairs and headsets. Consequently, the viewing is a solitary and intimate experience: each visitor is the recipient of the confidences of one widow, as if her words were addressed only to the viewer, an impression reinforced by the intimacy of wearing headphones. This experience reproduces the intimacy in which Varda recorded these conversations with her small MiniDV camera.

Still, we can't fully ignore the other visitors. We have to exchange chairs and headphones. The setup of the chairs in the room replicates the arrangement of the small monitors: they form a rectangle around a void echoing the central monitor. Moving from chair to chair, we thus mirror the solemn choreography of the widows, all dressed in black, who on the central screen are slowly moving around an altar-like stand on the beach. Although each portrait-film has its own autonomy, these some three-minute-long portraits are short enough that we can pick up a conversation at any time. Furthermore, we are free to see as few or as many as we like. In this sense, our circuit in the room from chair to chair and our more or less random choice of portraits carry out the final montage and design our emotional journey. Although the viewing is an individual and solitary experience, we also share it with the other visitors, or, as Bellour put it, this personal experience is "all the more troubling because it turns into a collective one."[19] The writer Marie Darrieussecq described it the following way: "You turn to your neighbor, a lump in your throat, but she is smiling or dreaming. Seated on these fourteen chairs, we are all at the same time thinking the same thing, but in a different way."[20] On the other hand, this arrangement creates a sense of community that enhances the subjective experience of the viewers. With *Les veuves de Noirmoutier*, Varda gives voices to silenced women's experiences and creates a display in which each of the elements reverberates with its topic. This is something that few multimedia installations attempt or achieve. A couple of years later, Varda's powerful installation *Hommage aux Justes de France* (*Homage to the Righteous of France*, 2007) also gives voices to those who have none, likewise linking the individual and the collective, the personal and the political.[21]

Varda's Cinema Shacks

Over the years Varda has made several *cabanes* or cinema shacks. The first cinema shack was made for her first large monographic exhibition, *L'île et elle* in 2006, commissioned by Hervé Chandès, the director of the Fondation Cartier pour l'Art Contemporain.[22] And a cinema shack was also among the very last works she created. It is extremely difficult to find an English equivalent for *cabane*. In French, *cabane* relates to several kinds of simple small

Figure 4. Agnès Varda, *Ma cabane de l'échec* (*My Shack of Failure*, 2006) renamed in 2009 as *Une cabane de cinéma* (*A Cinema Shack*). © succession varda

constructions crudely built of natural, found, or salvaged materials. Although it refers to shacks, sheds, huts, or cabins built for adults' shelter, storage, or leisure, the term is also very closely associated with special self-constructed children's places such as secret hideaways, forts, or treehouses. Varda's first shack was initially titled *Ma cabane de l'échec* (*My Shack of Failure*) before she renamed it for its second showing in 2009 at the Lyon Biennale as *Une cabane de cinéma* (*A Cinema Shack*). *Ma cabane de l'échec* started out as a way to recycle 35mm prints of one of Varda's commercial failures, *The Creatures* (*Les créatures*, France/Sweden, 1966), shot on the island of Noirmoutier. Her last shack, *Une cabane de cinema: La serre du bonheur* (*A Cinema Shack: The Greenhouse of Happiness*, 2018), was made of the 35mm film reels of her film *Le bonheur* (*Happiness*, France, 1964). In between she also made a cinema shack for her show at the Los Angeles County Museum of Art (2013) with two prints of her 1969 movie *Lions Love (. . . and Lies)* (France/USA).

These shacks are not little; they are, rather, small houses that visitors are invited to enter, to wander around, and to inspect the celluloid strips. Until 2017, Varda's production company Ciné-Tamaris took care of the distribution of Varda's and Demy's movies. Therefore, they had a large inventory of 35mm prints, among which were many reels of *The Creatures* that were waiting to be discarded. Gleaner that she is, Varda made use of these worthless prints and amortized their costly storage. Today, all of Varda's (and Demy's) films have been restored and digitized and are now usually projected from digital files. Additionally, Varda imagined and made models of some other "cinema shacks," with Super 8 filmstrips reproducing relevant sequences of the original films: a film tent for *Vagabond* (*Sans toit ni loi*, France, 1985) and a shipwreck for *La Pointe Courte* (France, 1955). These models were shown along with the models of *Ma cabane de l'échec* and *Une cabane de cinema: La serre du bonheur* (that was eventually exhibited the next year) at her exhibition at the Galerie Blum & Poe in New York in 2017. The models made are very small compared to the large-scale shacks. These small works present a playful interrogation of scale and our perception of grandeur that is similar to other works, such as *Patatutopia,* or her contrast of two printings of the same view of the Atlantic Ocean: *La mer immense* and *La petite mer immense* (*The Immense Sea* and *The Little Immense Sea,* 2003). *La mer immense* is a digital enlargement so immense that it can't be embraced with a single gaze. This large-scale image hangs next to *La petite mer immense,* a small silver print in a wonderful old gold frame that enhances the light and calm that emanates from the image.

The small shack models make one think of toy houses, and indeed, Varda associated the *cabane* strongly with the idea of childhood: "*Cabane* the word itself refers to childhood desires, to desires, always, to a rustic shelter."[23] In an interview for the second showing at the Lyon Biennale, Varda insisted even more on the link with childhood: "I believe that the cabane is an abode that everyone has known since childhood from the shelters one makes in the garden. Sometimes children make cabins from cardboard boxes; they place a sheet of fabric on top. The cabane is a little nest, a place to relax or a corner of solitude. Or rather, one hides, or wants to be alone, or even to hide in twos or threes."[24] Her words resonate strongly with Gaston Bachelard's contemplations of places and reveries. Bachelard had been Varda's professor at the Sorbonne and left a deep impression on her. He is possibly the only philosopher to whom Varda has ever referred directly in her work. She usually evokes Bachelard in regard to the biblical story of Jonah and the whale, but she must have felt also a profound affinity with the importance that Bachelard gave to daydreaming and poetic reveries.[25] His 1957 book, *The Poetics of Space,* focuses on small intimate locations within the house: the special spaces of solitude, repose, and reverie such as drawers, wardrobes, reading nooks, corners, or nests: "The house shelters daydreaming, the house protects the dreamer, the house allows one to dream in peace."[26] Bachelard doesn't write about huts or sheds as such, but he examines all kinds of hiding places in the house where one can retreat in order to dream and imagine: "In the house itself, in the family sitting room, a dreamer of refuges dreams of a hut, of a nest, or of nooks and corners in which he would like to hide away."[27] Reveries have always been central to Varda's creation. At the beginning of *The Beaches of Agnès,* she thanks "all these people willing to enter [her] reverie, something imaginary," whereas toward the end she says, while sitting on a pile of canisters in her cinema shack, "When I'm here, it feels like I live in cinema, that cinema is my home. I think I've always lived in it." Her shacks made out of recycled prints ended up being her "shack of reveries, the perfect shelter for a filmmaker," the ultimate expression of her life and domain.[28]

Her shacks are also at the crossroads of several contemporary artistic practices. On one hand, her use of filmstrips is reminiscent of certain forms of expanded cinema from the 1960s to today, from Peter Kubelka or Paul Sharits to Jennifer West, who work with filmstrips as material objects and not as a to-be-ignored medium for the projection of images on a screen.[29] On the other hand, Varda's shacks call to mind contemporary visual artists like Tadashi Kawamata, famous for his tree huts and nests. He builds impermanent, site-specific structures from materials found in situ (such as reclaimed lumber, beams and boards, logs, chairs, doors, barrels, or crates), on facades, on roofs, or in trees in parks.[30] We might also remember Stéphane Thidet's *Le refuge* (*The Refuge*, 2007) that Varda filmed in her five-part documentary *Agnès Varda: From Here to There* (*Agnès de ci de là Varda*, France, 2011).

For the second showing of her *Une cabane de cinéma* at the Lyon Biennale, Varda added another shack, *La cabane de plage qui est une cabine de projection* (*A Beach Cabin That Is a Projection Booth*), which was eventually converted into a new installation: *Dépôt de la cabane de plage qui est aussi une cabine de projection avec sa vidéo "La mer Méditerranée, avec deux r et un n, entre Sète et Agde"* (*The Depository of the Beach Cabin That Is a Projection Booth with Its Video "The Mediterranean, with Two Rs and One N, between Sète and Agde,"* 2010). This transformation, from a beach cabin to a depot or depository of the elements for building a shed, points to an even higher degree to the structure's precarious and provisional nature. Varda, being Varda, is well aware of the luxury of reveling in reveries in her refuge and the fact that, at the very same moment, many people in the world are without any shelter. The video, *La mer Méditerranée, avec deux r et un n, entre Sète et Agde*, projected in the cabin depot, is a compilation of shots—strollers on the beach or love-making trapeze artists—but these peaceful scenes are disrupted by violent

Figure 5. Agnès Varda, *Dépôt de la cabane de plage qui est aussi une cabine de projection avec sa vidéo "La mer Méditerranée, avec deux* r *et un* n, *entre Sète et Agde"* (*The Depository of the Beach Cabin That Is a Projection Booth with Its Video "The Mediterranean, with Two* R*s and One* N, *between Sète and Agde,"* 2010). © succession varda

news footage of wars, earthquakes, tsunamis, displaced people, and migrants. The coastal whale shelter built in *The Beaches of Agnès* (as an homage to Bachelard and as an incarnation of safety and happiness) reappears in the video as an angry beast "because the world is sick."[31]

While shooting *The Gleaners and I,* Varda discovered artistic gleaning, but she never forgot those who have to glean leftovers and trash out of necessity. Her first shack was an artistic project breathing new life into discarded objects, but she didn't forget those who do not have shelter. Already in *L'Opéra Mouffe* (*Diary of a Pregnant Woman,* France, 1958), the young pregnant filmmaker had borne in mind that the homeless people on the rue Mouffetard had once been beloved newborn babies. Similarly, when Varda was invited to participate at the 2012 edition of the contemporary art event

Estuaire in Nantes, she did more than just create an installation in homage to Demy's *A Room in Town* (*Une chambre en ville*, France, 1982), set in Nantes. She also produced a resolutely political installation, *La chambre occupée (paroles de squatteurs)* (*An Occupied Room [Words of Squatters]*). Here, she recorded conversations with refugees and squatters that are screened on monitors placed in objects, like a mattress or a stove, representing basic human needs: water, food, heating, a space to sleep.

Still and Moving Images

The dialectic between still and moving images, photography and cinema (or video), preoccupied Varda during her whole career. In 1995 she wrote:

Photography and Cinema . . . these two ways of capturing life, one immobile and silent, the other in motion and sound, are not really enemies but simply different, even complementary. With photography we have movement that has been stopped, or inner movement immobilized. On the other hand, the cinema gives us a series of successive photographs in a length of time that animates them. . . . But there is another way of combining these two visions: you could film the photographs themselves and show them on the screen. You can add to the fixed image the possibility of seeing them in a determined length of time. Make what is fixed come alive by the active gaze.[32]

Thus, it was only logical that Varda would continue to explore possible interplays in her video installations that would offer new means to intertwine the still and the moving, the fleeting and the fixed, as matter and subject. Varda made two "photo films": *Salut les Cubains* (*Hello Cubans*, France/Cuba, 1964) and *Ulysse* (France, 1983), not to mention her television series *One Minute for One Image* (*Une minute pour une image*, France, 1983).[33] Except for the short prologue, *Salut les Cubains* consists of over one thousand black-and-white photographs taken during a sojourn to Cuba in 1962 and animated with a rostrum camera. In contrast, *Ulysse* revolves around a single photograph. "Ulysse," Varda explained, "is the

Figure 6. Agnès Varda, *Corbusier's Terrace* (*La terrasse le Corbusier*, 1956) and *Les gens de la terrasse* (*The People on the Terrace*, 2011). © succession varda

name of this little boy in the middle of the photograph I took in 1954, on a beach in Normandy. Twenty-eight years later, I explore this image, my memories and the memories of those who have posed. What is an image? And thus, it is a film about one image."[34] *Ulysse* is a journey through memories and the past, a reflection on the picture and what it meant at the time to the photographer Varda and to the protagonists portrayed in the photograph. In the film, Varda constantly reframes the eponymous photograph figuratively and also literally, through frames within frames or photocollages. Retrospectively, this breaking open of the limitation of the frame, or the constrictions of the borders of the image, can be seen as an anticipation of her multiscreen installations.

Indeed, in 2011 *Ulysse* was shown as an installation and as a companion piece to two other installations, *La terrasse le Corbusier* and *Les gens de la terrasse*. Both installations oppose a printed photo to a projection: the photograph *Ulysse* from 1954 and the movie from 1982; the snapshot *La terrasse le Corbusier* taken in 1956 on the roof terrace of Corbusier's Cité Radieuse in Marseille and the short movie *Les gens de la terrasse* imagined around the snapshot. On one hand, *Les gens de la terrasse* tells a story about what could have led up to the constellation of people on the terrace. On the other hand, it also gives a behind-the-scenes perspective, a kind of making-of, recounting the different stages that led to the short film. In Varda's words,

Questioning a still image, a snapshot, led me to investigate the mystery of one captured instant. What were some people doing together in the same place at the same moment? They even may not know each other, and I know nothing about them. From watching one silent image shot in 1957, I imagined what happened at that instant, and in 2007 I created a screenplay that could be true and made a short film, played a game. Any other screenplay could be possible.[35]

These diptychs made it possible to show how moving images can propose investigations that bring out the imaginary potential of a still image.[36]

Photography and cinema are not only two different ways to capture life but also complementary means to stimulate the imagination. Varda's films are a realization of her imagination around a photo, but for Varda a photo as such is a site for reverie, as she explained the project of her television series *One Minute for One Image*:

As an ex-photographer and filmmaker, fascinated with the effects of the word on the image and vice versa, I thought of suggesting every photo as a place for reverie; it seemed to me that a bit of silence and a voice that communicates its personal impressions would stimulate the imagination of each and every person. When I say reverie, I refer as much to the emotions as to the horror, the fascination, the charm, the admiration, the pleasure, the nostalgia, the complicity in humor, in short, an active reverie, the little film inside every person's head.[37]

In some other video installations Varda turned the narrative investigation of the still image into a purely visual exploration. *Bord de mer* (*The Seaside*, 2009) also combines photography and video. It consists of a huge panel of a still photograph depicting waves breaking on the shore. On the floor there is a narrow band with a looped video projection of crashing waves on a sloping beach. The edges of the projection field end in a strip of actual sea sand.

Figure 7. Agnès Varda, *Marie dans le vent* (*Marie in the Wind*, 2014). © succession varda

Which form of representation—the photography, the video, or a trace of real sand—renders more vividly the crashing waves? The contrast between a frozen movement and motion in flow is also behind her series of photo-video triptychs *Portraits à volets video* (*Portraits with Video Wings*, 2009–14). The central panel is a photograph, usually a black-and-white silver print, flanked by two side panels with two video projections. In the center is a classic and calm portrait, a face with a still gaze, whereas the two wings are video recordings of movement.

The two most striking portraits with wings are *Alice et les vaches blanches* (*Alice and the White Cows*, 2011) and *Marie dans le vent* (*Marie in the Wind*, 2014). Alice is a little girl standing in a field in front of a big cow; in the background, two cows are partially obscured by the large cow in the front. The girl seems to be observing the cows, though her gaze is fixed, whereas the two videos projected on either side show the slow, steadying movement of massive cow bodies (fig. 8).

The central still of Marie captures her tousled hair and a wildly rotating toy windmill she is holding in her hand, while on each side wind turbines are slowly spinning with hypnotic regularity. "Movement is not always where you expect it to be," Varda wrote. "A frozen portrait of a woman in the wind moves more in our eyes than the moving windmills surrounding her."[38] Our fascination wanders back and forth: what captures movement better and stimulates our imagination more, the unmoving image or the slow-paced flow of motion?

The viewing of these works is contingent on another kind of temporality that Roland Barthes has called "pensiveness." Comparing the viewing experience of still images and moving images, Barthes remarked pointedly that watching a movie doesn't give you the time to "add something" to the images: "In front of the screen, I am not free to shut my eyes; otherwise, opening them again, I would not discover the same image; I am constrained to a continuous voracity; a host of other qualities, but not pensiveness; whence the interest, for me, of the photogram."[39] Barthes didn't discuss any forms of experimental cinema, or what is known today as slow cinema, which are forms that likely would have challenged his characterization of movies. However, what Barthes underscored in regard to the still image is also at stake in Varda's installations. Even if some of the videos present an unfolding linear narrative, they are so short that viewers, if they desire, can watch them more than once. What is pensiveness for Barthes corresponds to Varda's articulation of active reverie. Her exhibitions and installations are sites for the wandering mind. What we make of them depends on our own way of seeing, on the time we give ourselves to close our eyes so that we can "add" something to it.

La cabane du chat

Thanks to Hervé Chandès, the director of the Fondation Cartier pour l'Art Contemporain, since 2016 there is a permanent *cabane* in the garden of the foundation that houses Varda's 2006 video installation *Le tombeau de Zgougou* (*Zgougou's Tomb*): *La cabane du chat* (*The Shack of the Cat*). *Le tombeau de Zgougou* is a two-channel video installation dedicated to Demy and Varda's beloved cat Zgougou, who is buried in the backyard of Varda's home on the island of Noirmoutier.[40] The installation is a re-creation of a little burial mound of earth covered by sand. One video is projected on the reflective surface of sand on the grave, and another on the adjoining wall behind. The visitor who comes to see the installation is standing in front of the grave, very much as in an actual cemetery. The video for the grave comprises two parts, a series of images of Zgougou and a plaque identifying her as lying beneath the earth. During the second part, the grave is magically decorated with starfish and seashells through a set of images in stop-frame animation, while on an adjoining wall stalks of red and pink flowers appear to be growing.

The video on the wall then takes over, showing the grave in the middle of a small pine grove in Noirmoutier. An enormous bright red paper flower is affixed on the wall behind it. The camera starts to crane up and out, catching another big red paper flower in the top of a pine tree. The camera moves higher, revealing the shoreline nearby. The camera moves higher and higher, shifting seamlessly from a crane shot to a helicopter shot of the whole island before dissolving into a minuscule map of the island of Noirmoutier, where, as Varda says, the "little tiny cat, seen from a satellite, is like each of us, an invisible dot."[41] The films are accompanied by "Winds and Brass (with Strings)," the third movement of Steve Reich's *The Four Sections*, which echoes musically the seemingly incompatible moods of sadness and jubilation conveyed in the installation. For her last movie, *Varda by Agnès* (*Varda par Agnès*, France, 2019), Varda filmed a couple of children visiting the grave in the shack in the garden of the Fondation Cartier, where one boy expresses the central point: "I haven't seen many cemeteries. I know they are pretty sad. But this one is more. . . . Even though it's a tomb and we should be sad, it's more of a happy place with fun colors."[42] Varda has a wonderful gift of combining seriousness and playfulness, thoughtfully documented investigations and poetic imagination. Her movies were already invitations to posing questions; her photographic and videographic installations further these invitations to a voyage of personal reflections, emotional responses, or active reveries.

Next time you are in Paris, pay a visit to Zgougou's tomb in the *La cabane du chat*, and then stroll over to the Montparnasse cemetery and visit Varda's grave, where she is resting beside Demy. You can have a seat on the little bench that Varda had installed under the tree and let your thoughts drift away in some active reveries about this tiny woman and giant artist. Close your eyes and think about what she and her art might have added to your way of looking at the world.

Notes

I thank Julia Fabry, Rosalie Varda, and David Rodowick for their assistance with this article.

1. *Utopia Station* started in 2003 as an exhibition for the Venice Biennale and then in 2004 for the Haus der Kunst in Munich. The curators envisioned *Utopia Station* as a project extending over several years under different forms, such as virtual sites, gatherings, and seminars. It was active, in particular, for a couple of years on the e-flux publishing platform, where nearly 160 contributors have created posters for use in *Utopia Station*. "Utopia Station," e-flux, projects.e-flux.com/utopia/index.html (accessed 13 August 2020).

2. Raymond Bellour, "Varda ou l'art contemporain: Note sur *Les plages d'Agnès*," *Trafic*, no. 69 (2009): 16–19. Several segments of *Visages Villages* (*Faces Places*, France, 2017), which she directed with the photographer and muralist JR, can also be considered filmed installations.

3. Her works were shown at the biennales in Venice, Lyon, Basel, and Taipei; at the Fondation Cartier pour l'Art Contemporain (FCAC; Paris), Municipal Museum of Contemporary Art (SMAK; Ghent), the Centre Régional d'Art Contemporain at Sète, the Musée Paul Valéry (Sète), the Central Academy of Fine Arts Museum (Beijing), the Hubei Art Museum (Wuhan), the Centro Andaluz de Arte Contemporaneo (Seville), the Pazo da Cultura (Pontevedra), the Bildmuseet Umeå, the Los Angeles County Museum of Art (LACMA), the Centre Pompidou (Paris), and the Museé d'Ixelles (Brussels) and in the galleries Nathalie Obadia (Paris and Brussels), Blum & Poe (New York and Tokyo), and Sert Galerie (Chicago). And her works have been acquired by, among others, FCAC, Museum of Modern Art (New York), Musée d'Art Contemporain du Val-de-Marne, Fonds Régionaux d'Art Contemporain (FRAC) Alsace, and LACMA.

4. Claire Bishop, *Installation Art: A Critical History* (London: Tate, 2005), 6.

5. The exception that proves the rule is *The Shack of the Cat*, where her installation *Le tombeau de Zgougou* eventually found a permanent home. *Le tombeau de Zgougou* was not conceived as a site-specific installation and has been shown in many exhibitions around the world. I return to it later.

6. Sandy Flitterman-Lewis, *To Desire Differently: Feminism and the French Cinema* (Urbana: University of Illinois Press, 1990), 314.

7. Agnès Varda, artistic dossier, *Patatutopia*; my translation.

8. For a more detailed account of *Patatutopia*, see my catalog text: Dominique Bluher, "Vive la patate!," in *Agnès Varda: Patates et compagnie*, ed. Julia Fabry, Rosalie Varda, and Claire Leblanc (Ixelles, Belgium: Silvana Editoriale, Bruxelles, Musée d'Ixelles, 2016), 59–68; and Kelley Conway, "From Cinema to the Gallery: *Patatutopia* and *L'île et elle*," in *Agnès Varda* (Urbana: University of Illinois Press, 2015), 89–108.

9. Molly Nesbit, Hans Ulrich Obrist, and Rirkrit Tiravanija, "What Is a Station?," projects.e-flux.com/utopia/about.html (accessed 11 August 2020).

10. Georges Perec, "Approaches to What?," in *Species of Spaces and Other Pieces*, trans. John Sturrock (New York: Penguin Books, 1997), 206.

11. Perec, "Approaches to What?," 206.

12. Varda, *Patatutopia*; my translation.

13. In regard to "exposed editing," see Dominique Païni, "Du montage exposé: *Le triptyque de Noirmoutier*, 2005," in *Agnès Varda, L'île et elle: Regards sur l'exposition* (Fondation Cartier pour l'Art Contemporain, Actes Sud, 2006), 34–35.

14. See Raymond Bellour, "Un peu plus de réel," *Trafic*, no. 54 (2005): 5–12; Shirley Jordan, "Spatial and Emotional Limits in Installation Art: Agnès Varda's *L'île et elle*," *Contemporary French and Francophone Studies* 13, no. 5 (2009): 581–88; Marie-Claire Barnet, "'Elles-Ils Islands': Cartography of Lives and Deaths by Agnès Varda," *L'Esprit créateur* 51, no. 1 (2011): 97–111; Jenny Chamarette, "Spectral Bodies, Temporalised Spaces: Agnès Varda's Motile Gestures of Mourning and Memorial,"

Image [&] Narrative 12, no. 2 (2011): 31–49; Jenny Chamarette,
"Agnès Varda's Trinket Box: Subjective Relationality, Affect
and Temporalised Space," in *Phenomenology and the Future of
Film: Rethinking Subjectivity beyond French Cinema* (New York:
Palgrave Macmillan, 2012), 107–42; Delphine Bénézet, "*Les
veuves de Noirmoutier*," in *The Cinema of Agnès Varda: Resistance
and Eclecticism* (New York: Columbia University Press, 2014),
31–39; Conway, "From Cinema to the Gallery," 89–108; Rebecca
J. DeRoo, "Melancholy and Merchandise: Documenting and
Displaying Widowhood in *L'île et elle*," in *Agnès Varda between Film,
Photography, and Art* (Berkeley: University of California Press,
2017), 115–42; and Dominique Bluher, "The Other Portrait:
Agnès Varda's Self-Portraiture," in *From Self-Portrait to Selfie:
Representing the Self in Moving Images*, ed. Muriel Tinel-Temple,
Laura Busetta, and Marlène Monteiro (New York: Peter Lang,
2019), 47–76.

15. Agnès Varda, "*Les veuves de Noirmoutier*," in *Agnès Varda, L'île et elle*,
72; my translation.

16. While Demy was dying, Varda shot *Jacquot* (*Jacquot de Nantes*,
France, 1991) based on his childhood memories and including
extracts from his films and footage of him in his last months.
Demy passed away ten days after the end of the shoot, and Varda
completed the film after his death. She devoted two other films
to him: *The Young Girls Turn Twenty-Five* (*Les demoiselles ont eu
25 ans*, France, 1993) and *The World of Jacques Demy* (*L'univers de
Jacques Demy*, France/Belgium/Spain, 1995); and *The Beaches of
Agnès* contains several sequences in which she evokes the years
with and without him.

17. Varda, "*Les veuves de Noirmoutier*," 72. Intriguingly, in her last film,
Varda by Agnès (*Varda par Agnès*, France, 2019), Varda referred not
to Fra Angelico's *Crucifixion* (ca. 1420–23) but to Jan van Kessel's
Europe (ca. 1664–65) from *The Four Parts of the World* (1660), also
known as *Four Continents*, as a source of inspiration, as if she
was no longer comfortable with the strong feminist statement
implied by replacing venerated male saints with silenced widows.

18. "Entretien d'Agnès Varda avec Frédéric Bonaud, dans l'émission
Charivari," France Inter, 1 July 2004, quoted in Emmanuelle
Lequeux, "Agnès Varda: *Les veuves de Noirmoutier*," Collection
FRAC Lorraine, collection.fraclorraine.org/collection/print
/593?lang=en/; my translation.

19. Bellour, "Un peu plus de réel," 6; my translation.

20. Marie Darrieussecq, "Cinq photographies de veuves et *Les veuves de Noirmoutier*," in *Agnès Varda, L'île et elle*, 41; my translation.

21. See Sandy Flitterman-Lewis's remarkable article about this installation, "Varda: The Gleaner and the Just," in *Situating the Feminist Gaze and Spectatorship in Postwar Cinema*, ed. Marcelline Block (Newcastle: Cambridge Scholars, 2008), 214–25; see also her article in this issue.

22. Conway, "From Cinema to the Gallery," 89–108.

23. Varda, *Agnès Varda, L'île et elle*, 38; my translation.

24. "Une minute avec . . . Agnès Varda," Dailymotion video, 2:01, posted by Biennale de Lyon, www.dailymotion.com/video /xb79mq/; my translation.

25. See the alphabet section in Varda's book *Varda par Agnès* on *The Beaches of Agnès* where she evokes Bachelard and his lecture about Jonah in the whale's belly, unwillingly swallowed and possibly unwilling to come out. Agnès Varda, *Varda par Agnès* (Paris: Cahiers du Cinéma, 1994), 11, 34.

26. Gaston Bachelard, *The Poetics of Space*, trans. Maria Jolas (Boston: Beacon, 1994), 6.

27. Bachelard, *Poetics of Space*, 30.

28. Press release, Biennale Lyon 2009; my translation.

29. After a projection of his film *Adebar* (Austria, 1957), Peter Kubelka nailed the film on a number of wooden pegs, inviting the viewers to palpate the filmstrip and to examine each photogram. Eric Andersen unfurled the filmstrip of his "films" (1966) over the seats in the movie theater and asked spectators to pass the strip over to those seated next to them. See Hans Scheugl and Ernst Schmidt, *Eine Subgeschichte des Films: Lexikon des Avantgarde-, Experimental- und Undergroundfilms* (Frankfurt: Edition Suhrkamp, 1974), 37–39, 255. Paul Sharits's *Frozen Film Frame* (1971–76) series is composed of vertically arranged color film strips, pressed between Plexiglas plates. More recently Jennifer West has created cinematic installations such as *Film Is Dead . . .* (2016) and *Flashlight Filmstrip Projections* (2014/2016) with old film stock manipulated with everyday household substances (e.g., hot water, bleach, vanilla, salt, coffee, vinegar,

food coloring, or nail polish) to paint and erode the film emulsion and create colored splotches and patterns. In *Flashlight Filmstrip Projections*, it is the audience equipped with flashlights who project the filmstrip images on the walls or on other visitors.

30. In a recent issue of the French contemporary art magazine *L'Oeil*, Mathieu Oui discusses several *cabanes* made by visual artists. He starts his article by discussing Varda's *Une cabane de cinema: La serre du bonheur*. Oui, "Comprendre l'art des cabanes," *L'Oeil* 725 (2019): 74–77. FRAC des Pays de la Loire, one of France's public collections of contemporary art, has a very instructive dossier devoted to *cabanes* in contemporary art online. Lucie Charrier, "Cabane! Dossier thématique la cabane, l'abri, l'architecture dans l'art contemporain," FRAC des Pays de la Loire, fracdespays delaloire.com/public/pdf/peda_cabane_bassedef.pdf/. Varda's shacks could have also been part of the 2018 *Woman House* group exhibition of women artists at the museum Monnaie de Paris and at the National Museum of Women in the Arts in Washington, DC. Luc Vancheri and Gill Perry propose both compelling readings of Varda's shacks, exploring both different and complementary venues: Vancheri, "Les cabanes de Varda: De 'l'échec' au 'cinéma,'" in *Cinéma, architecture, dispositif*, ed. Helena Biserna and Precious Brown (Udine, Italy: Campanotto editore, 2011), 120–26; Perry, "Les cabanes d'Agnès," in *Agnès Varda Unlimited: Image, Music, Media*, ed. Marie-Claire Barne (Cambridge: Legenda, 2016), 157–70.

31. Agnès Varda, *Agnès Varda: Y a pas que la mer* (Sète, France: Musée Paul Valery/Editions au fil du temps, 2011), 67; my translation. By the way, the whale is also the emblem of the city of Sète, where the Varda family found refuge during World War II. Varda mentions the emblem but not the fact that Sète was her family refuge. Cap d'Agde is a seaside town about thirty minutes from Sète on the other side of the lagoons toward the border with Spain.

32. Varda, *Varda par Agnès*, 130–31; translation in Flitterman-Lewis, "Varda," 218.

33. *One Minute for One Image* comprises in total 170 short films (approximately ninety seconds each) first broadcast on public television in 1983. Varda had asked a dozen famous, unknown, or even anonymous photographers to create "imaginary albums"

of a dozen photographs that she paired with commentary by a diverse set of people including celebrities, other photographers, friends, and neighbors. Varda herself made two of these imaginary albums, in which she comments directly on a photograph. Agnès Varda, "Une minute pour une image," *Photogénies*, no. 1 (1983). The fourteen films made by Varda are now available on *Varda Tous Courts*, directed by Agnès Varda (Paris: Arte Video/Ciné-Tamaris, 2007), DVD, as well as in the box set *Tout(e) Varda: L'intégrale Agnès Varda*, directed by Agnès Varda (Paris: Ciné-Tamaris Video/Scérén-CNDP, 2012), DVD.

34. Varda, *Agnès Varda: Y'a pas que la mer*, 42.

35. Agnès Varda, "Photographs Get Moving, and So Do Potatoes," in *Agnès Varda: Photographs Get Moving (Potatoes and Shells, Too)*, ed. Dominique Bluher (Chicago: Reva and David Logan Center for the Arts, University of Chicago, 2015), 6.

36. Regarding Varda's interrogation of the still and moving image in her multimedia work, see Raymond Bellour, "'Cinévardaphoto' dit-elle," in Varda, *Agnès Varda: Y'a pas que la mer*, 49–57; Shirley Jordan, "Still Varda: Photographs and Photography in Agnès Varda's Late Work," in *Agnes Varda Unlimited* (Cambridge: Legenda, 2016), 143–56. The essays published in the catalog for the exhibition *Agnès Varda* at the Bildmuseet, Umeå, Goeteborg, in 2013 also revolve around photography. Christa Blümlinger created a very insightful montage of texts of Agnès Varda on the relationship between photography and cinema. The English translation is Blümlinger, "Agnès Varda: From Photography to Cinema and Vice Versa," *L'Atalante*, no. 12 (2011): 68–75.

37. Quoted in Blümlinger, "Agnès Varda," 73; translation modified.

38. Varda, "Photographs Get Moving," 6.

39. Roland Barthes, *Camera Lucida: Reflections on Photography* (New York: Hill and Wang, 1981), 55.

40. For some inspired descriptions of and comments on *Le tombeau de Zgougou*, see Laurence Kardish, "*Le tombeau de Zgougou*," in *Agnès Varda, L'île et elle*, 22–23; the English original is reproduced in the artistic dossier of *Le tombeau de Zgougou* and in Chamarette, "Agnès Varda's Trinket Box," 133–36.

41. Varda, *Agnès Varda: Y'a pas que la mer*, 77; translation mine.

42. It reminds me also of the group of children in *Ulysse* who are
     comparing the photo and the painting that the boy Ulysse made
     after Varda's photography. Some children consider Varda's photo
     more real, whereas others find Ulysse's painting pretty and even
     funny.

Dominique Bluher is lecturer in the Department of Cinema and
Media Studies and associate faculty in the Department of Visual Arts
at the University of Chicago. Her writings on French film theory,
French cinema, and autobiographical films have appeared in many
books and journals. She curated two exhibitions and retrospectives
of Agnès Varda: in 2009 at the Carpenter Center of the Visual
Arts (Harvard) and in 2015 at the Logan Center for the Arts at the
University of Chicago. She is currently preparing a monographic
exhibition of Varda's installations that will take place at Silent Green,
Berlin, in the summer of 2022.

Figure 8. Agnès Varda, *Alice et les vaches blanches* (*Alice and the White Cows*, 2011). © succession varda

Figure 1. Agnès Varda's scouting photographs for *La Pointe Courte* (France, 1954). Courtesy of Rosalie Varda

Agnès Varda: Photography and Early Creative Process

Rebecca J. DeRoo

Agnès Varda often described her career as encompassing "three lives": "photographer, filmmaker, and visual artist."[1] She trained in photography at the École de Vaugirard before turning to cinema in the early 1950s.[2] Her early work in the late 1940s and 1950s as a photographer for Jean Vilar at the Avignon Festival and Théâtre National Populaire is well-known.[3] Yet it has been often repeated that Varda knew little about cinema when she started her directorial career (a story she herself perpetuated);[4] how photography shaped Varda's early cinema remains a growing area of study.[5] This article excavates material from Varda's archives to demonstrate how, at the beginning of her cinematic career, she drew extensively on her training as a photographer as a way of working creatively. In particular, I focus on how she used photographs to conceive and plan her early films *La Pointe Courte* (France, 1954) and *L'Opéra Mouffe* (France, 1958). Even when not used as prototypes for specific film shots, the photographs illuminate previously unseen aspects of her work and concerns.

Photography also made sense economically. Varda did not have a producer or state subsidies for either film; it was efficient to

Camera Obscura 106, Volume 36, Number 1
DOI 10.1215/02705346-8838613   © 2021 by *Camera Obscura*
Published by Duke University Press

develop film shots, themes, and motifs in advance. Both films are focused on particular places: La Pointe Courte, a Mediterranean fishing village near Sète, and the rue Mouffetard in Paris's 5th arrondissement. Both films combine fiction with observational and documentary elements exploring the life, economies, and social dynamics of each place. Varda knew La Pointe Courte well, having lived nearby in the 1940s, and she said she went to the rue Mouffe-tard market often; she used photography to investigate the places and people further. Her photographs manifest her careful study and formal composition and demonstrate the sheer scope of her planning.

La Pointe Courte

Varda made extensive location scouting photos (*photos de repérage*) around La Pointe Courte to plan film shots and themes. Her archives also reveal prints of film shots, and she sketched specific compositions in her film shooting script. She sometimes num-bered the thousands of images in a reference system.

La Pointe Courte presents two fictional stories in counter-point. The first is the story of an unnamed fictional couple becom-ing unraveled. "She" is from Paris; "He" is from La Pointe Courte and is showing her his boyhood village as they decide whether to stay together. The second is the story of the villagers, whose local trade and economy depend on fishing in waters that have become polluted and threatened by authorities' prohibitions. These are fictional stories, but the film contains neorealist elements with sequences depicting the villagers' daily lives and labor.[6] Varda's scouting photographs focus, for example, on the geometric pat-terns of rows of wooden barrels, stacked timber, and arcs of boats' hulls with vertical masts; wood and fishing equipment come to be associated with men in the film (fig. 2). Varda also created photo-graphic studies of women drying laundry outside; she developed this in the film with white sheets billowing on laundry lines in the wind, close-ups of women's fingers maneuvering clothes pins, and long shots of the women chatting as they work.

Some scouting photographs resemble surrealist scenes:

Figure 2. Agnès Varda's scouting photographs for *La Pointe
Courte* (France, 1954). Courtesy of Rosalie Varda

empty streets with looming shadows and doors open to dark, mys-
terious interiors.[7] Other photographs focus on textures: grains of
sand washed up on the beach, prickly edges of a broken basket, or
details of wooden boards, with rough grain and jagged edges creating abstract compositions (fig. 1). This close examination of wood
and texture appears throughout the film. For example, the credits
of *La Pointe Courte* are presented on a close-up shot of a wooden
board, whose knot and rings evoke La Pointe Courte's pond and
shore. The credits are followed by a slow tracking shot down an
empty street, with laundry on lines dancing in the frame.

   Some of Varda's early scouting photographs are almost
completely abstract: wooden frames with dynamic play of light

Figure 3. Agnès Varda's scouting photographs for *La Pointe Courte* (France, 1954). Courtesy of Rosalie Varda

and shadow or luminous reflections and waves in the water (fig. 3). Although these specific shots do not appear in her film, this approach is sometimes represented there, as the camera roams over wooden boat frames and fishing nets, over walls, through empty streets, and to murky, oily reflections in storage buckets and barrels (fig. 4). The camera is often detached from a character's perspective and moves across the details of the village in formally composed shots. Some critics found her focus on formalism surprising and in tension with the film's neorealist depiction of villagers' daily life and labor, though others, such as André Bazin, championed Varda's singular vision.[8]

Varda has indicated she was influenced by Bertolt Brecht, whose ideas she encountered through Vilar, and Philippe Noiret and Silvia Monfort, who play the couple in the film, were actors in Vilar's Théâtre National Populaire. Inspired by Brecht, Varda instructed the actors not to convey emotion through gesture or expression;[9] they often stand and speak rather rigidly, and the emotional dynamics of the couple are conveyed metaphorically. Through sound and image, She is associated with trains and metal, and He is associated with organic materials such as wood and fishing nets.

Varda's photographs and shooting script reveal her devel-

Figure 4. Agnès Varda's scouting photographs for *La Pointe Courte* (France, 1954). Courtesy of Rosalie Varda

opment of a well-known sequence in the film (with directions and notes on the left, dialogue on the right, and sketches interspersed). The couple is arguing and discussing why he had not returned to his childhood home sooner. She suggests that it wouldn't have mattered to him whether he returned with or without her. A shot of felled tree limbs, which Varda sketched in the script and noted to repeat, conveys the emotional upheaval (figs. 5 and 6; see photographs in fig. 4).

He responds that "what I've found here is mine only." Her strained response is conveyed by her position in front of metal gears with tightly wound rope, with the tension underscored by the sound of an electric saw, which Varda noted by hand on the shoot-

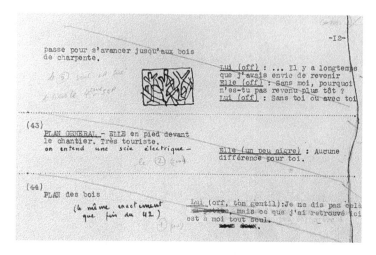

Figure 5. Agnès Varda's shooting script for *La Pointe Courte* (France, 1954), with sketches of shots she had photographed (see fig. 4) and handwritten notes. Courtesy of Rosalie Varda

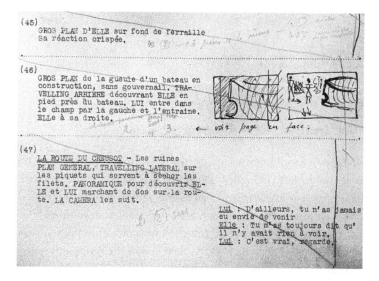

Figure 6. Agnès Varda's shooting script for *La Pointe Courte* (France, 1954), with sketches of shots she had photographed (see fig. 4). Courtesy of Rosalie Varda

ing script. To portray the couple's fragility and dynamics, Varda sketched and noted the close-up of the mouth of a wood-frame ship under construction, without a rudder, and then a shot of her standing alongside, before he takes her arm and leads her along. Varda's photographs and notes demonstrate how closely she attended to the interplay of dialogue, sound, and symbolic image.

The scouting photographs enabled Varda to develop her ideas and plan shots economically, working with a minimal budget since she did not have external funding and was not eligible for an advance loan or subsidy from the Centre National de la Cinématographie. Along with envisioning the film with photographs, she used personal funds, borrowed materials, and formed a cooperative with actors and technicians who worked for shares in the film.[10] She filmed on location from 10 August to 31 September 1954 (226), and she later explained, "I had imagined every shot, prepared everything with photography and drawings" (40).[11]

L'Opéra Mouffe

As with *La Pointe Courte*, Varda pursued photographic study in advance of *L'Opéra Mouffe* to develop the conception of the film. She took photographs in late 1957, choosing specific images to create a photographic notebook. The film is named for the rue Mouffetard market or La Mouffe; the film's subtitle, *Notebook of a Pregnant Woman* (*Carnet de notes d'une femme enceinte*), suggests this early photographic book.[12]

In contrast to the scouting photographs for *La Pointe Courte* that often align with the film's shots, this photographic book more broadly demonstrates her study of the area and development of *L'Opéra Mouffe*'s themes. Parts of the rue Mouffetard neighborhood were slated for urban renovation at the time because they were classified as slums (*îlots insalubres*).[13] Her film goes on to contrast the street's market abundance with the homeless, hungry population living there. Furthermore, the film moves between interior sequences of a woman's liaisons with her lovers and street scenes with symbolic close-ups of produce at the market reinforcing the themes of fertility and fecundity.

Figure 7. Agnès Varda, photographic study for *L'Opéra Mouffe*
(*Diary of a Pregnant Woman*, France, 1958). © Agnès Varda,
1958

Varda created a number of photos of homeless people in
her initial study. She later recounted how some of the people died
during the winter of 1957–58, between the making of the photo
book and the film shooting, so she included some of these photographs in the film as a memorial to lives lost. She also reproduced
several in her autobiographical 1994 text, *Varda par Agnès*.[14]

But the photographs depicted here are not well-known.[15]
Without giving them titles or numbers, Varda simply pasted and
taped them onto pages of her notebook, occasionally making brief
handwritten notes. One photograph (fig. 7) presents a man in a

darkened café, where his reflection in the mirror behind him as well as the shadowy figures working recall Eugène Atget's interiors. The artificial light and blurred window make it difficult to determine whether this is during regular hours or whether the figure has been drinking throughout the night. In the film, Varda goes on to explore alcoholism, depicting people sleeping in the street or leaving bars, tipsy in daylight hours. Varda's wordplay in the film score's lyrics intertwines the film's themes with the notion of *ivresse*—being intoxicated with passion and literal drunkenness.

In another photograph from the notebook (fig. 8), Varda depicts the facade of a *charcuterie* (butcher shop), identifiable by the metalwork hogs as well as the vernacular signage. The second story of the building contains paintings reminiscent of earlier times, in which women are associated with fruit, abundance, and fecundity—themes she would develop in the film through shots of actual produce at the market.

A third photograph (fig. 9) evokes Man Ray's surrealist street photographs, in which he found sexual metaphors in objects observed. (In the film, Varda goes on to reference Man Ray's *Le Violon d'Ingres* [1924] explicitly, and she uses symbolic, even surrealist close-up shots of ripe fruit to suggest fertility and sexuality.) Here, Varda presents a humorous image. The gentleman walking—his stooped posture echoing the chalkboard sign's drooping arrow—is oblivious to the bright, fertile lemons illuminated in the sunlight.

Another photograph (fig. 10) depicts homeless people living amid the rubble of a demolished building, presumably a site being renovated in the neighborhood. Varda's handwritten note signals that outside the frame there are *chambres à louer* (rooms for rent)—possibly suggesting the amorous liaisons of the film's lovers while also underscoring the cruel irony of the urban renovations that left local populations displaced. This is Varda's critical look at the urban modernization of Paris that benefited certain segments of the population (an expanding middle class in the period following World War II) at the expense of others. This urban and social critique of a society of abundance is typical of Varda's broader work, including her *Daguerreotypes* (*Daguerréotypes*, France, 1975) and *The Gleaners and I* (*Les glaneurs et la glaneuse*, France, 2000).

Figure 8. Agnès Varda, photographic study for *L'Opéra Mouffe* (*Diary of a Pregnant Woman*, France, 1958). © Agnès Varda, 1958

Figure 9. Agnès Varda, photographic study for *L'Opéra Mouffe* (*Diary of a Pregnant Woman*, France, 1958). © Agnès Varda, 1958

With these photographic studies, Varda developed the film's central concerns. Although she was ultimately unable to interest producers in the film, she went ahead.[16] She has recounted how she filmed using a borrowed 16mm camera, standing on a folded chair in the rue Mouffetard while pregnant with her daughter Rosalie.[17] Her unusual efforts convey how limited her budget was and suggest the importance of her preliminary photographic work so she could film as efficiently as possible.

Varda drew on her training in photography to visually conceive and develop her early cinema, a practice particularly useful when working with budgetary constraints. This practice anticipates her multimedia work of the twenty-first century, in which she combined photography and moving images. While her films and late-career artistic work are widely accessible, this discussion of treasures from the archive highlights Varda's largely unseen corpus of 1950s photographic studies as a legacy, a major dimension of her early work that fuels new understanding of her creative process.

Notes

I would like to express my gratitude to Agnès Varda and Rosalie Varda for permission to reproduce the archival images in this article. I thank the reviewers of this article for their thoughtful reading.

1. See Varda's disc, "Les Trois Vies d'Agnès," in *Tout(e) Varda* (Paris: Ciné-Tamaris, 2011).

2. Varda studied at the Sorbonne and the École du Louvre as well. She created visual artwork in the twenty-first century, astutely analyzed in contributions by Dominique Bluher, Nadine Boljkovac, and Sandy Flitterman-Lewis in this issue.

3. Varda discussed these photographs in *The Beaches of Agnès* (*Les plages d'Agnès*, France, 2008) and in *Varda by Agnès* (*Varda par Agnès*, France, 2019).

4. Varda recounted: "In the 1950s, to be a director, first you had to be an apprentice, then third assistant director, second AD, first AD, and then at 40 or 50 you became a director. But I just suddenly wrote a script at 25. I'd never been an AD, never gone to film school, and I knew nothing about cinema. I never even went to the movies. In my mind I just suddenly saw this film that would be good to make." See Varda's film commentary, "Souvenirs et propos sur le film: Entretien d'Alexandre Mabilon avec Agnès Varda, *La Pointe Courte*" (New York: Criterion Collection, 2008). For consistency, I quote her films' English subtitles in this article.

5. For Varda's own meditations on select photographs, see the disc "Les Trois Vies d'Agnès" in *Tout(e) Varda* and her final film, *Varda by Agnès*. For her films whose narratives focus on photographs,

such as *Ulysse* (*Ulysses*, France, 1982), *Salut les Cubains* (France, 1963), and *Ydessa, the Bears, and etc.* (*Ydessa, les ours et etc.*, France, 2004), see the disc "Varda tous courts" in *Tout(e) Varda*.

6. Critics at the time and since have compared Varda's film with Italian neorealism and see her cultivating a neorealist aesthetic through location shooting, inclusion of nonactors (the workers and villagers), and use of local dialect. André Bazin, for example, wrote that the fishing village in *La Pointe Courte* recalled Luchino Visconti's *La Terra Trema* (Italy, 1948). Bazin, "*La Pointe Courte*," *La Cinématographie Française*, no. 15 (9 May 1955). See also Alison Smith, *Agnès Varda* (Manchester: Manchester University Press, 1998), 1. On how Varda both invoked and challenged conventions associated with neorealism, see Rebecca J. DeRoo, *Agnès Varda between Film, Photography, and Art* (Oakland: University of California Press, 2018), 19–48.

7. Thanks to Lalitha Gopalan for suggesting that these scouting photographs recall the work of Eugène Atget, who inspired surrealist artists.

8. Critics such as Jean-Louis Tallenay and André Bazin praised the film, though Bazin admitted mixed feelings about the film's combination of neorealism or naturalism and highly composed shots, stating, "Perhaps Agnès Varda could not forget . . . her talents as a photographer." Martine Monod, for example, expressed concern about "a certain aestheticism" weakening the film. Bazin, "*La Pointe Courte*: Un film libre et pur," *Le Parisien Libéré*, 7 January 1956; Monod, "Naissance d'une cinéaste," *Les Lettres Françaises*, 12–18 January 1956. In praise of *La Pointe Courte*, see, e.g., Jean-Louis Tallenay, "*La Pointe Courte*," *Radio Cinéma Télévision*, 22 January 1956; and Bazin, "*La Pointe Courte*," *La Cinématographie Française*.

9. Varda, "Souvenirs et propos sur le film"; Kelley Conway, *Agnès Varda* (Urbana: University of Illinois Press, 2015), 17–18.

10. Agnès Varda, *Varda par Agnès* (Paris: Cahiers du Cinéma, 1994), 40. See also Kelley Conway's excellent contribution in this issue.

11. "J'avais imaginé chaque plan, tout préparé par des photographies et des dessins."

12. *L'Opéra Mouffe* is an essay film; on the role of the photo book in the development of the essay film genre, see, e.g., Nora Alter

and Timothy Corrigan, eds., *Essays on the Essay Film* (New York: Columbia University Press, 2017). On the title's various meanings and wordplay, see Rebecca J. DeRoo, "Pleasure, Pain, and Subversion in Agnès Varda's *L'Opéra Mouffe* [*Diary of a Pregnant Woman*] (1958)," in *Plaisirs de Femmes: Women, Pleasure, and Transgression in French Literature and Culture*, ed. Maggie Allison, Carrie Tarr, and Elliot Evans (Bern: Peter Lang, 2019), 37–54.

13. Conway, *Agnès Varda*, 34.

14. Varda, *Varda par Agnès*, 116–17.

15. Varda includes fleeting details of two images in the film *Varda by Agnès*.

16. Varda, *Varda par Agnès*, 114–15. She was invited to present the film at the 1958 Universal Exhibition in Brussels.

17. Varda, *Varda par Agnès*, 114–15.

Rebecca J. DeRoo is associate professor in the School of Communication at the Rochester Institute of Technology. She cocurated the 2016 retrospective *Agnès Varda: (Self-)Portraits, Facts and Fiction* at the Dryden Theatre, George Eastman Museum. Her book *Agnès Varda between Film, Photography, and Art* (2018) was a finalist for the Kraszna-Krausz Book Award. This research was supported by grants from the American Association of University Women, the American Philosophical Society, and the National Endowment for the Humanities. Her first book, *The Museum Establishment and Contemporary Art* (2006, 2014), received the Laurence Wylie Prize in French Cultural Studies.

Figure 10. Agnès Varda, photographic study for *L'Opéra Mouffe* (*Diary of a Pregnant Woman*, France, 1958). © Agnès Varda, 1958

The tree was coming back to life.

Figure 1. Agnès Varda's pruned tree, as featured in the
opening sequence of *Agnès de ci de là Varda* (*Agnes Varda: From
Here to There*, France, 2011)

"Virtual Varda": Sustainable Legacies, Digital Communities, and Scholarly Postcards

Colleen Kennedy-Karpat

The meditations on absence and presence that follow a person's death realign our memories and continue our relationship with that person's legacy. This process holds as true for public figures as it does for personal acquaintances, although few public figures integrated as strong a sense of intimacy with their public as Agnès Varda did during her long career as a filmmaker and artist. Quite by accident, I found myself writing about this public-private confluence in the unusually personal response to Varda's death on social media and in published tribute essays; these thoughts went into a conference paper delivered in April 2019 at Istanbul Bilgi University as part of an event dedicated to female agency and subjectivity in film and television.[1] While in my initial proposal I planned to discuss Varda's film *Visages Villages* (*Faces Places*, France, 2017)—specifically, how her late documentaries frame her relationships and use this framing to reveal her agency—I

Camera Obscura 106, Volume 36, Number 1
DOI 10.1215/02705346-8838625   © 2021 by *Camera Obscura*
Published by Duke University Press

never imagined that I would have to wrestle with such questions in the immediate aftermath of her passing.

Relationships persist even after death, and sharing the experience of mourning can also spark new friendships among the bereaved. Keen to maintain the momentum of the 2019 conference, in the months that followed Feride Çiçekoğlu and her colleagues at Bilgi invited me to help coordinate a symposium dedicated to Agnès Varda's legacy under the aegis of a new initiative aimed at exploring the interconnections between sustainability and gender equality. Thus, "Gender Equality and Sustainability: Agnès Varda's Sustaining Legacy" quickly began to take shape. We set a date in late March, to mark the anniversary of Varda's death; we sent out the call for papers and read the wide, warm responses; we invited and confirmed keynote speakers Sandy Flitterman-Lewis and Homay King; we built the final program and we began seeking a publisher for the volume to come.[2]

Yet in February 2020, as the date approached and we were dealing with these familiar tasks, an unfamiliar and rather menacing specter cast a pall over our progress. By early March the spread of COVID-19 had already prompted event cancellations and postponements in academic circles, leaving organizations scrambling to address or mitigate the upheaval of the global pandemic. With less than two weeks remaining until the symposium, we had to decide how to move forward. Bolstered by enthusiastic support from Bilgi University's administration, we announced the decision to keep the original date and move the proceedings online; within hours of sharing this news, our correspondence came up with the perspicacious nickname "Virtual Varda." This title renewed our determination to establish a format that could fulfill our mission in the midst of unprecedented disruption.

It helped us tremendously that Agnès Varda makes an apt subject to anchor this shift to digitality. Her late-career foray into digital video combines a sense of departure with a strong impression of continuation, just as a well-rooted trunk might sprout new branches. This natural metaphor is made literal in the opening narration of her 2011 documentary miniseries *Agnès de ci de là Varda* (*Agnès Varda: From Here to There*, France), which begins each of its five episodes with shots of a tree in the courtyard of Varda's home in Paris (fig. 1). This sequence creates a precise synecdoche for the "here" of the title and thus provides clear contrast to the changing locations out "there" that comprise each episode. In voice-over, Varda explains how, after a very thorough pruning, the tree regained its lush greenery over only three months, a striking regrowth in a fraction of the time it took to gather and edit her travelogue—whose viewers, Varda adds, will experience the series over several days, while on-screen the tree's regrowth takes just two minutes. Juxtaposing a fixed, specific space in the visual track with narration that insists on the subjectiveness and malleability of time strikes an inspiring balance between stability and change, and it also shows how comfortable Varda was in seeking this often tenuous balance.

Such inspiration is sorely needed in the current moment of the global pandemic, as many of the changes happening to, through, and around us in the academy are impairing rather than improving our sense of continuity with existing practice. How will we teach, and how will we continue learning through our own research? Some of the problems will no doubt stay the same; money and time will certainly persist as perennial obstacles to original research, and indeed, the pandemic will likely exacerbate the already unequal distribution of these resources. This is especially true for our teaching, which seems to have vanquished the threat of MOOC-ification only to contort itself, under duress, into approximations of the same forms that so many educators have long and ardently resisted.[3] The public reckoning of what has been lost or irrevocably altered in this forced embrace of online instruction has barely begun. Yet even if many traditional classroom practices are well worth defending against the entrenchment of virtual pedagogy, we must also recognize what might be gained as a result of this widespread surge in online capacities. Just as Varda's digital turn invigorated an already vibrant career, digital development can help overcome some impediments to the academic work of teaching and research.

Geographic distance and disconnections affect how we share our research at least as much as how we undertake it. But the stringent and prolonged policies of isolation in response to COVID-19 have inspired new, or perhaps simply newly attractive, ways to close geographic gaps among colleagues. The breathtakingly swift adoption of online platforms that can handle dozens of people connecting simultaneously is not without problems, but this shift in perspective has the potential to go beyond a short-term stopgap to respond to long-percolating conversations about how scholars share their research and which scholars are granted this privilege. Some, for instance, have already begun to question the paradigm of the annual, pandisciplinary megaconference. Sustainability was a common motivator for these discussions before the pandemic, as in a special session at the International Association for Media and Communication Research conference in June 2018 titled "Reimagining Environmental Sustainability for the Academic Conference," even though it's tough to overlook the irony of hundreds of scholars traveling to a conference only to question the sustainability of this very activity.[4] Our Varda symposium, considered honestly, might have been envisioned more sustainably from the start as a virtual one. But crisis allows us to pursue significant change by forcing open many of the cracks that had already been forming in old habits. I should note, though, that this movement rarely needs to push an event's organizers as far as it does the anonymous brokers who would assess these events' academic value.

Rethinking "Gender Equality and Sustainability: Agnès Varda's Sustaining Legacy" as "Virtual Varda" may have been born more of immediate utility than of revolutionary potential, but it is important to recognize that the former does not preclude the latter. Our experience produced compelling evidence that scholarly communities can survive and even thrive despite a severe restriction— if not (yet) wholesale abolition—of face-to-face conferencing. Online connection allows us to introduce and, eventually, integrate even the farthest-flung colleagues into our immediate scholarly circles and routines. We find ourselves sharing our time even if, individually, we occupy different times: morning coffee, after lunch, wrapping up the day. Like Varda's courtyard tree, our personal space can be fixed while subjective time is multiplied, though on these digital platforms we substitute a more lateral multiplication for Varda's emphasis on recorded duration. The resulting expansion of perspectives comes together in a kaleidoscope of pixelated videos, all arrayed on a single screen.

Beyond virtual space, moving online also prompted a significant rethinking of time, namely, the question of how best to plan its use within the constraints of the platform. The mental crash and burn dubbed "Zoom fatigue" is real (indeed, we may not have grasped just how real during those early weeks of isolation) and must somehow be accounted for.[5] What had been planned as a full day of panels on-site, with their attendant refreshments and socializing, we transformed into a Varda-focused, live-streaming content binge: two keynotes of thirty minutes each, plus ten presentations held to the barest double digits on the clock, all sequenced over four hours on a Saturday across time zones. The relentlessness of this succession of papers required team moderation with designated chiefs and backups throughout the program, a measure that proved necessary during our (fortunately brief and few) moments of technical difficulty.

Moving online also turned out to be a serendipitous lens for examining Varda's legacy. Already a master of building unity through diversity, Varda further reinforced this recurring theme in her embrace of digitality. The enhanced mobility and flexibility of digital filmmaking are qualities that vividly underscore Varda's strengths as an artist. Her generosity and genius, particularly as a documentarian, are grounded in the spirit of *partage* (sharing) that she declares in her final film, *Varda by Agnès* (*Varda par Agnès*, France, 2019), to be a driving force of her oeuvre. This core principle of *partage* also inspired us to press ahead with our plans; when limiting physical contact becomes key to our collective survival, the very act of sharing is loaded with a sudden, poignant nostalgia, but also renewed urgency. We committed ourselves to *partage* to better honor Varda herself. This shift also promotes more sustainable connections, as contacts established online might be more comfortably continued online—which is no small consideration for scholars who, like us, are based outside the Anglosphere and Western Europe. We were further buoyed by an enthusiastic response from our speakers, panelists, and university administrators at Bilgi in launching (and, perhaps, continuing) "Virtual Varda" in lieu of our symposium in Istanbul, finding swift and sure support that validates this community-building impulse and suggests an auspicious future for Varda studies.

Taking an even broader view, the insights produced by considering Varda's work in this online format visualize a path forward for other scholarship as well. Following Dominique Bluher's study of postcards in Varda's work, these virtual forms that academics are now exploring under a state of emergency might have durable appeal as a kind of scholarly postcard: a necessarily constrained yet effective way to develop and maintain social and professional networks by sharing research.[6] If the megaconference functions largely (if presumptuously) as an annual or biannual record of the state of a given field, and if journals and smaller, multiday conferences produce more detailed dispatches from specific subfields, then our experience with "Virtual Varda" suggests that there is room to consider online conferencing as a collection of scholarly postcards, each presentation offering a standing and infinitely shareable record of research that is publicly available. These scholarly postcards neither negate nor replace established conferencing practices but introduce a complementary format that has the added benefit of boosting public outreach (fig. 2).

Online platforms may have an inherent advantage in their ability to reach new and broader audiences compared to in-person conferencing; however, as with the physical postcard, both platform and audience are primed more for sound bites than for detailed communication. Citing Bjarne Rogan, Bluher noted that most postcards "provide very little information since 'their main function is to keep up reciprocal social contacts' and to give 'a sign of life or a confirmation of friendship.'"[7] This tracks with our experience in online conferencing, and other forms of technology have similarly adopted this social function of postcards in daily life. Bluher likens postcards to text messages in that, for both, "communication is the first and most important function" (289). But unlike text messages, openness is built into the postcard form: sent without envelopes, they arguably invite readership beyond the addressee and reach out to anyone whose interest might inspire a quick read (297). Similarly, the increasingly widespread use of online video meets all kinds of audiences—both academic and public—exactly where they are. The same is true for presenters: while no technology offers fully democratic accessibility, for many scholars the barriers to participation for an online event are far more easily surmountable than those in place for an in-person conference.

The live-video postcards that made "Virtual Varda" a success thus present a model of accessible and sustainable practices for building more resilient and inclusive academic communities. The community spirit of this event and in Varda's series *Agnès de ci de là Varda* may not offer a panacea for social isolation, but the shared structural reliance on the postcard serves as a vibrant reminder of the stakes of seeing through this global crisis. Connections matter, and in seeking ways to overcome our isolation through virtual contact, we can take inspiration from Varda's unshakable faith in the human ability to connect. This faith, expressed so clearly in *Agnès de ci de là Varda,* makes an implicit promise that no matter how these connections began, if we pursue them, they will persist even after we open our worlds to one another once again.

Notes

My heartfelt thanks to Feride Çiçekoğlu for the invitation to join forces for this worthy cause, along with the rest of the organizing team at Istanbul Bilgi University: Aslı Tunç, Zuhal Ulusoy, and Pınar Uyan, whose steadfast, collective support made "Virtual Varda" possible. Special thanks to technical support staff Burak Şungar and Ekin Ersin, who made sure we were prepared to host the international event online and oversaw the proceedings from Istanbul.

1. The proceedings volume from this event is Diğdem Sezen, Aslı Tunç, Ebru Thwaites Diken, and Feride Çiçekoğlu, eds., *Female Agencies and Subjectivities in Film and Television* (Palgrave Macmillan, 2020).

2. A full summary of the proceedings for "Gender Equality and Sustainability: Agnès Varda's Sustaining Legacy," including active links to selected talks, is available at *Gender Equality and Sustainability: Agnès Varda's Sustaining Legacy*, Istanbul Bilgi

University, 2020, ftvvarda.bilgi.edu.tr. An expanded proceedings volume is forthcoming, titled *The Sustainable Legacy of Agnès Varda: Feminist Practice and Pedagogy in Cinema and Visual Arts.*

3. Massive open online courses (MOOCs) offer instruction in a variety of subjects over the internet, often with few or no restrictions on who can register to participate and with highly variable institutional support for professionals teaching such courses. For an overview of current scholarship, see Ruiqi Deng, Pierre Benckendorff, and Deanne Gannaway, "Progress and New Directions for Teaching and Learning in MOOCs," *Computers and Education* 129 (2019): 48–60.

4. A description of the special session is available at oregon2018 .iamcr.org/sustainable-conference.html (accessed 28 April 2020).

5. Julia Sklar, "'Zoom Fatigue' Is Taxing the Brain. Here's Why That Happens," *National Geographic*, 24 April 2020, www .nationalgeographic.com/science/2020/04/coronavirus-zoom -fatigue-is-taxing-the-brain-here-is-why-that-happens/.

6. Dominique Bluher, "Varda's Gift of Postcards," *Área Abierta* 19, no. 3 (2019): 287–306.

7. Bluher, "Varda's Gift," 294, drawing on Bjarne Rogan, "An Entangled Object: The Picture Postcard as Souvenir and Collectible, Exchange and Ritual Communication," *Cultural Analysis* 4 (2005): 1–27.

Colleen Kennedy-Karpat holds a PhD in French from Rutgers University and teaches film studies in the Department of Communication and Design at Bilkent University in Ankara, Turkey. She is the author of *Rogues, Romance, and Exoticism in French Cinema of the 1930s* (2013), which won the NeMLA Book Award. Other writing has appeared in *Adaptation, Journal of Popular Film and Television,* and several edited anthologies, including her coedited collection *Adaptation, Awards Culture, and the Value of Prestige* (2017). She studies adaptation, film genre, and national cinemas.

Figure 2. Professor Feride Çiçekoğlu, coorganizer of "Gender Equality and Sustainability: Agnès Varda's Sustaining Legacy," sends a virtual postcard in the form of her introduction to the online event, unofficially renamed "Virtual Varda," on 28 March 2020. Courtesy of Feride Çiçekoğlu

Keep up to date on new scholarship

Issue alerts are a great way to stay current on all the cutting-edge scholarship from your favorite Duke University Press journals. This free service delivers tables of contents directly to your inbox, informing you of the latest groundbreaking work as soon as it is published.

To sign up for issue alerts:

1. Visit **dukeu.press/register** and register for an account. You do not need to provide a customer number.

2. After registering, visit **dukeu.press/alerts**.

3. Go to "Latest Issue Alerts" and click on "Add Alerts."

4. Select as many publications as you would like from the pop-up window and click "Add Alerts."

read.dukeupress.edu/journals

Printed and bound by CPI Group (UK) Ltd, Croydon, CR0 4YY

13/04/2025

14656476-0001